BREAD AND WATER

BREAD AND WATER

A Spiritual Journey

JENNIFER HAINES

ORBIS BOOKS

Maryknoll, New York 10545

The Catholic Foreign Mission Society of America (Maryknoll) recruits and trains people for overseas missionary service. Through Orbis Books, Maryknoll aims to foster the international dialogue that is essential to mission. The books published, however, reflect the opinions of their authors and are not meant to represent the official position of the society.

All Bible quotations are from the *Revised Standard Version* unless otherwise indicated.

Queries regarding rights and permissions should be addressed to: Orbis Books, P. O. Box 308, Maryknoll, New York 10545-0308.

Manufactured in the United States of America

Typesetting by Joan Marie Laflamme

Library of Congress Cataloging-in-Publication Data

Haines, Jennifer.
    Bread and water : a spiritual journey / Jennifer Haines.
        p.   cm.
    ISBN 1-57075-098-X (alk. paper)
    1. Haines, Jennifer.   2. Spiritual biography–United States.
3. Christian biography–United States.   4. Prisoners–United
States–Biography.   5. Government, Resistance to–Religious aspects–
Christianity.   6. Peace–Religious aspects–Christianity.   7. Rocky
Flats Plant (U.S.)   I. Title.
BR1725.H16A3   1997
277.3'0825'092–dc21
[B]   97-3386
                                                              CIP

To
Rhonda Schroeder

Contents

Preface

"You shall love the Lord your God with all your heart, and with all your soul, and with all your strength, and with all your mind; and your neighbor as yourself" (Luke 10:27).

That's more or less what this book is about. It's the story of my personal spiritual journey. So it's a story of relationship–with God and with people. And relationship belongs to the realm of confidentiality. I feel that I have a right to talk freely about myself, but not about others. So I've protected the privacy of most of the people who enter into this story–including all those who are members of our nation's security, legal, and penal systems– by not using their names. I hope this doesn't sound impersonal. It's an effort to be as respectful as possible of individual persons who have touched my life.

Prologue

It was early, too early really for being abroad on the city streets, but it was my morning prayer time, and I wasn't quite ready to give up spending it out-of-doors, in spite of the advancing season. Stars still shone in the morning sky, though the turquoise of early dawn was sifting through them.

"Do you have the time?"

He had come up quite quickly from behind me.

I don't think that I did, but I had left the Catholic Worker house only minutes before, so I must have been able to tell him something. He seemed satisfied and dropped back.

Suddenly, his arms were around my waist, lifting me off my feet. I struggled and squirmed, but, though he wasn't tall, he was a good deal stronger than I and clearly in control.

There was no time for either fear or thought. Only the grace of God could have directed my response. I started talking to him, saying over and over again things like, "You don't need to do this. You don't want to hurt me. You're strong. You don't have to prove anything by hurting me. You don't want to do this. . . . "

He carried me down an alley and dropped me into an areaway beside an abandoned building. Then he was on top of me, starting to undo the buttons of my pants.

The greatest grace was that it never even occurred to me to want or try to hurt him. I held his wrists, but it was as useless as my struggle to break free had been. I kept repeating the same things over and over again, softly, gently: "You don't want to do this. . . . "

Miraculously, he listened. He stopped undressing me. He started talking. At first, he blustered: "Just wait until I get my breath back." Then he argued: "I don't want to hurt you. Just let me do it. All I want is a little loving." Then he apologized: "I'm sorry. I didn't mean to do it. I never do things like that. I'm high. Please forgive me."

I forgave him. At some point, he asked me to let go of his wrists, and I did. He was still lying on top of me. I comforted him. I patted his shoulder. But when he started to fondle me, I said "no," and he stopped. He stood, and I sat up.

He didn't want me to look at him, afraid that I'd call the police. I told him that I wouldn't look, I wouldn't call the police, I'd never do anything to hurt him, he didn't have to be afraid of me. He said, "I'm terrified." My heart cried for him.

"Couldn't we just be friends and talk for a while?" he asked. I replied that I didn't think I could as long as he wouldn't let me look at him. He climbed out of the areaway but seemed reluctant to leave. We talked a little more. Finally, I announced, "I'm coming up." He answered, "No, wait there a few minutes while I go." I did. He left, saying, "Good-bye." I called, "God bless you."

When I climbed out, the alley was deserted. I found the shoe I'd lost, walked on to the place where I'd been headed for prayer, and prayed for him.

Later that same day, I was discussing pacifism and nonviolence with a friend of a friend. "But what would you do if someone attacked you personally?" he asked.

I now knew the answer to that question. Praise the Lord for grace!

—— ✂ ——

The personal spiritual journey is an ongoing adventure. We never know where the next step will lead, but simply take step after step in our best attempt at faithfulness, leaning on what little we've come to know of God so far, and growing in faith as we gradually trust enough to step beyond what we know. Eventually, we may come out on one of those scenic overlooks from which we can survey a stretch of the path, making out pattern and direction.

This book is a view from such an overlook. It picks up my journey at the point where God called me to embark on pilgrimage. "Pilgrimage" meant giving away my possessions, saying good-bye to my friends, leaving my whole past history behind, and setting off into the unknown. It meant depending on God for absolutely everything, from daily guidance through physical sustenance and survival itself. It meant living precariously, without roots or securities or predictability. I thought, back in 1981, that it would mean moving around the country, praying, and perhaps witnessing here and there at nuclear weapons facilities. In fact, it turned out to mean a great deal of prayerful presence at the Rocky Flats nuclear weapons plant near Denver, and in assorted jails and prisons across the country.

But, of course, 1981 was not the beginning. I discovered that I had a religious prayer vocation in the mid-1970s, when I was a Quaker living and working in Philadelphia. I had been brought up in the "unprogrammed" Quaker tradition, which gave me an enduring appreciation for silence and a rich heritage of pacifism and concern for social justice issues. But it hadn't taught me much about God. It wasn't until my junior year in college that I suddenly realized God had been touching me from infancy through human love and especially the unconditional love of my mother. Some years later, in 1973, I started a daily devotional hour, which opened the door to personal relationship with God through prayer, which is the door to everything. The next year, I moved into intentional community, was introduced to the writings of Thomas Merton, and followed excitedly the rapid unfolding and flowering of my spiritual life.

Still, it's hard to imagine what had prepared me to recognize my vocation. I was so sure of it by 1977 that, if I had been a Catholic then, I probably would have run right out and entered a convent. As it was, I made private vows to God of poverty, chastity, and obedience. I knew that I was called to the life and work of a monk, the work of hidden prayer, and at the same time to a ministry of presence to people. Prayer in the midst of the world. I had no idea how to live such a vocation apart from the ongoing guidance and grace of God, day after day and year after year.

By 1976, I was already blessed with a rapidly expanding worship community, including a charismatic Protestant church and a Catholic prayer fellowship, both of which fed me deeply. The Catholic deacon became my first spiritual director. And God launched what I look back on as an intensive campaign to overcome my resistance to the complexities of Christian faith. I preferred to continue knowing God as Spirit and Creator, and Jesus as a great human teacher. But about six months of internal and external nudgings, testimonies, insights, and even a healing finally brought me to the recognition that my deliberate deafness to the authentic Christian experience of millions of people was pure arrogance. I simply surrendered: "Okay, God, I give up. I believe that Jesus is divine." Surrender to God's invitations and promptings has been the key to my growing spiritual life from the beginning, always catapulting me into new depths of spiritual reality.

In 1977, I became aware that my next step was a membership commitment to a church family. I moved to inner-city DC to join Sojourners, a Christian community with a biblically based concern for peace and social justice. There, I gradually began to understand how central vulnerability is to my vocation, and to sense the need for prayer in the heart of the city—silent, hidden prayer which somehow, in the mystery and power of God, becomes a refuge and point of healing for human brokenness and alienation and misery.

I had a vivid experience of such prayer one day when I opened myself to all the pain of everyone on our street—and throughout the neighborhood—and all over DC—and found myself imaging the city as one huge, open, festering wound, raw and bleeding. The pain was almost more than I could bear. I had to pour it out to God—in the most powerful, impassioned, yearning intercessory prayer that I had ever known. I saw then that the heart and wellspring of intercession is pain. To love is to make ourselves vulnerable to pain. In intercession, we carry the pain of the world to the love of God and the love of God back to the hurting world.

A monastic vocation also draws us into contemplative prayer, in which we simply love and open ourselves to God. I was more of a beginner at that.

The nuclear weapons issue engaged my attention on the side, as it were. I didn't see it as necessarily more important than other peace and justice issues, but it became the particular place where God called me to witness to God's sovereign power and transforming love.

— ✖ —

It Is the Advent of Our Lord

The sky is dark against the stars
   and night sounds scamper away
stillness wraps 'round
   that place of silence in our hearts
   where triumphant caroling
   hastens in the Lord
we wait, breathless and patient

a turning sword cuts deep there
   slicing out the dross
we gasp and grasp the pain
   and find in our hands
   the wounded hand of the Lord
grace pours in
   enough for tomorrow

      Friend, I give you the night.
      Have you heard?
      The Lord has come.

A light bursts into the morning
it is the Son
hastening to the death of birth
and the birth of death
to give his life to us
   in a million daily gestures, signs, and promises

his love enfolds
   and deep in my heart grows a pain that knows
   such love in reflection
   dimly in a mirror
I cringe

–"Get thou behind me, Satan"–
stand tall, welcome in the light of the world

> Friend, I give you the day.
> Have you heard?
> The Lord has come.[1]

---

[1] "It Is the Advent of Our Lord" by Jennifer Haines, first published in *Sojourners*, December, 1981. Reprinted with the permission of *Sojourners* (2401 15th St., NW, Washington, DC 20009).

1

Initiation

I got my first glimpse of the Rocky Flats Nuclear Plant on December 23, 1981. I couldn't exactly *see* it, because the plant proper, inside its security fence, is surrounded by a huge buffer zone of empty land, which is hilly on the eastern side, hiding the buildings from the view of passers-by on Indiana Avenue. A small group of us stood vigil on the traffic island there, outside the barbed-wire cattle fence that marks the boundary of U.S. government property and between the inbound and outbound lanes of the access road that carries workers to and from the plant. It was late afternoon, when the day shift heads home, and most of what we could see was a double line of bumper-to-bumper traffic emptying endlessly out of the plant.

I held a large sign I had made, which looked exactly like a Christmas card. A Christmas star shone down on the one word, "Peace." A warm and seasonal greeting, I thought. One departing worker leaned out of his car window to yell, "Go back to Russia!"

— ✂ —

It was cold on Christmas Day. We had stood vigil at the east gate at dawn, while Peter walked onto the property, and now were at the west, with the sharp peaks of the Rocky Mountain front range at our backs and the plant spread out before us a mile and a half away. I still couldn't see much, though, because of the gathering dusk. We had brought candles but couldn't keep them lit in the wind. We sang together. And then the four of us—Ann, Hedy, Kris, and I, strangers to one another until a few days earlier—crossed the property line and walked down the access road toward the plant. The singing of those worshiping with us grew faint behind us. Wind surrounded us, and deepening darkness. We prayed—prayed for the peace of the world in the light of Christ.

Headlights approached and blocked our path. Security guards.

"Do you know you're trespassing on government property?"

We intended to carry our peace message into the plant.

"If you don't leave, you'll be arrested."

We didn't leave.

We were taken to a guard station, where we were pat-searched, photographed, and asked for personal background information to fill in the blanks on assorted forms. I was friendly and courteous and would answer no more than my name—already clear that it was not my job to help the system to incarcerate me. I believe that incarceration is wrong: inhuman, unchristian, and an inappropriate societal alternative to conflict resolution. So I would submit to its being done to me but would not participate in the work of doing it myself. I didn't mind if someone wanted to go looking for that information, but I also suspected that I could be jailed just as effectively without it.

We were given a copy of the court injunction under which we would be charged. "Trespassing" on federal facilities "in the custody of" the Department of Energy is a petty offense, punishable by up to a $1,000 fine, unless one crosses a "barrier," which makes it a misdemeanor, punishable by up to a $5,000 fine plus a year in prison. Symbolic little gates had been erected across the access roads at the Rocky Flats property line for the sole purpose of constituting a "barrier" in the legal sense when closed against people like us. The "preliminary injunction," which had been issued by the U.S. district court after massive demonstrations at the weapons plant in 1978 and 1979, added a further threat: *any* "trespass" now amounted to contempt of court, punishable by the heavier penalties. We had known that that was what we were facing.

We were handcuffed behind our backs and strapped into seat belts for the twenty-two-mile drive downtown to the Denver city jail. Pretty total helplessness. My crocheted hat brim had fallen over my eyes; I couldn't adjust it, so I missed most of the scenery.

That jail is quite an introduction to incarceration! It's officially a "pre-arraignment detention center," designed for very short stays, and thoroughly inhuman. You're locked into a cinder-block cubicle with a steel shelf for a bed, a mat, sheet, blanket, metal toilet/sink fixture, toilet paper, and the clothes you wore in. Everything else is taken away from you. You can't brush your teeth. You can't comb your hair or fasten it out of your face. You can't change your clothes. You're allowed soap and a towel for a daily shower. That's it for personal hygiene. After however many days of this (three, in our case, because of the holiday weekend), you go straight to court. What an affront to human dignity!

You try to sleep in a series of naps, between the fluorescent lights that stay on in the cells day and night, and the noise of heavy, electronically operated steel doors clanging open and shut, as women are booked in and bailed out at all hours and officers yell down long, cinder-block corridors that magnify and reverberate every sound. You leave your cell for about twenty minutes for each meal, at something like 5:00 A.M., 10:30 A.M., and 3:30 P.M., but the food is hardly worth it, especially for a vegetarian. I never ate much there. If you receive a visitor, the visiting room gives you ten minutes on a telephone through Plexiglas. The rest of the time, if there happens to be a Bible available, you can read. Most of the cells have out-side windows. The women contrive to talk under the doors, and you hear some heartrending stories. You feel the pain of the mentally ill, those sepa-rated from children, those kicking drugs, those unable to make bond, those unjustly accused: all the human misery of a relentlessly circumscribed world.

On the morning when the outside world went back to work, two U.S. marshals came to collect us for court. Another experience of prisonerhood: we were chained together in pairs with long chains that wrapped around our waists and fastened to handcuffs in front. How much security is really necessary to transport four nonviolent women whose "offense" was prayer on government property? We were locked into a caged van in the basement of the jail and not released from it until securely within the basement of the courthouse. The restraints were removed inside the marshals' holding cell, while a second marshal held a drawn pistol outside the door. Surreal.

In the federal system your first court appearance is before a U.S. mag-istrate, who determines whether you can afford a lawyer, offers you repre-sentation by a public defender if you can't, and sets a bond. We didn't want a lawyer, because we wanted to be free to speak for ourselves, and we were agreed on refusing a bond. A cash bond discriminates against the poor, and a personal recognizance bond requires a promise that my un-predictable future may not allow me to keep. We expected to spend our pre-trial time in jail.

The Denver County Jail is a step up from the city jail. A prisoner can be kept there for as long as two years, so there are provisions for personal hygiene and such amenities as a library and commissary. We were photo-graphed and fingerprinted in the receiving area before being escorted back to the women's building, which is·a separate wing of the jail. Someone asked for a wrist and attached a plastic ID bracelet to it.

In the women's building we were strip-searched one by one, ordered to shower, deprived of everything we had worn in except our underwear and socks, and issued uniforms, canvas shoes, bedding, a towel and wash-cloth, a toothbrush, tooth powder, and soap. All procedures were punctu-ated by long waits in holding cells. It was particularly eerie to watch through the wire mesh as each of my friends disappeared into the "book-in" room and reappeared homogenized—dressed identically to everyone else, with her wet hair in a towel. The same thing eventually happened to me. Each of us was assigned to a bed in a large, open dormitory that slept about twenty-five people and was dominated by a television.

What gift that one of the women welcomed us immediately and took us under her wing! She offered us the first necessity, a comb, and whatever else we might need until we could buy our own from the commissary. Indeed, I've almost never been among women in any jail or prison who aren't friendly, helpful, and generous. They know what it's like to be restricted and deprived, and their compassion is quick and general.

The very first thing that I learned in jail was that there is absolutely no difference between prisoners and non-prisoners. Prisoners are just ordinary people. So are the officers. As my years of experience mounted, I became more and more convinced that the line between captives and captors is utterly arbitrary. It's not at all uncommon for a jailer to be engaged in the very activity, say public drunkenness or selling drugs, that a prisoner in her or his charge is being punished for. And many people are locked up for behavior that society in general apparently endorses in secret, particularly getting away with a little undeserved financial gain at someone else's expense. There's no justice at all in determining which people do, and which do not, get held accountable.

I also quickly accumulated evidence about the "effectiveness" of punishment. Of the first one hundred or so women with whom I talked, I guessed that not more than two had been influenced by the jail experience to change their behavior in any significant way. For all the rest, if guilty, either the crime had been an accident or mistake (as murder often is) that was already regretted and unlikely to be repeated, or it was part of a lifestyle that would continue in any case. And I saw, over the years, more and more of the directly negative effects of imprisonment, which fosters anger, antisocial attitudes, low self-esteem, irresponsibility, and even the techniques of criminality.

However, it's not surprising that the most important things I learned were about myself. One striking lesson followed from noticing that I rarely talked about nuclear weapons in jail. My conversation always ran to God and faith and love and nonviolence. *That*'s where my life is grounded and what it stands for. Though my resistance to nuclear weapons arose from my faith–the weapons are a denial of God and a sin against all of creation–they're far from the central issue for me. I'd felt compelled on Christmas Day to express my non-consent as strongly as I could, sensing vaguely that taking a risk for what you believed somehow added power to its message value. But I was already beginning to see that risks and message value and power are all irrelevant. We're asked to do nothing more than to be who we're called to be in God and to do what we're called to do, and our faithful lives will end up speaking for God in themselves. The positive consequences of our faithfulness are as little our concern as the negative ones. All results are in the hands of God.

— ✳ —

Two dormitories faced each other across a long corridor, with banks of tiny-paned windows in the inside walls. There were many tiny-paned outside windows, too, and I drank in many sunsets. The doors were open from breakfast-time, about 7:00 A.M., until 9:00 P.M., except for a brief period in the afternoon. At 3:00 and 9:00 we were required to be on our bunks for roll call, and when everyone was accounted for, the doors were locked. My stomach twisted every time a key turned in that lock, depriving human beings of one more degree of freedom, dismissing us, shutting us away from the world. It was years before my gut stopped feeling it physically.

We were never allowed in the other dorm or in "max," the maximum-security area at the back end of the corridor, though women from both dorms were allowed in a "rec room," where there were some tables and books. The radio in the rec room was as obtrusive as the TV in the dorms, and the incessant noise was the most oppressive thing about the jail for the four of us. I learned to sleep at least through some of it, getting started before either the lights or the TV went off at night, so that I could be up for prayer a couple of hours before breakfast, which was the only quiet time. The rest of the day I wrote letters or visited or tried to read the Bible through a haze of distraction.

My first brush with jail authority came over a rule that I had trouble remembering: no more than one person was allowed on a bed. I was forever sitting on people's beds, which were the handiest things to sit on in the dorm, and one of the officers in particular kept calling me on it. I kept being surprised. What was I being warned about? Oh, the bed thing!

Six weeks passed before we had to face the work issue. The four of us were agreed that we would not work for the jail. We could not support with our labor an institution that we believed to be wrong. When we arrived, no unsentenced women were being required to work, but eventually the sergeant reorganized the job assignments to include everyone in the building. We ended up in max.

That was an improvement, overall, in our situation. We were locked into individual cells at night, but during the day the doors were open to a common area, which was separated by an iron grille from the rest of the jail. It was much quieter than the dorms; we had more personal space and autonomy; and there was room for exercise for the first time. I started a discipline of trying simply to be quiet, without activity, all morning. I sat on the upper bunk by the window and let my spirit breathe.

Cool, fresh air blowing gently in across my face. My heart flying out the window to embrace the beauty of God's creation. The pain of bruised and broken lives washing through me. Prayer overflowing–yearning, crying prayer without words. God praying in me.

I had already learned a lot about how monastic the jail environment could be. Even in the noisy dorm my heart poured out for the hurting people around me in intercession. The emptying of self that makes room for prayer was facilitated by jail restrictions even more than it generally is by my own discipline: all my little projects and agenda were swept away. There were very few activities available that I was willing to entertain, so my attention was freer than usual for God. And max was largely free of external distractions as well. I certainly hadn't chosen my environment, and was awed by the all-embracing providence of God, which meets us on every level at once and leads us by the strangest paths to precisely where we need to be.

The max arrangement lasted about three weeks. Then the jail wanted the cells for others and returned us to a dorm. We were assigned to cleaning the bathroom. That was a hard job to refuse. We're all ardent cleaners of our own living space, and we were happy to clean for the other women, though the question of whether we weren't also doing it for the jail lingered. Not feeling certain of refusal, we carried the tension of compliance.

But by then another rule had become unconscionable for me: the one that forbade entry into other living areas than your own. Whatever reasons the jail may have had for the rule, it was a violation of community to which *I* couldn't be a party. The issue had become very concrete for me, since I now had a friend in max, the woman who had been across the corridor from us on the south side when we had been on the north. She loved coffee. Coffee was one of the few things we were allowed to carry out of the dining room. So I asked Hedy one evening at dinner if she'd be willing to get some coffee—neither she nor I drank it—to supplement what I could get to take back to Stella. Hedy wanted to visit, too. We could talk and pass the coffee through the grille. But we had barely greeted Stella when an officer ordered us out of there and into her office.

"*What* were you doing back in max?"

"Taking coffee to Stella."

"*We* can take her coffee. You know you're not allowed back there."

"I know it's against the rules. But Stella is more important than the rules."

"Will you do it again?"

"Yes, I'll go back there whenever it feels right to me."

"Will it make any difference if I tell you not to?"

"No."

I hadn't thought this through at all, but the answers came readily, with conviction and a welling up of freedom. I discovered in my spontaneous responses to her questions how very sure and very free I was. The system had no hold on my conscience. I was absolutely at liberty to do what I believed to be right no matter what it said.

She got a different answer from Hedy, who was willing to refrain from returning to max.

She turned back to me. "I'm going to lock you up."

I had never felt freer in my life.

She put me in an observation cell, one of two or three in the front of the building that were designed for mental patients or others who needed to be closely watched. It had no window on nature, but it had large Plexiglas windows in the door, so there was no visual privacy. Further, it was in the working part of the building, where people were constantly passing by, and not quiet even at night. It made me feel like a laboratory specimen or an animal in a zoo. Of all the degrading rituals that you're subjected to in jail, one of the worst is tours, and it was worse still in observation. Curious faces peering in at you, wondering what kind of a deviant you might be, almost tempted you to do something crazy, to break out of yourself and put on a show.

There was deeper pain for me there, too. When a friend came back from a visit in tears, I yearned to put my arms around her, but I couldn't even get her attention through the Plexiglas. I felt so helpless! Full of love and compassion, I was shut away from all humanness–except, of course, that God was there, and I could always pray. I wonder if I would know anything about the power of prayer if I hadn't kept getting thrown up against those situations in which there was nothing else that I could do.

My stay in observation was brief. I was there only overnight before my trial and two more days before sentencing. The trial date was March 1. The judge had reduced the maximum penalty to six months in prison and/or a $500 fine, so that a jury trial was not required by law. Before the judge, the prosecutor called witnesses who readily established that we had "knowingly and wilfully" violated the court injunction against trespassing. We didn't contest it. Our attention focused on the evil of nuclear weapons and the imperative to turn to God for our security. Some of us presented closing statements. The judge pronounced us "guilty."

At sentencing, those with previous records in this jurisdiction were given six months in prison, and the rest of us four months, all suspended, and we were each given a year's probation. That meant that if we violated any of the conditions of probation within the year, we could be made to serve the prison sentences. Officially, we could be resentenced to as much as the maximum for the charge.

I protested. "I'm not willing to accept probation, because I can't promise to abide by it." In fact, I was already clear in my own mind that I would celebrate Easter on the Rocky Flats property if I were physically able.

"I'm not asking you whether you'll accept it. I'm *sentencing* you to it," the judge retorted. She ordered us released as soon as the paperwork had been completed.

The paperwork was brought to us in the marshals' holding cell, and my position caused some consternation for probation department personnel, who were used to routine compliance. I not only wouldn't sign; I wouldn't even provide an address. Someone went back to consult with the judge. The judge ordered us released.

I spent the greater part of the next five and a half weeks living and helping out at a hospitality house for homeless women and families in downtown Denver. I felt very good about the work and especially glad to enable the woman who primarily held it together to take a week's vacation.

—— ✖ ——

Easter fell on April 11. I had been looking forward to it eagerly. I had already tasted the power of celebrating the illuminating, redeeming, commissioning love of our Lord in a place of darkness, and I couldn't imagine a more prayerful or joyful commemoration of Easter. I planned to walk into Rocky Flats along the railroad spur that entered it from the south, at least partly because there was a good chance that my prayer wouldn't be interrupted for the mile or two before I reached the access road. I was excited to plan the celebration for dawn, since sunrise has always been my most profound Easter symbol. About fifty people gathered for a sunrise service at the point where the tracks cross the public road; their love and prayers saw me off. A friend had given me the perfect gift, a potted Easter lily, to carry to the security guards.

What a glorious morning! Birds called. Morning light spread over the countryside. The bomb factory is set in a very beautiful corner of God's creation, where serene pasture land rises gently to the stunning mountains lifting suddenly into a great expanse of sky. I'm perennially thrilled by the beauty. I was blessed by about forty-five minutes for prayer, brimming over with the joy and peace and freedom of wholeheartedly worshiping God.

Security guards were waiting for me on the access road. They told me that I had to leave. I said that I wanted to walk on in. They replied that I couldn't. We were all very friendly and gracious. I'm sure I smiled a lot. I gave them the Easter lily, and they accepted it, which delighted me. They gave me the formal warnings, the copy of the court injunction. I was arrested.

Things were becoming familiar. The procedures at Rocky Flats. The city jail. The U.S. marshals with their business suits and handguns and chains. The magistrate's courtroom. I was assigned to the same judge whose probation I had violated. The Denver County Jail.

I was glad to be reunited with a friend from my earlier stay there. We visited and prayed together. I was assigned to an utterly insignificant job—cleaning the water fountain—which I chose not to do for the jail, though sometimes I would clean it for the other women who used it. The jail chose not to take note of whether I did it or not.

All winter we had been cooped up inside, but now, on warm days, we might be allowed out for an hour in the yard. It was deeply nourishing for me to touch the grass and walk under the open sky.

I felt free to ignore the rule against visiting in the dorm I wasn't living in, though I tried not to flaunt my noncompliance, so that the officers wouldn't have to make an issue of it if they didn't want to. Once I practically ran into an officer by accident on my way out of the "wrong" dorm, and she acted hurt. "Jennifer, why do you *do* this to me?" I was puzzled. She wasn't a victim, was she? *She* was the one in charge. But I guess she didn't feel the freedom I did. I hadn't meant to hurt her and was sorry.

Another officer on a different occasion wasn't hurt at all. She called me out of the "wrong" dorm and promptly locked me up. I was sentenced by the "conduct adjustment" committee to some number of days of punishment time in max and then returned to the dorm.

The "bed thing" came to a head. Even though I could now remember the rule, I had trouble obeying it. It made so little sense! And I was so unafraid of punishment that it didn't seem to matter whether I complied or not. I was inclined to go ahead and sit on a bed until warned, and then move. The officer who was consistently bothered by it was becoming very frustrated with me.

Then it hit me like a ton of bricks one evening in prayer that I was being unkind to her. This was not a rule that I *had* to break. Therefore, I had to comply. What I had been doing amounted to game-playing, almost to teasing. How unworthy of a Christian! Deeply humbled, I begged forgiveness and determined to reform.

—— ✄ ——

Show me your face, Lord
    wandering through ten thousand souls
    peering out from tear-dewed eyes
    huddled in the dark corners of poverty
my fingers grope for the obvious
my brain spins its wheels
    in endless convolutions upon the incomprehensible
my heart beats, beats, beats
    silently unravelling the central truths
    my mind's too sharp to see

God breathes fire into agony
    beyond acceptance
    to power
God dies
    and pours into my uselessness
    passionate prayer
I fall, falter, fail
    frustrated in my inability
    to do or be
and God is there
    instead of piety, accomplishment, or worth
God's own self cries in me
    I am.

—— ✄ ——

I was tried before the judge on May 14. She asked the prosecutor some pointed questions about how long a preliminary injunction could remain in effect, and he referred her to some case studies. As she was taking a recess to consult them, I and my supporters in the courtroom tasted the possibility of a reprieve. But she returned with the expected "guilty" verdict.

At sentencing three days later, I stood at the rostrum while the judge summarized the charges, convictions, and penalties and lectured me about restricting the expression of my beliefs to legal channels. I already knew that I was facing four months for the probation violation and up to six months for the new contempt of court charge. She pronounced sentence:

> It is adjudged, pursuant to conviction in case number 82-CR-84, that the defendant is hereby committed to the custody of the Attorney General, or his authorized representative, for imprisonment for a period of six months. It is further adjudged, pursuant to conviction in case number 81-CR-249, that probation is revoked and the defendant is hereby committed to the custody of the Attorney General, or his authorized representative, for imprisonment for a period of four months, the two sentences to be served consecutively.

I was still standing there waiting for some word of suspension or mitigation when the reality began to sink in that she had finished. I had been sentenced to ten months in prison! She had thrown the book at me. I had been prepared for the possibility, of course, but was rocked by the reality. How do you make it through ten months in prison? I had no idea. With God's help, I had to assume that I would somehow endure. One day at a time.

—— ✕ ——

The marshals came for me very quickly, in a matter of days. They booked me out of the jail and into their custody. They took charge of my property. I had become little more than a piece of government property myself, accounted for by a paper called a "body receipt," which changed hands as I was transferred from one jurisdiction to another. In the usual chains—one for each prisoner—in the usual caged-and-locked van, some men and I were driven to an unfamiliar expanse of open country, where we waited by an isolated airstrip with other official vehicles carrying or prepared to carry prisoners. The airplane flew in and landed. A carload of marshals with rifles deployed themselves in a circle around it and us, their weapons at the ready. Could this be real? It looked like a scene from a movie.

Prisoners were disgorged from the plane into the custody of the waiting vehicles. Prisoners were boarded. It was a large plane, perhaps a DC-10, entirely given over to the transport of federal prisoners, and almost full. There are several such planes. They hop across the country all week long, picking up and discharging prisoners. If your pick-up point and destination don't happen to fall on the same leg of the airlift, you're delivered to a county jail along the way until a plane or a bus or a van comes through that's headed in your direction. Transport can take weeks or even longer, and be extremely punishing.

There are no federal prisons for women anywhere near Colorado. The judge had recommended Pleasanton, near San Francisco, so I wasn't surprised to be told on the way to the airlift that that was where I had been designated. After thirteen hours in chains, and several stops here and there along a generally westward route, I was delivered to the Los Angeles jail for women, the Sybil Brand Institute.

Los Angeles? I had an overwhelming sense of having fallen off the edge of the earth. I had been whisked half a continent from home to a place where no one who cared about me would ever think to look. I might as well have been nowhere.

One of the marshals who had received me from the airlift had been angered by my refusal to provide information for her form. She threatened, "You need to tell me your birth date if you're going to be housed anywhere but in this van, and *I'm* not waiting around all night for you to change your mind." Long pause. I suppose she hoped both that I believed she meant it, which I didn't, and that it would have made some difference to me if I had, which it wouldn't. Anything she chose to do would be all right with me. I could see that that was my freedom; with no agenda, I was unthreatenable. She finally gave up, drove me to the jail, and someone invented a birth date to satisfy the computer.

I don't like confrontation. My natural desire is to build bridges, to make everybody happy, to calm troubled waters. I like people. I'm always friendly and courteous. It felt strange to be drawn more and more deeply into a world where my love for an all-loving God led me to do and say things that brought anger and retaliation down on me. I suppose that I was able to do it–that is, was free to be faithful in such situations–precisely because there was no ego-gratification in it for me.

And I did understand the system's reaction. I saw, more and more, how threatened it was by my imperviousness to threats. The system is designed for control; it uses threats and punishment as tools for control, and when the tools fail to control, it recognizes its helplessness and is enraged. At least, some individuals are enraged. Others are less invested in the system and more free to be personal.

I received a wonderfully affirming response just after I arrived at the jail from some passing official, whose curiosity was aroused by my appearance. He asked the marshals what I'd been convicted of, was not enlightened by "contempt of court," and so asked me what I'd done.

"I violated a court injunction against trespassing on the property of a nuclear weapons plant."

"Ah. I thought it must be something like that. Keep up the good work."

The rest of my time there was a desert. The jail was huge and oppressive. I was put in a cellblock with small, crowded cells fronted by bars.

There was no privacy, very little space, and almost nothing to do. But by far the worst aspect was the attitude of the officers, who treated us as if we were imbeciles and vermin. Petty rules were rigidly enforced. We were marched to the dining room, single file, eyes straight ahead, no talking. For evening "roll call," we were ordered to stick our wrists bearing the ID bracelets out through the bars of our locked cells, while an officer walked down the corridor checking each one against her roster. What utter dehumanization! Their complete dismissal of us as persons was summed up for me one night when they passed out the mail at the very end of the evening, and then promptly turned off the lights.

My lifeline was a scripture song that I'd learned in Denver County Jail at one of the weekly prayer fellowships led by outside Christians:

> Break forth into joy, O my soul!
> Break forth into joy, O my soul!
> In the presence of the Lord
> there is joy forevermore.
> Break forth, break forth into joy, O my soul!

I spent so many hours singing that song that it now brings back memories of the Sybil Brand Institute.

The marshals left me there for two weeks. On June 3 I was delivered by van to Pleasanton. Federal prison. The facility had been built for youth not many years earlier and was quite attractive physically. A very small compound of well-manicured grass and flowers was ringed by one-story, redwood-roofed buildings, beyond which was a large rec yard with a track. A double, barbed-wire-topped security fence enclosed the whole. I drank in the fresh air as I walked across the compound.

New arrivals were automatically assigned to the dorm officer as orderlies. In the morning I refused a work assignment and was soon being escorted to the lieutenants' office. The same graciously smiling young lieutenant who had given me a lecture the night before, when I'd declined to provide the usual information in R & D (Receiving and Discharge), presented me with an incident report and called someone to take me straight to detention. Goodness! That was fast! I was struck again by the fine line between freedom of movement and physical captivity. Here I was again, locked in a cell—with a cellmate who smoked. Within a week I had been sentenced to a recommended "disciplinary" transfer (recommended to the regional office of the Bureau of Prisons, which is responsible for prisoner designations and transfers).

I had known that all sentenced federal prisoners are required to work, so it was no surprise that I was in trouble for refusing. But it had been quite a whirlwind! My first day in my first prison landed me in detention, and my first, "moderate severity" incident report earned me a transfer. I learned later that such an exceptionally heavy punishment required the specific approval of the warden.

The redeeming grace, though, was that person after person asked me why I made the choices I did, and every conversation gave me an opportunity to talk about faith and security in God and the power of prayer. I didn't do it on purpose; that's just what came pouring out. Talking about God always tends to inspire and uplift me, and I loved all the personal dialogue with all the people who approached me with questions.

The detention unit at Pleasanton was small and crowded. Practically as soon as I'd been sentenced by the "disciplinary" committee, I and another woman awaiting a transfer were moved to the nearby Contra Costa County Jail. That meant starting all over again with all the book-in procedures, losing access to my property, and being confronted anew with demands for information that I was not willing to provide. The information issue was somehow a big deal there. I was threatened with isolation if I didn't cooperate, which I rather suspected that the jail was serious about, and it was. I ended up skipping the general population altogether and being locked directly into solitary.

I didn't mind solitary itself. It was quiet. The most punishing deprivation was a frosted and unopenable window, so that I couldn't see outside at all. When you're separated from your property, money, *and* fellow prisoners, you have to do without some very basic personal hygiene items, such as deodorant and shampoo. Providentially, after ten days or so, I received a money order in a letter forwarded from Pleasanton. My time was very empty. I was allowed a Bible and writing materials but wrote few letters in the limbo of not knowing when or where I would be transferred. I tried to use the time in positive, God-centered ways, but I confess that I was stretched by it.

One bright spot in what turned out to be a rather barren month was an officer who gifted me with some genuine human concern.

"How can you stand to be shut up back here all the time?"

"One chooses to stand it. You might as well be as happy as you can."

We talked. She asked me what I most missed, and I confessed that it was the out-of-doors.

The next day, she let me out. I was allowed out of the cell for one hour in forty-eight to shower, and I could use the day room and the telephone then. From the day room I had seen the concrete courtyard, with its high, gray walls and view of nothing but sky. Still, you could walk in it and breathe the air. She invited me to go out, and then let me stay out for as many hours as I wished. I was deeply touched and grateful.

When Pleasanton eventually picked the two of us up, it returned us to its detention unit for one final week. Then we were called out very early one morning for the long drive to MCC (Metropolitan Correctional Center) San Diego. MCC, a downtown "highrise," was very new at that time; it was built by the federal government for the primary purpose of pre-trial detention. It's a maximum-security facility, with the highly restricted movement and extremely limited opportunities for constructive activity typical of jails. (Jails are municipal and county facilities. Prisons are state and federal facilities specifically designed for sentenced prisoners; they anticipate longer stays than jails and are generally somewhat more tolerable.)

After three days of "normal" life in the general population, I was called into the case manager's office to discuss job assignments. He knew all about my position from the case manager at Pleasanton. I reiterated it. He wrote an incident report, and I was locked down, initially in a room on the women's floor with a view of sunsets and sailboats on the bay. I was allowed to keep my property and could bring books into my cell from the common area. I had a right to use the area for forty-five minutes of exercise each day, but my coming out required everyone else on the unit, whose doors were normally open to the area during most of the day, to be locked in, so I turned down the opportunity about half the time.

The "disciplinary" committee sentenced me to fifteen days of "disciplinary segregation" (DS), which is punishment time in lockdown, including the loss of both "non-essential" property and privileges, such as phone calls. Eventually I was transferred down to the detention floor, but even while my situation was still relatively comfortable, I was feeling the strain of having been so restricted for so long. I was not looking forward to months more of it. Then I suddenly received a very exciting piece of mail.

People are important to me, and I respond to everyone relationally, rather than on the basis of roles, so I had written to the judge after my sentencing to explain something more of my beliefs and the reasons for my choices; I wanted her to know that my noncooperation with the legal system's expectations, and especially the probation that she had sentenced me to and that I had ignored, was no reflection on her and that I understood and respected where she was coming from. I had hesitated to write again, from Pleasanton, because I knew that her desire was for me to do easy time; it wasn't her responsibility that my prison choices tended to lead to the opposite effect. But she had surprised me by writing to me, asking to hear how I was doing, and so I had told her.

Now, out of the blue, I held in my hand a formal order, mailed by the clerk of the U.S. district court, for modification of my sentence.

Sentence modification is a legal possibility that at that time (the federal law is different now), any defendant could pursue, and almost all did. I chose not to, because the legal machinery of the court, even though I got caught in it when I tried to be faithful to God's calling for me, is really irrelevant to what I'm all about. I'm not interested in defending myself, or protecting my rights, or securing justice or even mercy for myself through the courts. The whole foundation of my life is to trust all those things to God—including God's action through other people; I believe that gospel living calls each of us to be concerned for the rights and needs of *others*. I was essentially passive with respect to the legal process, submitting to its consequences, while directing my own attention, action, and conversation toward the things of God.

So this order was like (perhaps *was*) manna from heaven. It was made on the judge's own motion, entirely at her initiative, and it modified my sentence so that the two terms ran concurrently instead of consecutively. That reduced the total sentence from ten months to six. I didn't know exactly what it did to my release date, because there were complicated calculations involving credit for jail time served before sentencing; "statutory good time," which was awarded automatically at a standard rate of days per month, but which could be taken away as punishment, so I didn't count on it; and "work good time," which I was clearly not earning. It looked as if my earliest possible release date now fell in September. Hooray! I asked the case manager if the prison had received its copy of the order. Not yet.

Some weeks later the case manager came by to ask if he could borrow my copy; the prison still hadn't received one. Sure.

It was very shortly after that that an officer opened my door to announce, "You're leaving. Get your things together."

"Leaving? To where?" I wasn't halfway through my second DS sentence.

"To the streets, apparently."

"To the *streets*?!?"

I couldn't believe it. It was August 18. I couldn't possibly be being released this early. But I got my things together.

In Receiving, I was issued my civilian clothing. Somebody gave me money for the bus, since there hadn't been time for the usual procedure of purchasing the ticket in advance. I overheard a clerical person, who saw me being processed out, commenting on the sentence computation: "I must have done it right." Barrier after barrier dropped behind me. I was through the front door. I was standing on the city sidewalk.

I believed it.

The walk from the prison to the Greyhound station is only two or three blocks. I was back in the "real" world, restored to full freedom of movement, on my way home!

The only possible explanation I can figure out for that early release is that she *didn't* do it right. Maybe in the rush she gave me credit for all that "work good time" that I was so assiduously not earning. I'm not about to complain.

2

Discernment

August 22, 1982, was the first Sunday after my release from prison. I had shocked Ann and Al–pleasantly, of course–by appearing without warning at their door in Arvada, a Denver suburb, a couple of days earlier. Now we were standing in a circle of friends on the traffic island at the west gate of Rocky Flats, praying.

This was the regular Sunday afternoon prayer vigil. It had grown out of the mass demonstrations in 1979, where faith-based people became convinced of the need for a specifically faith-based witness. Every Sunday since then, stalwarts from the Denver Catholic Worker community and the Arvada Mennonite Church and others had been gathering here, witnessing to God's peace and security with their presence as they worshiped God and prayed with one another, mostly in silence. I had started joining the group on my first Sunday out of confinement in March, and valued its prayers during the long months when I could be present only in spirit. There was no more natural place for me to be on this sunny afternoon.

Bright yellow "no trespassing" signs dotted the simple fence in front of us. A large blue sign identified the Rocky Flats Nuclear Plant (one of our group kept itching to add the word "Bomb" to the title so that passers-by would know what really went on in there), belonging to the U.S. Department of Energy and operated by Rockwell International. Its primary function was the processing of plutonium, received from places like Hanford in Washington State, into products called "plutonium triggers," which it sent on to the Pantex plant in Amarillo, Texas, for final assembly into hydrogen bombs. The trigger of a hydrogen bomb is basically an atom bomb, like the one that destroyed Nagasaki. That's what Rocky Flats was producing.

The cluster of buildings in the distance gave the impression of a low-lying town dominated by a water tower. The access road at our feet stretched toward it, straight and empty and bordered by waving meadow grass. I could see where the railroad spur came in from the right and curved to follow the road. Only the road itself extended the federally controlled property on which the plant was built as far as State Highway 93, where we stood. The pasture land on both sides was privately owned and still used for grazing cattle.

The plant drew me like a magnet. As our prayer service concluded, I found myself walking to the fence, gazing down the road, and feeling almost physically the pull to keep on going, on over the property line, on into the heart of the bomb factory.

I wasn't at all sure that that was what I was supposed to do.

I turned to the group for help with discernment. People cautioned further consideration and time to regain perspective. Their advice certainly made sense. My eager spirit quieted somewhat. And not being sure that I had to walk in was reason enough to refrain from doing so.

Anna asked, "Why don't you come live at the Catholic Worker hospitality house?"

It sounded like a great idea. Within days, I had moved in.

That turned out to be the beginning of more than a year of rather intense discernment about my vocation. God had a lot to show me, and I seem to be a slow learner.

I was already adjusting my image of what it meant to be "on pilgrimage." I wasn't exactly moving around the country. I seemed to keep coming back to Rocky Flats. But I was unrooted and unattached. I was free to go wherever God led. If the guidance I was receiving from God kept amounting to "The next place I want you to pray is Rocky Flats," I was free to do that. After some years, I finally accepted that I was called to pray there indefinitely, and I still felt the same sense of living lightly, ready to pick up and go whenever and wherever God might beckon.

Pilgrimage living brought with it tremendous gifts, the greatest of which was the discovery that how much God provides for us is limited only by how much we trust God, within our calling, to provide. I like to provide for myself, to carry my own weight. Some degree of self-sufficiency is compatible with the callings of most people, and I had proven my competence at it in earlier years. But when God called me to give up everything and depend totally on God, I tried to be obedient, and everything was provided. God put people in my path who offered me food, shelter, and other necessities. I didn't have to ask. People sent me money in the mail. The most spectacular gift of that sort was a $1,000 check from a total stranger who knew nothing about me or my circumstances—part of an expansive "thank you" to my father for his university teaching.

The invitation to join the Catholic Worker community included another kind of gift, the gift of a place to fit in, to be of service, to round out my vocation. I thought at first that the life and work with the homeless would itself be that rounding out, the active complement to my contemplative prayer. But I discovered quite quickly, with Anna's perceptive and understanding help, that that kind of hospitality is not part of my vocation. Much as I value it, I have too structured a personality to be able to live comfortably and flexibly within its ambiguities: the need to be an authority as well as a friend for the guests in the house, for instance; the need to take responsibility in areas where you have limited control. The tensions were too difficult for me to sustain over time, and I became agitated and easily upset. I had to acknowledge that I couldn't do hospitality well. This valuable work was not for me.

What *was* for me?—as a complement to the prayer. The question percolated.

I spent a large chunk of the fall and early winter traveling among family and friends in the east and especially visiting with my parents, who had bought me the bus ticket. By the time I returned to Denver, I had missed a huge snowfall. I had also missed Christmas at Rocky Flats.

Nonetheless, I was ready to walk in again. I was beginning to realize that I had to let go of planning, to wait quietly for God's leading, but I also had a sense of appropriate times and seasons. I arrived at the first Sunday vigil of the new year prepared to discern whether this was a day for celebrating God on the property. By the end of our regular vigil, I felt clear. I walked through the open gates—which were typically closed when we were present, but happened at the moment to be buried in piles of snow—and down the access road toward the plant.

I was arrested. The court injunction against trespassing had been repealed—at the initiative, I suspected, of the judge who had sent me to prison under it—and I was charged with simple trespass, a petty offense.

But the really amazing new wrinkle in the situation came from the magistrate, the same one who had seen me twice before. After offering me a personal recognizance bond and hearing again my refusal to promise to return to court, he announced:

"I'm releasing you."

The date of the next hearing was established, and he made it clear that I was ordered to appear. That was all.

What a treat to have my fresh air and free movement handed back to me so unexpectedly! My friends and I rejoiced. It required me, however, to face the question of my conscientious response to court orders in this novel situation of having the freedom to choose.

I have serious objections to the legal system, especially its adversarial structure and claim to supreme authority. I separate myself from the court's assumptions when I decline to participate in its process. And the way in which I naturally reach out with caring to individuals, including everyone within the system, expresses the Christian values I embrace, values that honor relationship above law and reconciliation above justice. In fact, the magistrate's choice to step beyond the law's demands and release me without a promise—though I suspect that his own reasoning was essentially pragmatic—affirmed in itself the values I stand for.

But what response to the court's *authority* was required of me? I wasn't sure, so I appeared for the hearing. At its conclusion, another hearing was set, and I shared with the magistrate my hesitations about coming back. He said something like, "Oh, I know you'll be back." And I suddenly knew that I wouldn't. He was counting on the court's assumption of authority, and especially its punitive power, to manipulate my behavior. I felt dirtied and compromised by his expectations. No, I couldn't come back simply because he ordered it. It was not authority enough, not reason enough. I needed to act in a clearer way on my dependence on a higher authority—the One who created all human beings equal and gives inner guidance to govern our choices.

I wrote the magistrate a letter explaining why I wouldn't return, and I didn't return, and he issued a warrant for my arrest.

The U.S. marshals didn't need an address. They knew about the Catholic Worker, which is conveniently located only seven or eight blocks from their office. I had no intention of running or hiding. My intention was to go calmly about my business as if the court didn't exist—which is actually quite a challenge when you're expecting to be dramatically interrupted at any minute. Two marshals were waiting for me one morning as I returned from a walk. We knew each other. Anna offered them coffee. They declined. It was very, very cordial and polite. I ended up back in the Denver County Jail.

I was already becoming acquainted with the staff there and making friends. I wasn't doing it deliberately. I just like people. I try to understand where others are coming from, and I don't expect them to agree with me. I do expect them to punish me for breaking their rules, so that never becomes an obstacle between us. In fact, it becomes a point of contact. People keep asking me why I can't just go along with the system, and their questions lead to many significant conversations. The women's building officers would sometimes wander by to visit me, especially when I was locked down, simply to talk. Anything relational always made my day.

I was a little concerned over the obvious power that my imperviousness to threats gave me. Of course, the only power for good is God. Our responsibility is to stand in such surrender and obedience to God that we become clear channels for the power of God's love to act through us. But we must never forget that the power is God's. If we claim any of it as ours or try to use it ourselves, we shut God out and turn the power away from God's good purposes. So I prayed to stay surrendered. At first, I was surprised that new kinds of confrontations seemed to come up every time I returned to the jail, but, considering how different my values are from those of the system and how value-laden all my choices are, conflicts were probably inevitable. By the time my trial date arrived, I was in an observation cell, being punished with both lockdown and loss of privileges.

My case had been assigned to a different judge, who automatically gave me a jury trial. I don't offer a legal "defense," but I spoke in closing about the idolatry of our trust in weapons. The verdict was "guilty." The sentence was a $500 fine, suspended on the condition that I not be arrested within six months. There was no reference to my contempt of court in refusing to appear for the hearing before the magistrate. I was released. The sudden lightness of everything made me feel as if I were walking on air.

——— ✖ ———

Lent had become an important season for me. I love its anticipation of Easter. I had found helpful and centering ways to fast, such as eating one meal a day, during Lent at Sojourners. This year, it came to me that the most meaningful Lenten discipline would be a weekday prayer vigil at Rocky Flats.

I chose the east gate, because I could get to within about four miles of it by local public bus for 35 cents each way. (I was living almost without money, and weighed every expense carefully.) I chose the hour of the afternoon shift change, with some quiet time preceding it. I would leave Denver right after lunch, change buses in Arvada, walk the four miles, partly along roads and partly across empty pasture land, stand vigil at the gate for two or more hours, greeting the homebound workers during the shift change, and then reverse the process, arriving home around 7:30. I ate a sandwich supper while waiting for the bus.

It certainly was meaningful—and a serious discipline. It was an ordeal in more ways than one. I valued the out-of-doors and the exercise, and grew very fond of the pasture path, but central Colorado is still cold at that season, and Rocky Flats is noted for very high winds. Heavy snow might make me skip the shortcut through the fields, and the extra mile or so by road seemed interminable. Sometimes it would take all my physical energy and endurance to make the trip, leaving me exhausted by evening. I refused to miss a day.

The presence at Rocky Flats was even worse. I faced there all the emotional pain of our willingness to maim and poison and murder and annihilate one another. The plant became a massive symbol for me of the evil in the human heart. I know that there is no such thing as an evil person. Good and evil are within all of us. But whatever evil is in any heart crucifies Christ and thwarts God's loving purposes for humankind.

The enormity of the evil intention that's incarnated in nuclear weapons is almost beyond my comprehension. I felt the pain so intensely at times that I could hardly bear it. We hurt one another so much! We hurt God so much! We do it in so many ongoing, unthinking, institutionalized, daily ways! I stood there in the presence of evil and let in the pain. The wellspring of intercession. I prayed.

One momentous day, God lifted me from the danger of drowning in the pain. From the east gate, you look across the plant to the mountains. And it hit me, "Even God's *mountains* are bigger than this bomb factory!" God, of course, is a great deal bigger than that. Love is always bigger than evil, always big enough to embrace it, and even to transform it into love. That is the way of God's working in the world.

—— ✗ ——

I'm not entirely certain of my Easter morning motives. I had an agenda, and I'm afraid that I may have let some planning creep in ahead of God's leading. I wanted to worship on the Rocky Flats property, to celebrate a sunrise service that wouldn't be interrupted, and that part was all right. It's easy enough to do. There's a lot of property. I was given a ride, before dawn, to the north side of the plant, where there aren't any access roads. I walked in from the highway a short distance through the fields and sat down to pray.

It was snowing when I arrived, and there wasn't a ghost of a sunrise, because heavy fog had settled around me as I prayed–though that was all right, too. The sunrise is merely a symbol. I eventually guessed that it must have happened and brought my prayer to a close. Perhaps I should have turned at that point and walked back off the property.

But I wanted to see the security fence. I never ordinarily got a chance to walk that far. I had vague wonderings about whether it might be possible to walk all the way in from the public road and climb the fence without being spotted and stopped on the way. I wasn't planning to climb the fence. I just wanted to see. I was planning to walk on around to the west access road and out to Highway 93. I didn't expect to get that far unchallenged. But I was prepared to leave when asked to leave.

My expectation of challenge increased as the fog lifted and I discovered that I was on high, open ground in full view of the plant. The walking was easy, not broken with steep drainages the way much of that countryside is. I walked and walked, increasingly surprised at being still undetected, especially since Rocky Flats security people were getting to know me well enough that I could predict that they had been waiting for me, probably since dawn. I reached the security fence, which is bordered on that side by a road. If I had wanted to climb it, I had the opportunity. But I was ready to leave, and turned westward.

A security car appeared on the road ahead of me, and things started happening very quickly.

"Do you have any identification?"

"No."

"You must have come cross-country."

"Yes. And I'd like to keep on going."

"This is as far as you're going to go. In about two minutes, there'll be seven cars here."

A second car arrived. I recognized one of the guards. A third. The fourth brought two men I knew, who were higher-ranking security people and deputized as U.S. marshals so that they could make arrests. We saw quite a bit of each other. Not only did we have time for conversation at Rocky Flats and on the long drive to the Denver jail, they would return at my trial to testify against me. One in particular I considered a friend by now, and I greeted him.

But he was angry–angry, I found out later, because he *had* been waiting for me since dawn and was frustrated by my apparent elusiveness.

"Jennifer, I'm getting tired of this. I'm placing you under arrest. Put your hands behind your back."

Someone else cuffed me while he read me my Miranda rights (your right to remain silent, your right to a lawyer). I guess I wasn't walking off the property after all.

After the photographs and the pat search, he put me in the passenger seat of his car and took his own seat to fill out forms.

"You know, Jennifer," he remarked, his usual good humor resurfacing, "I had a dream about you last night. I dreamt you walked away, and I didn't have to arrest you."

"You know, I would have."

"Why didn't you?"

"You didn't give me a chance."

"Not this far in."

But I wondered, in the gruffness of his reply, if there weren't some regret that he hadn't given me a chance.

That was the only time that I was ever prepared to leave the Rocky Flats property when asked to leave, and it was the only time that I wasn't given at least three opportunities to do so. Interesting.

The marshals held me in the Weld County Jail, one of quite a few local jails that they used for detention of defendants in the U.S. district court in Denver. Though I cooperate with everything I can, I quickly discovered that this jail's regimen of requiring prisoners to stand at our cell doors for "face count" violated my sense of personhood. I was locked down for refusing. After some number of days of punishment time in isolation, I was released, and promptly refused to stand for "face count" again. The punishment time was doubled. Jail staff kept trying to talk me out of it. They were flabbergasted by the amount of punishment I was willing to endure for something that seemed to them so small. Of course, the consequences are always irrelevant to my choices, since my one goal is to be as faithful to God and to my own integrity as possible, so it was far from small for me. And I could see that it was precisely my acceptance of suffering that became the foundation for my strength.

I was also beginning to glimpse how God was using my willingness to suffer as a spiritual challenge to those whose job it was to punish me. Most of them didn't want to. In general, they liked me. They were caught between their own compassion and the demands of their job. That pushed them to ask themselves questions about their values and priorities. I didn't ask the questions, and I didn't see the answers. But I saw bits of the struggle, and I know that that's the way to growth for all of us.

At the same time, there were perspectives from which I was not particularly suffering. I was meeting God in the circumstances of my life (strange and unreal though they often appeared to me), attending to my work, which is prayer, and doing my own learning and growing. One of the great advantages of a prayer vocation is that *no* external circumstances can interrupt it. My deepest pain lay in seeing how my choices kept increasing my physical separation from people who cared about me, which tends to be harder on the others than on me, since I feel profound closeness with loved ones in prayer.

I was tried before the judge who had sent me to prison, again on the less serious trespassing charge. She declared me "guilty." No reference was made to my violation of the condition of my previous sentence. The new sentence was a fine that was suspended without conditions (equivalent to "time served").

The sentences were getting lighter and lighter!

—— ✄ ——

Now I really had to come to grips with the question of how best to enable and express my prayer vocation in a lifestyle. Where was I supposed to be living, and how was I supposed to be structuring my daily routine? I had pulled back from working at the hospitality house but was still trying variations on the theme of living there and being personally present to individuals. I had tried some time away in an apartment during Lent. I had given the question a lot of thought in jail. Answers eluded me.

I did feel clear that prayer had to remain in the center of my attention, so that an independent lifestyle in which I supported myself and prayed on the side didn't seem to be an option. Being a beggar was terribly uncomfortable to my independent personality, but I could see with increasing clarity not only that it was appropriate to my vocation but also that it was good for me spiritually, humbling my pride and emphasizing my interconnectedness with the human family. The folks at the Catholic Worker house kept encouraging me to see my spirituality—including both my hidden prayer and my witness at Rocky Flats—as a complete and sufficient contribution to its life. That was appropriate to my vocation as well, but it was very hard for me to accept, mostly because I'm so aware of my inadequacy, especially in prayer, that it never feels as if I'm contributing enough.

I decided to allow myself some personal retreat space in the hope that direction would emerge. The apartment that I had borrowed earlier, an inexpensive one near the Worker, was available. The $1,000 had arrived with perfect timing to give me the freedom to pay rent for a little while—putting the rest of the money in the Worker house account. I moved in, tried to yield myself to the "uselessness" of prayer, and listened for God's will for me.

A month stretched to two, and I still felt muddled. Maybe I needed an even more radical retreat, more separated from the ordinary agenda and distractions of my life, more fully immersed in God and what God might be trying to show me. A friend had suggested St. Benedict's Monastery in the Colorado mountains—a contemplative community of the same order to which Thomas Merton belonged—so I wrote to ask if they had room in their guest facilities for the fall. No, they were booked up. It might be possible to camp on monastery land. I wrote back to ask about things like drinking water and toilets. There was nothing. It would be totally primitive. I had no experience of primitive camping, but the emerging sense that the monastery was right for me refused to be discouraged. I would go.

I collected equipment. I borrowed tents, one for me and a separate one for food. I bought containers for drinking water. I planned and assembled an extraordinarily simple diet that would last a month without refrigeration or cooking (mostly granola, dried milk, and fruit). Friends drove me to St. Benedict's in early September.

The monks were wonderfully hospitable. The bit of land they offered me was splendid, a flat, grassy area among trees beside a dancing stream, far enough off the road for privacy and two miles or so from the monastery buildings. I set up camp and dug a latrine.

Simplicity inspired all my choices. My discipline was to walk to the monastery twice a day for services—lauds and Mass in the morning and vespers in the evening—and to do almost nothing else: no reading except the Bible, no writing except for limited journaling (setting aside correspondence is a major discipline for me in itself), no activities except for walking and a bare minimum of survival tasks. I ate two cold meals a day. I never lit a fire. I bathed every fourth or fifth day in stream water that I had warmed in the sun. I kept warm through nights that dropped far below freezing by snuggling into my sleeping bag as soon as I got back to camp from vespers, and walking to the monastery as soon as I got up in the morning.

I found myself absolutely glorying in every bit of it. I fell in love with the monastic worship—slow and centered and deeply reverent—recognizing immediately my own home in it. I was touched in new ways by the symbolism and ritual of the Catholic Mass.

I already knew that I was in love with nature, and I basked in it practically every available minute. I would sit by the stream for hours, watching and listening to the singing water. I would take long hikes up into the mountains, along the road, along the stream, on footpaths, and through unbroken country, exploring and just breathing it all in. I climbed all the ridges around the monastery, and would sit on high outcroppings of rock absorbing the view. The valley commands breathtaking vistas, including some of Colorado's 14,000-foot peaks. I marveled to watch the seasons change from late summer, through a panorama of fall color, into intimations of winter with heavy frost and one light snow. Brilliant stars greeted my morning walk to Mass.

I avoided conversation as much as possible and praised the Lord for the isolation of my hermitage, which gave me more solitude than the guest houses and enfolded me in the quiet peace of nature. What unexpected blessing!

I became so quiet myself, so empty, so open that I was truly drawn into the heart of God more deeply than ever before. And God gifted me with three indescribable mystical experiences, that I'm going to try to describe anyway.

One was my baptism. What can I say? I knew that that's what it was. I had never received a church baptism, because Quakers believe that sacraments are spiritual experiences between the believer and God that need no outward form. This was the spiritual experience, beyond a doubt. On October 1, the feast of St. Thérèse of the Child Jesus, I was walking to lauds, walking toward the morning star hanging low over the mountain ridge behind the monastery, walking toward the gradually approaching dawn. And something broke open inside me. I wrote in my journal (referring not to a vision or an external presence, but to an inner, spiritual awareness):

And the Lord met me on the road to Mass, and I knelt in the dust and received his baptism—his death and resurrection—"it is no longer I who live, but Christ who lives in me" [Galatians 2:20]—and I stand rooted to the spot, worshiping, while day breaks—and I want to sing a new song to the Lord, my own song, and, behold, the Lord has already given it to me— "It Is the Advent of Our Lord" . . . —my mind has been full of Advent lately, and yesterday I spent time with Luke 2: "the time came for her to be delivered. And she gave birth to her first-born son and wrapped him in swaddling cloths, and laid him in a manger" [Luke 2:6-7]—the manger of my heart—my tears flow—God is so wonderfully good to me. . . . And, would you believe, Mass turns out to be a baptismal service!

The second encounter was so awesome that I didn't even attempt to write about it at the time. I was walking back from vespers, through the lingering glory of sunset and the gathering dusk. I was trying to practice simple Buddhist mindfulness—being present where you are—attending to each blade of grass and maturing seedpod along the road as I passed. Suddenly, it was as if the veil between material and spiritual reality were growing thin, dissolving, and about to part like mist, and I knew that in a moment I'd be standing face to face with God in the field to my left–not an anthropomorphic presence, but sort of an intensity of being. The intensity and the overwhelmingness were so great that I must somehow have stepped back within myself, afraid of being lost in the encounter (I *would* have been lost, which is precisely the purpose of prayer, but our ego so clings to an ego-controlled image of self that it resists the surrender to God in which the ego disappears and the true self, the self created in the image of God, is liberated)–and the moment of opportunity was gone. That one really rocked me. I was used to knowing God through God's actions. The possibility of meeting God directly is truly as overwhelming as scripture suggests. I'm sorry that I wasn't equal to the opportunity.

The third experience was extraordinarily gentle. I was lying in the grass, gazing up at sun-dappled leaves against the sky, caressed by every detail of the beauty and luxuriating in the stillness and freedom from demands (my own demands of myself are the tyrant in my life), when I began to be aware, ever so lightly, of God's enspiriting presence sustaining me. What I think I remember is more than I recorded at the time: a tangible sense of God's love for me, never before experienced, like a taste so subtle and so unobtrusive that only great emptiness notices it. Its message was: "You're okay." I *felt* okay, acceptable, deserving of the gentleness and generosity that God so freely offers me and that I so rarely offer myself. I received the gift gratefully.

That retreat touched my life in such deep ways that it seems superficial to add that God also answered my specific questions. My vocation to the hermit's life, the life of solitary prayer, was affirmed within me. And my calling to the city, to prayer in the midst of the world, was vividly reconfirmed. City life is not my personal choice, and I harbor a little fantasy that I might be permitted sometime to live my vocation in an isolated hermitage by a wilderness mountain stream. Of course, the fantasy leapt to life in the place of my retreat, and every time I happened upon an old log cabin or a sheepherder's hut in the course of my wanderings, I wove it in: "Wouldn't *this* be a great place, God?" No. It would be a cop-out and barren. God's will for me to return to the city was utterly clear and directive. I *knew* it one evening after vespers and *saw* it in meditation the next morning before Mass:

> *I was there with all the poor of the city, people I know and people I don't know, events I remember and events I imagine, loving them, praying for them, feeling truly at home the way I did on my block in [Washington] DC. I came out of it struck with the realization that I seek the face of God, and these are the faces God shows me–the face of God for me.*

How to live that inner-city prayer ministry was shown to me as well. Another retreatant catalyzed the vision for me: "Why don't you start a contemplative house for the Worker?" Flashbulbs went off in me. Every-thing suddenly fell into place in my mind. I would open a house of prayer, where I could live a monastic lifestyle, hopefully in community with oth-ers who might be drawn to join me, in the inner-city neighborhood of the Catholic Worker, which would offer retreat and worship space to busy people whose callings immersed them in active, social ministries. It was perfect. I set to work on it as soon as I returned to Denver.

I found a three-bedroom house to rent a few blocks from the Worker house. I received from Catholic religious orders small grants to get me started on rent and incidental expenses. Furniture was donated. I set up worship space, rooms for retreatants, and a monastic daily schedule for myself. Folks from the Worker prayed lauds with me most mornings, and I prayed midday prayer and vespers. I arranged for a priest to say Mass once a week.

At first, I thought that I should find part-time, income-earning work to contribute at least partially to the house's support. I had lots of time. I didn't have to be praying every minute. So I figured out the ideal job for my talents, interests, and schedule (afternoon preschool teaching), looked for it, found it (one that exactly fit in every respect and was Christian to boot), was offered it, and *then*–holding the concrete reality in my hand–*knew* that it wasn't for me. The "perfect" regular job wasn't for me, be-cause I *was* supposed to be praying all the time. There was no "comple-ment" to my prayer.

Praying full-time is incredibly difficult. I never really manage it. But I give myself to it as best I can. I find that I do the most growing in prayer when my circumstances give me more quiet, empty space than I want. I try to cooperate. The house of prayer felt natural and right for me. I liked the monastic schedule. I moved slowly, trying to be present to each mo-ment.

Earlier in the year, I had been blessed to find a new spiritual director. I had been hungry for direction for a long time, but I never know how to *look* for it. It requires a very particular relationship with a person whose journey is somehow similar to yours and who is in some sense ahead of you on the path, and all I know is that I can recognize the right person for me when he or she comes along. The right person was a Vincentian priest who had chosen to live in our neighborhood because his heart was with the poor. In the spring of 1983 he moved into the Catholic Worker house. He became part of the life of the house of prayer. And he gave me two insights about my spiritual journey that I'll never forget.

One had to do with the tension in me between action and contempla-tion. I felt very clearly called to the hermit's life of solitary prayer. At the same time, I felt unmistakably called not only to the city but also to wit-ness at Rocky Flats, which was a very public and social presence. I longed to resolve the tension, to get beyond feeling pulled in two directions at once.

Ted said, "I think it's your vocation to live in the tension." I knew instantly–sadly–that he was right. I would never be granted a resolution. It is precisely my work to hold together the polarities in my very being. And other polarities, too. Intercession is a bridge between heaven and earth that is possible only because the intercessor is stretched to live in both places. Even the basic, universal calling to follow God is a bridge: holding together our own erring nature with God's perfect grace.

The other insight related to letting go of my identity. Since 1973 I had been working deliberately at letting go of everything I was aware of being attached to, engaging deeper and deeper issues, until I had reached this very intimate place. Now I was discovering–even as I tried hard to be willing–how very threatened I felt. If I let go of my identity, who would I be? I shared my struggle with Ted, explaining, "The deepest layers of my identity that I'm aware of are of myself as a person of prayer and, below that, as one who loves. Below that, there is nothing."

He answered, "When you get down to nothing, then you will be face to face with God."

3

Disarmament

I walked all over Denver during these early years, getting my exercise and occasionally making a useful discovery along the way. The walk to the river across the Broadway viaduct, over the railroad switching yard, took me through a warehouse district where a produce wholesaler and a floral wholesaler faced each other across the street. Their dumpsters were gold mines. I would stop for fruit and vegetables and sometimes come home with an armload of flowers as well. One Sunday afternoon in early January, 1984, I found such a wealth of flowers that I shared them with everyone at Rocky Flats, including the security guards. I stepped over the little "barrier" to present my gift and then stepped back.

My great freedom to cross that line made me wonder: How am I ever going to stay out of Rocky Flats for three more months?

Yes, I felt right about the house of prayer, and I had made a commitment there through the first quarter of 1984. But Rocky Flats still drew me. I could easily walk in at any time. In fact, I felt so open to it internally that I suspected God of having provided external restraints in order to keep me from acting precipitously. Of course, I wanted to do what God wanted of me. It looked as if the safest discernment for me with respect to civil disobedience was to hold back from it for as long as I could. If I didn't do it until I couldn't *not* do it any longer, then I could be sure that it was an expression of God's will for me.

Corporate process contributed to my discernment again. The year 1983 had turned out to be one of civil disobedience at Rocky Flats. Almost every month, without any overall coordination, an individual or small group had crossed the property line in one way or another. I had been present for many support vigils and had attended many court sessions.

Now, at a mid-January meeting, our Sunday afternoon prayer group was suddenly beginning to talk about carrying our regular corporate worship onto the property together. There was much spontaneous excitement about the idea, which seemed very right to me, and I could hardly imagine not participating. So when we set the date for Palm Sunday, April 15 this year, I knew that I could stay out of Rocky Flats at least until then.

I was reevaluating the house of prayer. Qualitatively, it fully enfleshed the vision that had been given to me on retreat, but quantitatively, the scale was wrong. Only a few people used it regularly for either worship or retreat. No one had joined me in monastic community. The house was too large, under the circumstances, and too expensive. I had never intended to have so much space primarily for my own use, nor would the Rocky Flats portion of my calling permit me to be tied down indefinitely to a responsibility that rested on me alone and required my daily, physical presence.

The approaching Palm Sunday witness seemed to offer a natural point of transition. I decided to close the house at the end of March, trusting that it had somehow served its purpose. As usual, it wasn't until later that I found out where it had been leading. Experience of the house of prayer had emphasized for folks at the Catholic Worker house the value of that kind of quiet refuge. They could afford to rent the cheap apartment I had used the previous year and re-create there a worship and retreat space on an appropriately reduced scale.

Meanwhile, Ash Wednesday saw me beginning a weekday vigil at Rocky Flats again. I moved to the west gate, primarily for the continuity of presence there with the Sunday vigil. It was more expensive, since I had to use a regional bus that cost three times as much as the local, but I was learning to ask for help with my specific needs, and I gradually came to appreciate that people who could more readily give money than time were pleased to be able to participate in my witness by contributing to its cost. The walk from the bus stop was shorter now, less than two miles. The time at the Flats was somewhat shortened, too, circumscribed by the bus schedule.

But my prayer was vastly expanded. All I knew at first was that I somehow met God at Rocky Flats in a particularly powerful way. I was awed by God's majesty as never before, and poured out my soul in worship. And that worship overflowed into love and yearning, heartfelt prayer for every human being in the vicinity, which meant primarily the workers in the plant. I prayed for them as for any of my friends, for God's blessing and presence and guidance in their lives. I didn't pray for the closing of the bomb factory, but I'm also convinced that it's precisely when we come to know God deeply and intimately that we choose to lay down all our weapons.

I thought, perhaps, that my prayer there had become so profound simply because I was supposed to be praying there—which may have been part of the reason. Our obedience does open us up in ever new ways to God. The other part, though, has been revealed to me gradually. It had been through facing all the pain of the year before, facing the reality of so mammoth an evil that it threatened to inundate me, and then recognizing how much bigger God is than all of it, that my understanding of the greatness of God had grown. The God whom I knew to be sovereign in a place of that much darkness is a God of awesome greatness indeed. My spirit fell to its knees in homage.

Through that growth in my awareness of God, without my noticing it happening, Rocky Flats was becoming for me a place of real and tangible hope.

I was also making friends. It was easy to meet the security people. They regularly monitored my presence at the gate and occasionally came over to talk with me. The departing workers were hampered by having to attend to driving in heavy traffic, but I smiled at everyone and waved to all who waved. I came to recognize those who were regularly supportive and thought of them as friends even if we didn't talk. Every now and then, someone would go to the trouble of parking and walking over to me for some real conversation. I treasured those interactions. Sometimes passers-by on the state highway would do the same. Of course, there were negative responses as well, but I smiled and waved at those people, too, and I tended to hear less and less from them.

The really golden opportunity for relationship was presented by my walk from the gate back to the bus stop. I was often offered rides, especially in difficult weather, either by workers departing late or by others driving by. Almost all of them had seen me standing vigil at the plant. Some were particularly interested to talk with me, and others were simply being kind. I appreciated both motives and accepted rides on principle, though I had no objection to walking. I was glad to become acquainted with people on their own terms, never asking workers about their work, and finding that I encountered a broad spectrum of opinion on many subjects.

Some of those relationships grew into enduring friendships. Eventually, that spring, one worker was picking me up practically every day. She would drive out at close to the end of the shift change and invite me to leave my vigil post to ride with her. She drove me all the way to Denver, to within a few miles of my neighborhood, on her way to her home in another part of town. We talked and talked—about our personal histories and daily lives, about struggles and questions, and especially about spirituality.

We started visiting in one another's homes and meeting one another's family and friends. We corresponded during my next prison sentence and went camping together the summer after I was released. We're still friends, though she has since left Rocky Flats and moved out of town. At one point, plant security berated her for picking me up, and she was incensed: how *dare* they try to tell her with whom she could associate on her own time and away from work! The bond of humanness is no small thing.

I had already discovered that when you choose to receive everyone as a friend, you live in a world without enemies. One day it hit me like a bolt from the blue that this business of making friends with everybody, especially with people who might not expect it (which comes naturally, without goal or design, to me) *is*, in itself, disarmament–the disarmament of the heart, on which rests the cessation of all hostilities. Disarmament is the ongoing work of my daily life!

— ✄ —

Our Palm Sunday service was scheduled to begin at an earlier hour than the regular Sunday vigil, because it was important to some of our group to arrive before the gates had been closed across the access road. Al, Anna, Bill, Marge, Peter, Shirley, and I walked through the open gates onto the traffic island on the Rocky Flats side of the fence and formed an unbroken circle with the large crowd of fellow worshipers on the state highway side. All of us sang and prayed together. We had planned a more structured worship service than usual and had agreed that we would be ready to leave at its conclusion. But Rocky Flats security people were not interested in waiting. We seven were drawn out of the circle and arrested.

In the morning, we appeared before the magistrate. We were all familiar with such proceedings. Having recognized ahead of time significant differences among us in our principled responses to the legal system, we had decided to affirm the differences, allowing each one to respond as he or she felt led. That freedom gave us more solidarity than I think any uniform group discipline could have created.

Most of our group were prepared to accept a bond because of commitments in the community, including the hospitality house and the soup kitchen, which would become a serious burden on others if they had to spend much time in jail. We expected to be offered personal recognizance bonds, which would be quite routine in such a case, and even more likely since any of us who had in the past made promises to return to court had kept them.

So it was a shock to hear the magistrate set a $500 cash bond for each of us. I would have refused bond in any case, and Al refused to put up cash. The others felt that, in order to honor their commitments, they would have to find or borrow the money. Since its purpose is to ensure one's appearance in court, bond money is returned at the conclusion of the case and thus represents a different level of involvement in the system from paying a fine (to the government, as punishment–which most of us were unwilling to do, since we believe the *government* to be in the wrong at Rocky Flats) or restitution (to the "victim"–in our case, Rocky Flats itself, which would have been unthinkable to all seven of us).

While the other five were given time to make phone calls and arrange for bond money to be brought to the court, Al and I were transported with some other prisoners to the Larimer County Jail in Fort Collins. One of our warders was the Rocky Flats security person who had arrested me the previous Easter. I reflected on the friendship that was gently growing between us under the surface of our official interactions: even if we remained always on opposite sides of the fence, we respected and even liked each other. And that makes the fence sort of melt away. The lines become blurred. The fence begins to make less sense than the friendship. How many times can you arrest and handcuff and testify against your friend? What you're defending becomes of less value than whom you're defending it against. Maybe eventually you discover that it isn't worth defending, because the concepts it rests on lose all their reality in the face of relationships, of being loved in spite of everything, of being respected exactly as you are.

Al and I were still waiting for processing in the receiving area of the jail when who should suddenly appear at the door, in the custody of the marshals, but our five co-defendants! What had happened?

Each of them had been able to arrange for someone to bring $500 to the court to post as bond. They had been called from the holding cell back into the magistrate's courtroom to complete the formal agreements and paperwork, and were signing the papers when—in response to a warning by the magistrate that bond money could be applied to the payment of fines—Anna asked a clarifying question: "Do you mean to say that if we're found guilty, the money that's been put up for our bonds could be used against us to pay our fines?"

The magistrate apparently lost his temper, withdrew all the bond agreements, declaring, "These people don't want to put up bonds!" and ordered everybody jailed.

Processing took a long time, especially for me, because I was locked in a solitary cell for some hours for refusing something or other. After everyone else had been taken upstairs, the officers finally returned to me. Every jail presents slightly different challenges, and here one challenge was a new kind of form. It was a medical authorization, giving the jail permission to make medical decisions on your behalf. It was routine. Everybody signed it. But I made a conscious decision about anything I was asked to sign for the system, and I could not sign this. No way was I willing to delegate such authority to the jail.

My refusal to sign the form meant that I was not *allowed* any medical treatment, not even anything from the nurse's cart, including dental floss and vitamins, or anything ordered through the medical department, including a vegetarian diet. How ironic!—to have a vegetarian diet actually available (in Denver County Jail I refused the meat, did without protein at most meals other than breakfast, and lost weight) and still have to do without! But I accepted the situation. I try to embrace the consequences of my choices, to be content with whatever I may have to endure, trusting God's guidance for the choices and God's grace for all that follows.

Overall, the jail was very new, relatively small and uncrowded, and more livable than any other I'd encountered. We four women were housed in a unit with eight single cells opening onto a common area. Since there was no one else in the unit, we could keep the television turned off (liberation!), and we enjoyed our two days together. Then the five who had intended to post bond were called back into court. The magistrate presented the bond papers again, stipulated that the bond money would *not* be forfeited in the event that fines were ordered, and completed the procedure. They were released.

I was moved by the jail into the other women's living unit–and was almost immediately called on my refusal to lock my cell door. The doors closed manually, locked upon closing, and were opened by an officer electronically. We were expected to lock ourselves into our cells several times every day. I was willing to be in the cell at the required times but was clear from the beginning that I would not lock a cell door against anyone, including myself. I was charged with a rule infraction and moved again, to a small maximum-security area, which turned out to be blissfully quiet, since I was the only one in it.

I was in a tender, receptive inner place, feeling very vulnerable without being fragile, very clear without being strong, very open without being insecure. Something about the emptiness and detachment of my environment lifted up my prayer vocation out of everything else in my life and drew me into it. I was absolutely immersed in God, and actually aware of it rather often.

On Easter morning I awoke to a world transformed into wonderland by six or eight inches of snow–and the memory of this dream:

> *I was hurrying to try to get on a plane, up a long escalator, and then suddenly the walkway had turned sharply, and I had stepped off the edge of it. I was unsupported, maybe two stories up over a hard floor, and not close enough to catch the railing in front of me. There was nothing I could do. I knew that the fall was long enough to hurt me seriously. I screamed, and I fell. (In nightmares of my childhood, such a fall would plunge me into the oblivion of wakefulness.) But I decided on the way that I needn't choose to expect to be hurt. I could land deliberately, carefully, on my feet, in a way that would break the impact. And that choice was somehow like invoking a miracle. The headlong, out-of-control rush slowed, was transformed near its end to a gentle, dance-like floating to rest. I stepped onto the floor and kept walking.*

---- ✄ ----

Two days later, Al and I were called out for court. Our friends must have had some notice of the hearing, for they were waiting for us in the spectators' section. It turned out to be our arraignment. We responded to the charges–I don't plead, which the magistrate records as "not guilty"–heard the "speedy trial" dates and the name of the judge to whom the case was assigned, and reiterated our non-interest in a lawyer. The magistrate then asked if we'd be willing to sign unsecured signature bonds, to which

Al answered, "Yes," and I, "No." He listened to my reasons for refusing, accepted our statements that the marshals had addresses for us, and announced, "All right then, I am ordering that you both be released. You will be notified by certified mail of your next court date. You are free to go."

My mouth dropped so far, figuratively speaking, that I practically had to pick it up off the floor. This was the magistrate who *knew* (at least, if his own past experience was any indication) that I would *not* return to court. And still he was releasing me!

Of course, there were practical considerations. He also knew that I wouldn't run, and it was really just as easy–and a great deal cheaper–for the marshals to pick me up at home as for the government to keep me incarcerated.

There was, additionally, a price demanded of me. My refusal to return put me in contempt of court, for which I could be punished independently of the original charge, so the unexpected release increased the seriousness of the potential consequences. But consequences are never my concern– and of no significance compared to my delight in watching the magistrate again transcend the legal requirements of his role to make a choice that reflected more personal understanding–even if not relationality or caring. He was, at least, acting as a human being rather than as a functionary of a machine.

Reunited with our friends, we all trooped downstairs to the courtroom that is used for defendants not in custody, where the other five had been scheduled for arraignment before the same magistrate. At the close of the routine formalities, Shirley requested, since Al and I had been released without bond, that the bond for the rest of them be reduced to personal recognizance and their money returned.

The magistrate answered, "You should know that bond is an individual matter, up to the discretion of the court. There is no requirement that it be equal. Bond will be continued in the amount of $500 each."

Now this was really too much! Had he heard what he'd just said? Bond is, indeed, an individual matter, but it's *supposed* to be related to the making of court appearances. His choices were backwards! He was imposing extra conditions on those who could be relied upon to return to court anyway and, effectively, *rewarding* me for my refusal to abide by *any* conditions.

Our case had been assigned to the judge who had already seen me three times. She set a status conference for May 14, at which my six codefendants appeared. She issued a warrant for my arrest.

I lived for almost a week in suspended animation, as it were, trying to ignore the existence of the court and yet knowing that every unrestricted step I took might be my last for a significant period of time. On Sunday, I returned from church to the news that the marshals had been looking for me, had, in fact, stopped by the Worker house twice. I was actually staying at the apartment then, but I didn't want to complicate their job unnecessarily or to give the impression of evasiveness, so I spent the afternoon hanging out at the house.

At about dinnertime, a marshal whom I knew came to the door, accompanied by a city policewoman. With uncommon scrupulousness regarding a female prisoner, he asked her to handcuff me and drive me the short distance to the city jail in her patrol car. On the way, she expressed admiration for what she knew of the Worker, and our conversation grew quickly warm and amiable. When something brought up her skin allergy to direct sun, I was sympathetic. By the time we got out in the basement of the jail, the internal conflict between role and relationship had clearly become too much for her. She apologized for delivering me to jail. I was deeply touched, but at a loss for a response. I think I sort of smiled and shrugged as I walked on into captivity. Next time, I decided, maybe I could say, "I understand."

In the morning, I stood before the judge. She was willing to consider releasing me until the trial, if she could be assured that I would appear for it. Of course, I had written to her to explain my position with respect to court orders. I had said that I expected to come to the trial, because of my commitment to my co-defendants (the trial couldn't proceed without me, so a nonappearance there would create a huge hassle for everybody), but that I wasn't otherwise willing voluntarily to come to court. I repeated my explanations in person, concluding, "So all I could say is that my expectation would be that I would come, but something could intervene; so I'm not willing to promise that I'll come."

She decided "that we should accept the statement that it is her present anticipation that she will be present with the other defendants, although she is unwilling to make a promise." The prosecutor did not object. The judge ordered me released, advising me, "The date is June 6, 9 A.M. The other parties will be here, and I hope that you will find your way here."

Will wonders never cease? *This* release was truly caring and relational—not that it was based on personal friendship, but that it *did* have my best interests at heart—and it was also entirely appropriate with respect to the legal system's practical goal of ensuring my appearance in court. I would move mountains to get to that trial now. I couldn't promise, because of not being in control of my future, but everything in me *wanted* to affirm the judge's values and concern. It's not surprising that the fulfillment of that desire was within God's will for me.

The trial itself was not easy for me. When your choice is to be silent and the choice of others is to speak, then what is spoken sets the tone of the proceedings, and it was not always the tone that I would have chosen. But I had had other opportunities to be myself in that setting. Both the judge and the witnesses from Rocky Flats knew me. I didn't have to prove anything. I respected the freedom of my co-defendants to express themselves in their own ways.

The judge had a point to make as well. It was obvious to me that her overriding concern was the prevention of illegal behavior. Her sentencing lectures repeatedly underscored it, and I interpreted her sentences themselves as successive attempts to gain my compliance. Alternatively, she now suggested that Rocky Flats might adjust *its* behavior toward the same end. Following the testimony of Rockwell International's security chief at Rocky Flats, she asked him:

The Court:　Could I just inquire whether . . . permission is ever given to a group who wishes to hold a short prayer service on the grounds of Rocky Flats, if you know.

The Witness:　Your Honor, I don't believe there has ever been permission to hold a prayer service. There have been in the past situations where demonstrations have been held on the Government property and permission has been granted for that.

The Court:　If someone wanted to hold a prayer service for half an hour, would you be the one that they would contact to do so, to get permission?

The Witness:　Either myself or the Department of Energy; and our answer to that would probably be no, for that's not official business on the property.

The Court:　Although you say you've allowed a demonstration on the property.

The Witness:　That's correct. In 1979 was one major one.

The Court:　Was that official business?

The Witness:　They went through a formal procedure with the United States Government to allow permission to come onto the property to profess their views at that time, and that was granted by the Government, with certain stipulations.

. . . .

The Court:　And if they made those arrangements as to date and place and so forth, then there would be no problem with their holding a prayer service?

The Witness:　If the Government authorized it, yes, as owners of the property.

The Court:　You had answered to [Peter] that he did request permission from you and you turned him down.

The Witness:　That is correct. I did that in concert with the Department of Energy.

. . . .

The Court: You know, as a judge whose time is needed on a lot of real criminal cases, has there been any consideration by your office to resolving this desire by a small group such as this to come onto the Flats property to hold their prayer service by considering, perhaps, in certain circumstances, certain times, allowing a prayer meeting?

Her idea was really a very good one, at least for me. I had moved beyond any fantasies about climbing the security fence. I knew now that prayer alone was the whole purpose of my presence at Rocky Flats. I wasn't trying to make any particular statement or to challenge the government to any particular response. I didn't need to escalate my behavior. I *did* need to pray on the property sometimes—specifically in celebration of major religious holidays—because that prayer was even more powerful than prayer at the gate. It was, in itself, a declaration of God's sovereignty over all creation, and especially over this piece of land, which God had created for productivity and on which the U.S. government had no right to trespass for ungodly purposes. It was an affirmation of my trust in the one true security, the only One stronger than nuclear weapons, and in the power of prayer. Those divine realities were so heightened for me by my standing on the very ground of menacing darkness that my prayer was heightened and deepened and empowered as well. I needed to touch God in that way. But I suspected that such passionate prayer would be just as possible for me if my presence on the property were permitted. Rocky Flats presumably didn't see it that way.

The trial concluded with our conviction on the simple trespass charge. A date was set for sentencing. That was a tense moment for me, because I had no intention of returning for sentencing, which I hoped that I had made sufficiently clear to the judge in my letter. In case I hadn't, though, I didn't want to remain at large on the basis of a misunderstanding and would have been relieved, in a way, if she had taken me into custody on the spot. She didn't. She didn't ask about or refer in any way to the issue of my return. We all went home.

The sentencing date was June 25. I had been continuing my weekday vigil at Rocky Flats since my unexpected release by the magistrate in April, and I couldn't imagine a better place to be at the time of sentencing. So I bussed out to the west gate first thing in the morning, with the intention of standing vigil there through the afternoon shift change. I didn't expect to be able to stay that long. I expected to be arrested. But as the day wore on, I wondered. Four o'clock was approaching, and the first early indicators of the heavy traffic soon to come were trickling from the plant. Maybe I would actually complete my vigil in the normal way and return home.

A car driving north on the state highway stopped on the shoulder, and two men walked over to me. High-level security people from Rocky Flats.

"Are you waiting for us?" they asked.

"No. I was looking forward to going home as usual."

I didn't go home as usual. The Rocky Flats people, who had been in town for the sentencing, had been hanging out with the regular marshals, who, they discovered, had a warrant for my arrest. "Oh, we know where she is," they had offered. "Would you like us to pick her up for you?" I spent the night, another of a growing number of such nights, in the city jail.

In the morning, I was sentenced, as each of my co-defendants had been, to a $300 fine, which I would not pay. I had no financial resources at all and could have signed an official declaration that I was a pauper, but I preferred to refuse the fine on the grounds that I would not help the government to punish me for an action that I believed to be right.

The more weighty consideration, under the circumstances, was contempt of court. I had refused to appear twice in the same case, which the judge felt she simply could not ignore. She asked several questions to determine whether there might be some excuse for my absence other than willful defiance of court orders, but there wasn't one. I had intentionally chosen not to appear. She lectured me on the seriousness of the offense. I thought at the time that I could probably be sentenced to up to a year in prison for it (I have never fully understood how the contempt-of-court statute operates), and a newspaper headline claimed that I was facing five years. Serious consequences, in any case. She pronounced me "guilty" and ordered me to serve five *days*.

The marshals returned me to the city jail, apologetic about leaving me in such an awful place for four days more; apparently, the county jails were crowded. I reassured them that I could surely endure *anything* for four days. The sentence was so minimal, so token! It was perfectly understandable that the judge felt she had to punish me; such convincing evidence that she didn't want to was gift.

The icing on the cake was an article about my sentencing that appeared in the [Denver] *Rocky Mountain News* on June 27. According to the reporter:

> "I like Jennifer," [the judge] said in her chamber after the hearing. "She's an educated woman. She's been a school teacher and I like her." After shaking her head for a moment, [she] added, "She sure has her own ideas."

4

Grace

By the summer of 1984 I had been lifted onto a mountaintop. That series of interactions with the court had been an incredible affirmation of the values I live by, of respect and relationship and caring, of the primacy of love and trust and humanness. I feel called to live those values in any case, regardless of what the world chooses or thinks and of what anyone else does or doesn't do in response. They are the heritage of all of us as God's children, created in God's image to do God's will on earth. I believe that the kingdom of God exists insofar as every one of us is converted to it and lives it, so my responsibility is to live it, trusting that God can do more through my obedience than even I know how to evaluate.

In fact, I have no interest in effectiveness, precisely because God is the only one who can determine what is or isn't effective in God's way of working in the world. My job is not to accomplish anything or to change anything. My job is simply to be faithful, leaving everything else to God. Not having goals or agenda is tremendously freeing–freeing for faithful-ness–because you're never tempted to figure out or circumscribe your choices with a view to what you think you might accomplish. And it tends to help you to step out of the way of God's action through you, because you know you're not *doing* anything at all, just being there; so when God acts, you know that it's God who's acting, and you have a marvelous sense of being privileged to stand around watching miracles.

But now I was also seeing others responding in kind: people whose roles were dictated by an entirely different set of assumptions were living the higher values, God's values, ennobling the roles, as it were, by living within them a greatness of spirit that transcended their own assumptions.

That somehow gave me a new kind of hope for the world. I don't gen-erally find evidence for hope in the world. I see in it too much brokenness and evil and suffering. My hope is entirely in God, in spiritual realities that I know to be true without evidence. Yet I'm occasionally gifted with glimpses into God's working in the world, and the reciprocal relationality of my recent court experiences certainly looked like such a glimpse. It said to me that if disarmament–that is, a mutual stepping through barriers to affirm commonality and relate as friends rather than adversaries–is possible one relationship at a time, then universal disarmament, no matter how unlikely it looks, must be possible. What an exciting potential.

The culmination of those experiences came in July when I shared them at the annual gathering of Quakers from my home state. The sharing was graced, and even the fact that I was able physically to be there seemed to be an act of God. But telling the story finalized it for me and somehow closed a door on a chapter of my life. I could not see a thing beyond it. I already was falling off the mountain emotionally, feeling blank and empty and directionless.

Shortly after my return to Denver, the flaw in my process approach to hope in the world landed on me like a heavy fog: There are too many people, always moving on and always being replaced by others. There wasn't any more chance of the values I live by having an impact on the world through individual relationships than through anything else that expresses them. *Then* I realized that I had somehow gotten hooked into an agenda for changing the world. I thought that I had let go of such things long ago, that I was content to live for God without evidence of my life having any effect at all. But it must have "snuck up" on me through all the positive feedback I'd been receiving. I had to let go all over again.

Letting go of false hope plunged me even more starkly into the hopelessness I saw all around me, including within myself. I still clung, without any doubt, to a spiritual hope in God, but I didn't *feel* it. I felt useless and prayerless and bereft of meaning. I looked out on a sick and dying world. Reality is not rose-tinted among the homeless in the inner city, in jail and prison, or at the gates of a nuclear weapons factory. All fall I struggled to find anew my place in the world (or my perception of the world) and in my own vocation.

— �֍ —

I don't remember my thoughts and feelings around the celebration at Rocky Flats on Christmas Day, 1984. I know only that I was ready to listen again for God's leading about prayer on the property. It seemed to be time. A few friends joined me at the west gate on Christmas morning. Our presence drew the usual attention from security guards, who closed the symbolic little gates across the access road and sat watching us from their patrol cars. So, though I had ample time for quiet discernment, my actual prayer on the property turned out to be very brief.

I spent about three days in Denver County Jail before being unexpectedly called back to court. I had appeared before a new magistrate, who seemed to be a genuinely caring person and had been distressed at my refusal of a personal recognizance bond. Now he had decided to release me anyway. He carefully advised me of the penalties for not returning to court, and I acknowledged that I understood. Later, I wrote to him, too, to explain my position and the reasons for my choices. I was delighted to receive a letter from him in response, which reflected both his active Christianity and his personal compassion. Touching a human being behind an impersonal role is always gift.

At the same time, I was well aware of the price that I might have to pay. I was already facing a year in prison for having crossed a "barrier" onto the Rocky Flats property, and the magistrate had assured me that I could receive an additional year for contempt of court.

A hearing before the judge was scheduled for January 10. One of the marshals came looking for me a day early, ostensibly to deliver a court order that changed the hearing time by fifteen minutes. We greeted each other amicably. I accepted the copy of the order. He wanted to know where I was going to be then.

"I go to Mass in the morning."

"Where would that be?"

I declined to specify.

"Where do you go after Mass?"

"I come home for breakfast."

Well, nothing about this arrest was a surprise. Breakfast did not fit into the program. I was whisked off to court within half an hour of the scheduled hearing time. From there, I was transported to the Larimer County Jail.

Larimer County was more crowded than it had been earlier, but it was still the most livable jail I'd experienced. It was light and airy, with long, vertical windows in each cell and large windows at the corners of the common area, looking out over fields and trees. There was an outdoor courtyard, all concrete with high walls, but open to the sun and boasting a ping pong table. The television in the common area was on all day long, but I could get some relief from it by retreating to my cell and closing the door just short of locked.

For no reason that I could identify, my good spirits started bubbling up again. I was happy, even "dancy." I was particularly struck by seeing very ordinary things as beautiful, such as the rough texture of my sheet or a strand of my hair catching rainbows in a sunbeam. Everything was easy. Everything was cause for thanksgiving. It was a special treat to watch hot air balloons rise past my window on weekend mornings. And then–wonder of wonders!–a pair of birds started building a nest in the tree branches below me! I recognized that, without trying or thinking about it at all, I was actually *being* rather than doing. Miracle.

Knowing that I need to be in a spiritual place other than the one I'm in is like standing on the brink of an abyss, looking across at the promised land. I have no idea of how to get there or how to cooperate with God's getting me there. And when God accomplishes it, I have no idea how it happened. I suddenly notice that I'm standing on the far bank, amazed. Gift and grace.

—— ✂ ——

There was something deeply symbolic for me about the judge to whom my case had been assigned. I had not appeared before him before, but my friend who had stepped across the "barrier" onto the Rocky Flats property on Christmas Day of 1983 had. He was sentenced to the maximum–a year in prison plus a $5,000 fine–which was suspended on the condition that he pay $200 *restitution* to Rocky Flats. He wasn't prepared for prison– I think that the judge must have sensed as much–and the restitution was horribly punishing. Impossible as it would have been for me to pay restitution myself, I actually contributed some money toward his paying of it in order to share with him a little of his deep pain. And something in the core of my being yearned to say to the judge, "I'll do that year in prison for my friend."

In a sense, I got my chance.

My trials were becoming increasingly perfunctory. The prosecution was learning how much it could get away with, especially since I never objected. Even the judge seemed to be less careful than the two I had met previously. On February 6, I was quickly convicted by a jury. The following week I was sentenced to a year in prison. There was no mention of contempt of court. But it did seem to me that this time the motive behind the sentence was pure punishment. The system, including this judge's particular efforts of the year before, had failed to deter me; its ultimate assertion of power is punishment. Thankfully, I was prepared for the possibility.

The marshals picked me up about ten days later, held me overnight in the Denver city jail, and put me on the airlift in the morning. I was ready to move on to federal prison, but nothing had prepared me for the intervening step. Oklahoma City, where there's a conveniently located federal prison for men, was then the stopover point for the airlift's two-day trips across the country from east to west and west to east. Later, it became the hub of daily loop trips in various directions. At that time, the marshals were still housing women in the old Oklahoma County Jail.

That jail was the pits. I have never seen worse. I couldn't believe that the federal government stooped to using it. We were locked into a metal box without so much as a skylight to mark the difference between night and day. The box was barely big enough for its furniture: bunks for twelve (it slept sixteen one of my nights there), a long metal table with metal benches, a shower, two toilets, and two sinks. There was soap (plus commissary if you had money). There was one incandescent bulb hanging from the ceiling. Food was passed in through a hole in the wall, which was covered and locked at all other times. You never left the tank. There was no exercise. There was close to nothing to do. The few books available were trash. A prisoner who could afford to provide her own TV or radio was permitted to, and someone had a radio, which filled the box with noise.

The jail made a boast of how cheaply it fed its population. I'm fine with beans and cornbread, but lots of meals had bits of meat in the beans, so I ate mostly cornbread. There were essentially no vitamins, no milk, no fresh vegetables or fruit. The matrons paid little attention to us. Even in an emergency, it was like pulling teeth to get medical attention. And the real horror was that women might be held there for *months* pre-trial.

Ten days was bad enough. It would have been longer if one of the matrons hadn't complained about us to the marshals, asking when they were ever going to get those "blankety-blank bitches" out of there, which was kind of her. We left by van on a Friday, instead of the following Monday, for Fort Worth, Texas.

But it was in that awful pit–thinking about how hopeless the world is, full of anger and woundedness and insanity–that I suddenly found myself with the answer to all the questions I'd been asking in the fall. The answer is that there *is* no answer, no reason to hope for any progress toward sanity; there's just love, blind, irrational love, never expecting to be able to do anything for anybody, much less for society in general, but just *being*– being what it is, expressing God–and that's enough. Love–God–doesn't need reasons or justifications, doesn't even need to be, in some kind of ultimate sense, the salvation of the world. My anguish in the fall had a lot to do with being unable to see how even love could be enough, but what I was doing wrong was seeing "enough" in terms of accomplishing something. No, it's enough simply that love *is*.

—— ✄ ——

A typical low-security federal prison looks like a rather crowded college campus, where dormitories are locked at night and during counts, but prisoners are not locked into rooms. There is significant freedom of movement during the day, regulated by rules, schedules, specific work and school assignments, and the ever-present oversight of staff. Apart from supervisory and security roles, prisoner labor runs a prison, at a starting wage of 11 cents an hour. During leisure time a variety of activities is available, from educational to recreational. In 1985, FCI (Federal Correctional Institution) Fort Worth was atypical only in that it was "co-correctional," housing both men and women.

My experience of it, however, was not typical. I barely made it past the initial strip-search in R & D before getting into trouble. I refused to sign the fingerprint card. I had been refusing that particular signature for quite a while, since it would amount to a direct participation in the work of my being incarcerated; I let people take my fingerprints but won't help. Here, it was enough to have me immediately escorted, through a labyrinth of basement corridors, straight to detention. Goodness! I had hardly done anything! Oh, well.

Life in a prison detention unit is utterly different from life in the general population. The unit is locked, and your cell door is locked. Meals are brought to you. PAs (physician's assistants) and the staff of your assigned living unit check in regularly. You're allowed out, by BOP (Bureau of Prisons) policy, for three showers and five hours of exercise a week. Any time you leave the cell, you're escorted by an officer. You may read and write, and a limited selection of books is usually available. If you own a radio or playing cards, you're allowed to use them if you're not on punishment status. That's about it.

My status was an enigma. I was told that I had to complete the intake processing in order to be released into the general population, and also that I was on "quarantine" until I completed the initial medical screening– though all the prisoners I'd arrived with had gone directly to the compound.

R & D staff acted as if I didn't exist. They refused to process my property into the institution or to receive any of my mail. That was the truly heavy punishment. I understood that *I* might not receive my mail until I had been given a chance to sign the authorization form for it. But the prison wasn't even holding it. It was returning it to the senders without explanation, and I didn't even know which of my friends were being given fresh cause to worry about me. Since I couldn't receive money, I couldn't buy stamps. I tried to be content with being so wildly out of control, but nothing hurts me more than the inability to save people who love me pain.

Fortunately, I was able to use a telephone, which met my top-priority need to let my closest friends and family know where I was and that I was okay. And I reached a spiritual breakthrough when, after about a week of struggle, I finally surrendered to God my need to protect my friends from being hurt on my behalf. All at once, I found that I'd recovered that depth of serenity I'd known in Larimer County where it was irrelevant that I was locked in. I'd again gotten beyond the prison's ability to imprison me. The key is to give oneself so fully to the present as it is that one loses any need or desire for it to be otherwise or elsewhere.

Still, it was a shock to learn, when one of my unit staff brought me the authorization form for my mail, that what the form actually said was, if you didn't sign it, you were supposed to *receive* your mail. The prison had been lying to me, withholding one of my basic rights on the pretense that my noncooperation was an obstacle. I had been trusting and patient, and now I felt manipulated and tempted toward anger. But I knew that, basically, the prison was trying to punish me for being noncooperative, and that my choice not to be punished always depended on my being able to take whatever it dished out without letting it get to me.

I was determined to avoid anger in any case. I've been blessedly free of it in general. I see it as a natural human response to helplessness in the face of injury, which we need to accept if it comes up in us but not get stuck in. It is a negative, violent, useless emotion, which can never serve God's purposes in the world, and so our challenge is to grow beyond it. The best way is to recognize that we're never really helpless, both because we always have control over our own response to a situation–which is the whole of our responsibility with respect to it–and because we can always pray to God, who is never helpless. What we're left with then is pain, and pain is okay. Pain flows with things as they are, absorbing the injury in them into oneself, where God transforms it into compassion, which heals and redeems.

I was cleared medically on March 18. The very same morning I was ordered to clean my room on a day when I'd decided not to do it, because it simply didn't need to be done every day, and so I was given an incident report for refusing. I felt sorry for the staff people who were hoping to see me in the general population and who couldn't understand how my choices gave me more strength and peace and freedom than the ones that would make more sense to them.

At the same time, I recognized that my refusal to participate in the prison system was only part of something much larger, which is my refusal to obey any order that doesn't make sense. The officer had said something about "learning" to obey rules, and my immediate thought was that I never intend to learn that and don't think anyone should. Echoes of Nüremburg. Even as a child, I'd had rules explained to me. They were expected to make sense. Rules that don't make sense are blatant coercion, disrespectful of human dignity.

So I remained in detention for the "disciplinary" process (I put "disciplinary" in quotes because it's really a punishment process): Any staff person can write an incident report (commonly called a "shot"), which charges a prisoner with a rule infraction. A lieutenant "investigates" the incident and decides whether to deliver the incident report. One or more unit staff people (Unit Disciplinary Committee or UDC) hold a hearing with the prisoner and decide whether to throw out the shot; to impose sanctions (punishment) such as extra duty, unit restriction, or loss of privileges; or to refer the incident to the higher-level Institution Disciplinary Committee (in recent years replaced by a Disciplinary Hearing Officer). The IDC (or DHO) automatically hears cases of the highest severity and can impose heavier sanctions, such as loss of "statutory good time," lockdown in "disciplinary segregation," and/or recommendation of a "disciplinary" transfer.

Before the IDC hearing, I was on "administrative detention" status (AD), which also includes people in protective custody and those on holdover or transfer status on their way to other prisons. The IDC sentenced me to three days in "disciplinary segregation" (DS) and the loss of five days of "good" time. I was transferred to a DS cell, behind a locked grille at the back of the detention unit, and then, the evening of March 28, released into the general population!

The next few weeks saw me in and out of detention over a variety of minor incidents. I was in an inner place of great lightness and freedom, which made it easy to appreciate people but hard to take the interactions with the prison seriously. When I'd refused to plead "guilty" or "not guilty" at my first IDC hearing, the captain had said sternly, "This is *not* a game." He seemed to be personally invested in the authority of the institution and affronted that I wasn't duly impressed by it. I thought, "Of course it is. You just expect everyone to play by your rules." But I didn't want to get caught up in the game. When you're very free, you can do anything, so you have to be particularly disciplined to choose only the right and godly things. I wanted to stay rooted in the relationships, in my caring and respect for all the people involved.

I was eventually released from DS to a job assignment as a unit orderly, which neither the unit manager nor the regular day officer intended to oversee. They were really bending over backward to enable me to remain in the general population. My contribution was to stay in my dorm during working hours, so that I wouldn't be either "out of bounds" or in anybody's way—which gave me welcome chunks of quiet time for reading and writing. But on the third day, in the unit manager's absence, I was called in to see the acting unit manager, who asked about my work, clarified that I was refusing to do my assigned job, and wrote me up. Detention again.

Admission to detention always involved a strip-search. For some reason, rather to my surprise, strip-searches didn't particularly bother me. The officer wouldn't touch you. She would order you to remove all your clothing and then to turn, bend, and so forth to show her everything she wanted to see. But this time, I was wearing a tampon, and I had reached my tolerance level for removing a tampon a long time ago at Denver County. I hadn't refused there, but the last time that I had cooperated, I had known that it would be the last time ever. It hadn't come up again until now.

I couldn't really explain my refusal to the concerned officers, or the acting captain, or the hospital administrator, who tried to talk me out of it. Even after I began to understand what the consequences were going to be, and my own logical self could hardly affirm that it was worth it, I just knew that, being me, I couldn't do it for them. I refused to undress again, to stand up, to participate at all in this thing that they insisted on. So the two officers, both women, undressed me from the waist down, stood me up, bent me forward, and spread my legs. The hospital administrator pulled out the tampon. They gave me a sanitary napkin and let me get dressed. No one looked at anyone.

I felt dazed and drained. In the detention office afterward, I looked up at the lieutenant, who met my eyes, rather reprovingly. I looked at the officer and said, "That wasn't a whole lot of fun, was it?" She looked at me, also sort of reprovingly, and commented, predictably, "It would have been a lot easier if you'd done it yourself."

When they put me in a cell, I just lay on the bed. For a whole day, I could do almost nothing but sleep and stare at walls. I had a stiff neck and shoulder, for no reason at all, which had never happened to me before. I suddenly felt old. I felt like a prisoner—meaning, someone who'd better not expect to be treated like a human being. But I couldn't complain; I had chosen to noncooperate. I tried to work on my feelings by writing, but it wasn't enough. For another day, I did almost nothing but sleep and stare at walls. I felt violated. I felt numb. I felt so deeply injured that I couldn't even find my feelings. I felt that I hardly had a *right* to my feelings, because I had brought the whole thing on myself. I was stuck. And so a prison psychologist came to visit me. Some other caring staff person must have sent for her. I was disinclined to talk with her, partly because I wasn't willing to complain (I had to talk that through with her before I could even start), and partly because I didn't know if I knew her well enough to feel safe with her when I was so vulnerable. I tend to expect psychologists to respond more out of their professional role than their humanness, and perhaps I had a similar expectation with respect to prison staff in general. But she was offering help that I badly needed, so I risked trust, and was rewarded. She was able to draw me out and help me work through the feelings—a great gift in itself—and it was gift, too, to realize that I *could* turn to prison staff in my emotional need. I'm hesitant to ask for favors in any case, and especially so in prison, where I'm not giving staff what they're asking of me. But it's really much simpler than that: we can be human for one another. *That*'s what I *do* give them, and it's just as appropriate from them to me—affirming again the values I cherish.

On May 1, the IDC sentenced me to a recommended "disciplinary" transfer, which would certainly mean that I would remain in detention until the marshals came to transport me.

It was only a few days later that I discovered my good spirits had returned. The vulnerability was gone, my equilibrium restored, and I was being touched with joy by little things again. And then I was totally astounded to be released from detention *again* on unit restriction. When the captain proposed it, I said honestly that I didn't know whether I could live with it or not—particularly with signing out and in when I left the unit at mealtimes—and he replied, "Well, let's try it one more time." All right. I could try it.

I chose to exercise during the hour I was allowed out for dinner. An officer stopped to chat with me on my way to the rec field.

"Do you think they like you or not?"

"Oh, I think they like me, and also they have to deal with my noncooperation."

"They like you. You wouldn't believe all the things I've heard this month, from staff. I've never heard such things before, about an inmate."

Goodness! How very affirming! God must somehow have been touching people through me. I was making choices intuitively, hesitant to claim that I knew God's will, but doing my best to stay true to my own integrity, to be loving, defenseless, and relational, to avoid anger and judgment. Such positive feedback confirmed that I surely must have been letting God act in it all.

Grace had clearly had a tremendous role in my life ever since my most recent arrest. I could see it in my spontaneity and gentleness toward myself, in my trust of my intuition and freedom from my own expectations, in the lightness and naturalness and ease with which my life and discernment were flowing. It seemed as if God had somehow accomplished the transformation in me of submerging my controlling, logical, rational, *doing* self into my intuitive, *being* self, so that my controlling self, my ego, *I* was no longer insisting on being in control. The dominant and directing aspect of my existence seemed now to be grace. Wow!

There was a wonderfully effortless quality to my love, which seemed to happen quite apart from me, from anything I was doing or even being. There was nothing going on but this love, springing up spontaneously, just being there, amazing me because it seemed to keep on being there toward everybody under all circumstances. A friend asked in a letter how I kept from getting angry at my keepers; she tried to see Christ in them and sometimes failed miserably. Well, to use her language, I wasn't trying to see Christ in people at all; Christ was just *there*; I met people, and valued the good in them, and loved them without thought or effort. Because they were lovable. Not even because they deserved love or God loved them or any other two-step reason. Simply because they were lovable.

I had been sure that my prayer life must be around somewhere, in the midst of everything, because of its evident manifestations in my outer life, and now it was surfacing in recognizable forms. My morning quiet time was becoming, again, more quiet, more centered, more prayerful.

It wasn't long before I stopped cooperating with the sign-out requirement of unit restriction. I wondered why I had ever started. Isn't signing out the most direct self-policing that the institution could ask of me? Isn't it doing the prison's work in a very blatant way? My reason had been personal. I had wanted to affirm the captain's choice to trust me, or at least to give me chances beyond the system's normal limits. I wished that I could have made it work for him, but was now clear that it wasn't right for me.

On May 15, after a wonderfully quiet week in a dorm by myself (one of the great advantages of prisons over jails is that there's enough space to get away from the television entirely), the unit officer noticed that she hadn't seen me at the sign-out sheet and asked me about it. I explained that I had stopped signing out. She called the lieutenant.

Knowing that I would be written up, and probably locked up, the next time I left the unit, I chose to go to commissary at dinnertime. I was treasuring the wide out-of-doors and the company of my friends, chatting in the long commissary line that looked out over the track and playing field, when a yard officer came looking for me. I was to report to such and such a station. I said good-byes to people I'd probably never see again, and went.

Walking into captivity is such a strange sensation! I was free until I reached the station, though the yard officer was keeping an eye on me; then I was escorted; and then I was locked in (greeted with cries of "Jennifer's come home again!"), quite sure that I had seen my last of the Fort Worth compound.

The lieutenants were becoming so friendly, pleasant, and even respectful that I was rather overwhelmed. It was hard to imagine what, from their point of view, there was in me to like. The captain was continuing to treat me with remarkable leniency, and I made a point of saying, at my next IDC hearing, that I thought he'd been more than fair and I appreciated it. I liked him in spite of all our differences, and suspected that he liked me.

But the truly revolutionary thrill was discovering that, for the first time in my life, I actually liked *myself*! This unaffected, spontaneous, happy person who was emerging in me was pleasant, easy, and fun to be with. In the past, I'd been proud of my achievements but never satisfied with myself, since I never measured up to my own high expectations. I'm not sure that I even had a sense of self apart from the totality of my achievements. Now I was finally meeting the person in me who simply *is*–and liking her. What a gift!

— ✄ —

May 20. I woke up this morning thinking, "I'm not in prison. What a silly idea! How can anyone as happy as I am be in prison?" And of course it's true that I'm not in prison, because I'm very free. Remembered someone's conclusion–perhaps mine–that when your faith is great enough to move mountains, then your insight is also great enough to know that the mountains do not need to be moved–and I'm experiencing something analogous about prison walls: I can walk right through these walls; I just don't need to. I'm not even physically restricted, because I choose to be where I am. It's sort of that, because I choose freely to be where I am, I know that I could choose to be somewhere else if it were right, but I don't, because it isn't. My choice is not constrained by my circumstances. Am I making any sense? I know that what I'm saying is sort of metaphysical. But it's present to me with a powerful reality.

— ✄ —

My last two incident reports earned me fifteen more days in DS, and DS time was suddenly made more punishing by the removal of all the personal-hygiene items, especially deodorant and shampoo, that I'd been denied in detention in San Diego but had gotten used to having here. It took me a little while to adjust to that, but then, just lying on my bed, being quiet, I found myself again simply liking the people who were punishing me, wanting them to be happy, praying for them the way I prayed for the workers at Rocky Flats. It was all embraced in a soft glow of grace–God's love–healing–and I knew that I was whole again.

I wrote the captain a letter affirming him and explaining myself a little more; told my unit manager and "correctional counselor"–both particularly caring people–that I liked them and was glad to have gotten to know them; had a lovely conversation with the regular day officer, who was a sweetheart; and was very glad to be giving my relationships the attention they deserved.

Before I left with the marshals for Alderson, West Virginia, on June 3, my counselor said good-bye with a handshake. I don't think that any prison staff person had ever treated me that much as an equal before.

5

Absolution

My journey over the past year or so seemed to have taken on a roller-coaster quality that was new to me. Though I'd always been sensitive and cried easily, I wasn't used to emotional mountains and valleys—perhaps because I'd kept myself so carefully controlled with my will and discipline that my emotions hadn't had much room to move. My sense was that trying to let go of responsibility had taken the cap off, that I'd somehow loosened up on myself enough to begin to experience a whole additional layer of my personality, an unpredictable, rather out-of-control layer that soared and plummeted.

The first five months of this sentence had carried me up another mountain. I was overflowing with joy, love, freedom, lightness, and spontaneity. Life had become dancelike. It felt as if I were bumping into God every time I turned around. At Alderson, I fell again; I don't know how or why.

Alderson was the first federal women's prison, built in the 1920s, I was told. I found it quite lovely physically. It resembled an *un*crowded college campus in a rural mountain setting. There were spacious lawns, old trees, and pretty, restful vistas. The buildings were of brick, with sash windows at normal heights and even wooden floors in places—a comfortable kind of architecture for me. Its security classification at that time was "administrative," which encompasses all levels from minimum to maximum, but it seemed to be a lot more relaxed (and less secure) than any other place I'd been.

I was not locked down when I arrived, on a Thursday evening in mid-June, after a week in the Douglasville County Jail near Atlanta, Georgia. The R & D staff didn't seem to care whether I gave them information or not. They had my files.

So I spent several days in the general population, enjoying the out-of-doors, the library, my roommates, and the other women at Alderson who were serving sentences for acts of civil disobedience in resistance to nuclear weapons. I had not met most of them before, but they were warm and instant community for me. Sitting on a bench at the brow of a hill, gazing over a quiet valley into the mountains, I reflected on how natural and unprisonlike this life was.

On Sunday, I wrote a letter mentioning that I had thankfully missed the first week's duty roster for "cottage" (a two-story dormitory building) clean-up and that I was ignoring the rule that everybody had to sign out and in every time she left her cottage. Alderson read all outgoing prisoner mail. On Monday, I was written up for refusing a cottage assignment that had been added to the duty roster and then for failing to sign out when I was sent over to R & D to pick up my property from Fort Worth. A lieutenant called for me that evening, delivered the incident reports, and had me locked down on the spot.

The maximum-security building, Davis Hall, sat at the back of the upper compound, rather menacingly surrounded by a high chain-link fence topped with coils of barbed wire. But the building itself was as appealing to me as the rest of the physical plant. The AD cells had ordinary windows that you could open and close, porcelain sinks and toilets, and ordinary wooden doors, which were opened in the ordinary way for the delivery of things like food trays.

An officer added my name to a list of special diets so that I would receive a vegetarian tray. I had discovered the availability of that option toward the end of my time at Fort Worth. Until then, I had been accepting the regular trays and avoiding the meat and gravy (plus much of the white flour and sugar), knowing that my diet was deficient in protein and often even in calories. I had fared better in the dining hall, where there was a serving line and more choice. Now I also was eating well in detention.

I was surprised to be handcuffed practically every time I left my cell. I had never encountered handcuffs inside a prison before. Here, they seemed to be standard for movement to pretty much anywhere except the shower. We were cuffed in front or to another prisoner. The cuffs were removed in the exercise yard, though not at "disciplinary" hearings.

During my first two days, I was graced with patience over the interminable waits for ordinary requests to be granted by the officers, and delighted to discover that the "library"—a single bookcase in the rec room, with the wild assortment of books that was usual in detention—had an unusually high proportion of gems, including not only the life of St. Teresa of Avila but also biographies of St. Francis of Assisi and St. Bernadette of Lourdes.

Then my UDC (Unit Disciplinary Committee) sentenced me to one week of cottage restriction on each of the incident reports and had me released from Davis Hall. I was out overnight and then locked down again in the morning for refusing an ad hoc work order from the cottage officer.

For about two more days, I experienced my cell as a monk's cell. I reflected on "outsiderness," that being apart, living outside of society's functioning and expectations and yet at the same time fragilely sensitive to its pain and contradiction and sickness and chaos, somehow enables one to carry it, perhaps to be a soul for it. Most people are so caught up in life's immediate demands that the larger picture is hidden from them, whereas a journey like mine seems to pick up the bits and pieces, the fragments of meaning from the individual lives, and hold them in some fuller wholeness of meaning—not anything of mine or of my doing, but I could see that the separateness is given to people like me so that somehow our lives can be vehicles for everybody's meaning.

But I was quickly slipping, for no clear reason, into an impoverished inner place where my vocation was swallowed up in my own neediness. I was already running out of patience. The officers didn't seem to notice even your most basic needs unless you asked, and I hated to keep asking and asking. The worst problem was that I was always hooked, when someone said yes, into expecting whatever-it-was, and then bent out of shape when it didn't happen. I wished that I could stop needing *anything*, making do with whatever was offered. But I wasn't willing to do without toilet paper or tooth powder or pencil-sharpening, especially since I knew that it wasn't the prison's intention to deprive me. I kept trying to work on my attitude but felt fragile, self-centered, and easily frustrated.

My most serious struggle stemmed from the requirement, not enforced at Fort Worth, that an inmate registration number be included in the return address of all outgoing mail. I had become increasingly uncomfortable with using that number, and had stopped giving it to people who asked for it. I'd complied in the past because the thing was readily available anyway, but now I realized that the point is that *I* don't identify my *self* by a number; what the prison does is not my concern. I was still putting the number on my envelopes, though, because I could hardly imagine that the principle was worth keeping my mail from going out.

But it was bothering me more and more. I was soon feeling violated every time I wrote the number next to my name. It wasn't *me*. I couldn't convince myself that it was unimportant. I tried sending a letter without it, and the letter was returned to me. I was told that policy required it. So not using the number would keep me from sending out any mail as long as I was at Alderson, and people I loved would suffer, and the prison wouldn't care. No alternative was acceptable. I felt trapped and helpless. But I gradually recognized that the only conscionable choice was to stop using the number and accept the consequences, trusting that whatever was necessary for me would have to be okay for everyone affected by it. Before long, I began to see a gift in that choice: I was running out of words, tired of listening to my own voice. I was ready for a deeper retreat, resting in some incoherence.

On June 24, I was unexpectedly released from Davis Hall because of a procedural error: the unit team had failed to give me a "disciplinary" hearing within its time limit, invalidating the shot. It was wonderful to reconnect with my friends. I was still on cottage restriction and had to sort out the self-policing question: to what extent was it my responsibility to bind myself to restriction? I would not sign out. But I do routinely go where I'm told to go, and I don't play games. So, in the absence of a compelling reason to be elsewhere, I stayed in the cottage. The ideal place was the back porch, where I could be alone, quiet, *and* outside. Leaving for "orientation" sessions and meals was allowed. And exercise was compelling. Early in the morning, on my way to breakfast, as it were, it was a gift to be able to walk for an hour around the upper compound under the stately old trees in the misty freshness of awakening day.

The prison was kind to me in ignoring the sign-out issue for nine days— my longest stretch in a prison's general population yet. Then it began confronting me, obviously trying a variety of approaches in an attempt to find one that might influence my choices. I was locked down until an IDC hearing, sentenced to ten hours of extra duty, and released in spite of my assurance that I would not do the work. The cottage officer ordered me to begin immediately and sent me back to Davis Hall the same evening. Next, I was given ten days in DS (disciplinary segregation).

Soon my visits to the compound were predictably brief, while punishment periods in lockdown lengthened. The lieutenants were tracking me on the refusal-to-sign-out issue. Any of them who saw me in the dining hall, or anywhere outside, might call the cottage to check if I had signed out, which I never had, and then ask the officer to write an incident report. It tended to happen within about twenty-four hours of my release.

So I saw a good deal of the lieutenants and was developing friendly relationships with them, but I was having a harder time with my unit staff, whom I didn't see quite enough of. They were in some ways as central to my life in detention as the officers, and were even less available. I learned early on that I couldn't expect them either to follow through on specific promises, such as giving me a phone call, or to attend to routine responsibilities, such as bringing me those items from my personal property that were allowed in Davis Hall. It was common that I would have to make the same request over and over again, frequently discovering that the staff person not only hadn't done anything about it, but didn't even remember that I'd already asked.

Prison had introduced me to a pervasive kind of helplessness in several realms. I had never before belonged to an oppressed minority, a lower class, with restricted rights and freedoms, discriminated against, looked down upon, and treated as less than fully human. I will never regret the learning. When you go through something yourself, you grow into true compassion for the other who is made to suffer it. I've often reflected on how different our legal and penal systems would be if judges, lawyers, and jailers had all experienced being thrown into prison and treated as we were routinely treated every day.

I wasn't handling it very well by now, though, falling farther and farther into the emotional vulnerability of a wounded child. When one of the case managers lied to me, denying a request on a pretext that I had good reason to know, and later confirmed, wasn't true, I felt so hurt by her harsh and unreasonable dismissal of me that it took embarrassingly long to remember that *my* responsibility was to *forgive* her.

One morning yet another instance of arbitrary rejection was suddenly more than I could absorb, and I fell apart, curling up in a corner of my bed in tears. For some time I couldn't pull myself out of it. I couldn't make myself eat lunch, not because I was sulking but because I was miserable. I refused a shower. I didn't want my light turned on in the evening. On following days I was able to accept meals, showers, and outdoor rec, but was very subdued. I did little and cried a lot. I felt tired and defeated. Everything hurt. Everything was difficult. Even the officers who cared couldn't do anything for me. *I* couldn't seem to do anything. I felt very alone in the general helplessness. Still, I kept trying to live my life. I kept trying to pray. I kept trying to smile at people if I could. Imperceptibly, the heaviness lightened, the pain eased.

Once the officers forgot to serve me dinner. I wanted to not care—to say, "Oh, well, what's a meal?"—but I couldn't. I pointed it out to the next person who came by, and eventually ate. Then, after I had cleaned the cell and settled in and gone to bed, they made me move. It's the little things that wear you down. You keep wanting to be above such stuff, or something, and when you can't manage it, you feel frustrated not only by the system's inhumanness, but also by your own vulnerable humanness. At least, I do.

Well, vulnerability itself is gift. The heart of both intercession and compassion. I *had* to stay vulnerable. But how could I manage both vulnerability and contentment? Contentment always seemed to me to be the ultimate spiritual answer to deprivation, and yet it also seemed to me that the people who made you suffer needed some indication that what they did was hurtful so that they would want and choose to change. Was it right that I swallowed so much of my pain?

The question was rather theoretical, though, because I wasn't swallowing it very successfully. People could see that I was hurting. And *I* felt altogether inadequate, immature, and hardly a shining example of Christian faithfulness. I didn't like myself for it, which made me feel worse. Everything was still pretty difficult.

The prison was closing in on me, as it were. The pervasive lying on the part of both prisoners and staff was driving me up a wall. I felt like an alien from another planet, struggling desperately to uphold a way of being based on selflessness, honesty, and caring, but I was so bombarded by the utterly different value system of the world around me that I was both losing my own centeredness and wondering if anything I said or did even communicated. What did my life here mean if everything I stood for was irrelevant to everyone else?

My life was further complicated at the end of September by the quarterly shift change for the officers, which had, predictably, brought quite a few people into positions of control over my daily existence who did not yet know me or have any particular reason to care about me. What new people often respond to first is the challenge that my noncooperation presents to their authority. I invite personal relationship with my very being, but it takes time to develop.

One of the current Davis Hall officers was a very rigid person with a friendly, Christian facade and no observable compassion or sensitivity. She handcuffed us for the short walk to the shower and locked us in the shower room—policy, apparently, but a shock to me, who had never encountered it before—and I quickly decided that showering wasn't worth it. I could keep just as clean, although with a good deal more trouble, by sponge-bathing at the sink in my cell. The floors on the segregation wing were tiled. I could wipe up afterward with toilet paper.

There was another problem, though, that was more serious. I had reached my tolerance level for cooperating with handcuffs about a month earlier. Ever since the marshals had first put me in chains at the Denver city jail, I had sort of wondered why I cooperated. It happened at a level largely beyond thought. I submitted to the system's control of my body, which I considered the only thing that it *could* control. I also tend to move accommodatingly, the way you naturally step out of the way when someone passes you in a narrow space. So when I was asked for a hand to be fingerprinted or handcuffed, I gave it.

But handcuffs are surely as thoroughly inhuman as anything we prisoners had to deal with. They were the most direct way, perhaps even worse than locked doors, in which we were treated as animals. I would never handcuff anyone, just as surely as I would never lock anyone into a cell. And I am conscientiously opposed to participating in doing to myself something that I believe to be wrong. Those many weeks in Davis Hall, during which the issue confronted me daily, brought me to the point where, one day, I deliberately stopped presenting my hands on demand.

I remained passive, in no way preventing the officer from picking up my hands and cuffing me. Any staff person would do it if the prison wanted me to go somewhere. Those who knew and cared about me were willing to do it in order to give me outdoor exercise. I was not hurt by their cuffing me; it's only what I do myself that can compromise my soul.

Those who didn't know me, however, were less inclined to be accommodating. As I had known all along might happen, some insisted on complete compliance as the price that I had to pay for exercise. I had an absolute right to exercise, but I also had a right to refuse it, and they would simply say that I had refused it. It was very painful for me to be denied my most nurturing available activity, but my freedom lay in accepting the loss. I could grieve and live with it. Any other choice, now that I was clear what integrity demanded of me, would have eaten away at my soul, and I *couldn't* live with that.

I still had a window. I could even sit in it, on the wide sill, looking out over the autumn-tinted mountainside, crying a little perhaps when my rec group was exercising below me, but willing to bear the pain.

There was a deeper pain, too, though, that was harder for me to embrace, because I didn't understand it. It was the absurd contrast between the severe punishment that I was enduring for something much less than a rule infraction and the total impunity with which others were actively permitted, and sometimes assisted, by several different officers, to break rules outright, particularly the one against cigarette smoking in disciplinary segregation. One officer who denied me rec would actually *distribute* cigarettes in seg. What did it all mean? I kept vainly trying to make sense of it, not recognizing the importance of my contribution in simply carrying the pain.

My next visit to the compound, in late October, was extraordinarily brief. While I was moving in to the cottage, the officer sent me next door for a set of sheets. I was aware that my not signing out would be obvious to her, but assumed that it would not be an issue under the circumstances. She knew exactly where I was. I was back in minutes. She confronted me immediately over my failure to sign out, ordered me to do an extra-duty assignment as punishment, and had me locked down again for refusing.

On the day of my IDC hearing, I was in a very vulnerable inner place. The incessant accumulation of frustration and pain—being punished and denied, being ignored and forgotten, being misunderstood, feeling alone and helpless—was almost more than I could cope with by now. Sometimes I felt as if I were drowning in it.

The IDC chairperson asked in a friendly way about my departure plans. My release date was no longer a myth of the dim, distant future. My calculations suggested that, considering all the statutory good days I had lost as punishment in the course of the year, it now stood at December 12; he had someone call the records office, who reported that it was December 9. As I tried to field the question of whether I might be home for Christmas, the tears that were already on the surface overflowed.

— ✄ —

November 7. Images from prayer:
  Some days ago I tried focusing my attention in quiet prayer on the cross, just the simple cross, in black silhouette on the horizon—and suddenly I realized that the cross had grown larger and come nearer to me until it had entered into me—it was in me, filling most of my empty inner space— and I was the cross on which Jesus died—the sin that killed him.
  The next day, focusing on the cross again, I knew it was there, but I couldn't see it, or anything, because of the thick darkness of the night. That was the day when I wrenched out a yes to God over the barrier of my nos, and broke down in sobs.

There were some days when internal distractions, as usual, made focusing impossible.

When I came back to the cross, I was at the foot of it, and it towered over me, lifesize, with the crucified One hanging on it, his feet by my shoulder as I knelt, and his blood dripping where I could catch it. Why, why, being so close, hadn't I stopped them? Why had I allowed him to be crucified?

I read about someone meditating on Mary at the foot of the cross, and returned there. It was small and simple again. I reached out to touch it and touched thorns. But I knew the thorns were on Jesus' head—and then I was touching his face—and then I was, as Mary in a pieta, taking him down from the cross into my arms, laying him in my arms and lap. . . .

I'm being drawn into prayer on my knees.

This was a new kind of prayer experience for me. The intent in contemplative prayer is to focus one's attention on God, but since one can't see or locate or visualize God, it's hard to keep mental distractions from overtaking all of one's inner space. In the past, I had sometimes tried looking at the back of my closed eyelids—which amounted to darkness—or imagining the night sky. Now, I was feeling a need for more visual help, so I was looking at a mental image of a cross.

None of the ensuing transformations were intended, expected, or initiated by me. They developed the way dreams do—with their own internal reality, which you realize only afterward is different from ordinary reality. There may have been some contribution from my unconscious as in dreams, but I think that, for the most part, I was being graced with visions, which are a gift from God. An image would be presented to me with such power that it required a response. And my response would open me to fuller understanding and relationship with God. The authenticity of the experience was compelling in itself and was soon verified by the tremendous spiritual growth that it catalyzed in me.

November 13. Thursday, the 7th, was the great day, the watershed day, the day I was reborn a new person—and I can't for the life of me remember what happened—in prayer, on my knees, after dinner—what I said or heard, what I promised or confessed or let go of or accepted. I remember only that until then I was buried in pain, and since then I've been free to walk with the pain and praise the Lord. I remember the beginning of the praise—walking in my room before dinner, pausing with my elbows on the top of my locker, feeling praise, like a new dawn, rising up in me, gently, wondering at it. And it was following the prayer, the rebirth, that I started writing.

That morning I had finally cried with complete abandon, because [an officer] was willing to listen, and a few words brought me to a scream, "I

*can't stand it!" and violent, noisy sobbing. That helped. But I was still
responding like a wounded and helpless child in the afternoon, when the
closing of exercise before our group got a chance to go sent me back into tears.
I don't know what God did, and only know with certainty that God did it.*

*November 14. I remember. There was this worm in me, a huge, corkscrew-
shaped worm of pride and selfishness and desire for attention and recognition, a petty, grasping self-centeredness—and God drew it out. . . .*

*I've been trying to understand about suffering—why the medieval
saints embrace it as a positive, not merely neutral, thing. St. Francis says
(see the "perfect happiness") it is both because it's the punishment our
wickedness truly deserves (and that we never receive from God) and
because our suffering is for the love of Christ and our pain at his suffering.
The Virgin Mary spoke to Bernadette of penitence, and Bernadette,
responding simply to her love for the lady, found that her suffering relieved
the suffering of the lady. St. Paul spoke of "filling up that which remains
of the suffering of Christ" [Colossians 1:24, paraphrased]. But why? Why
does our suffering relieve Christ's? Why, how, does our penitence help
God? Why do we do it for God and not just for our own soul's purging? I
could feel the desire to do for the love of God whatever helps God (at least,
I could conceive of it—I wonder, again, if I really love God at all), but I
couldn't understand how it could help.*

*Last night, I was praying the Jesus prayer. (I've gotten beyond my
hesitation in asking for the mercy that I know God is already giving,
because when our need is very great we cry out for what we can't do
without, even if it's only waiting for us to receive it—and I'm learning that
receiving, indeed, is far from easy.) As I prayed in the presence of the cross,
of Jesus hanging on the cross, I could barely choke out the words, I was
overcome with tears, because of the pain my own sins cause God—and I
finally understood that the crucified Christ is, right now, hanging there in
pain because I, with my own, personal, particular sins, nail him there,
right now and daily, that I hurt God directly—which the incarnation of
the crucifixion enables my limited mind to comprehend—and that my
penitence, my accepting and offering of suffering to God, with gladness for
the opportunity to suffer for God, somehow loosens those nails, undoes some
of the suffering I've inflicted on God. That's how it helps.*

*And I asked for forgiveness, and Jesus came down from the cross,
robed now and holding out his hand, to walk over to me with forgiveness
and blessing—and I could hardly stand it, could hardly receive it, because
I'm so utterly unworthy of forgiveness and blessing.*

*Afterward, it occurred to me that, of course, one is always unworthy
of forgiveness. That's precisely what forgiveness is all about.*

—— ✄ ——

Deep healing had been given to me in those confessional sessions with God. The visions were a materialized expression, as it were, of powerful spiritual encounters. As I had received baptism on retreat at the monastery, here I had received cleansing and absolution. They left me feeling essentially intact again, essentially functional.

My season of incoherence was over. I was journaling freely now, and I started writing letters–responses to months' worth of accumulated correspondence–which I intended to mail as soon as I was released from prison.

I returned to the compound on November 19, a Tuesday. And one of the women in my cottage made a very determined effort to keep me there. She insisted on signing out for me. That made me uncomfortable, but it was her gift, and I wanted to allow her to gift me. I refused to *ask* her to do it, though, so she kept an eye on me, especially around mealtimes. I found that I was relaxed and happy, not feeling pursued by the prison expectations that I was ignoring, and just being myself.

Since I had never spent enough time in the general population to receive a regular job assignment, I was relatively free until the cottage duty roster was posted on Sunday. I still felt some ambivalence about cottage chores. My assignment was to get the ice, pairing up with another woman each evening to fill a large cooler from the ice machine in the cottage next door. I suspected that I'd been given the task deliberately, in the hope that I'd be willing to do it, and I decided that I *was* willing. It served the prisoners directly and required no supervision. If it was done, it was done. I actually enjoyed doing it on Sunday.

But the next night the officer made such a point of asserting his oversight, giving me no space at all to do the job in my own way or for the women I lived with rather than for the prison, that I finally realized how utterly impossible it was to separate even cottage clean-up from the prison authority that had taken it over. I was particularly sad and disillusioned about the officer, because I liked him and had expected humanness and understanding from him. But the issue itself was now crystal clear for me, and I stated firmly that I would never do another cottage assignment again.

It took me a little longer to comprehend my right relationship to my friends in the cottage, who thought that I was hurting myself by my noncooperation and would gladly have protected me by doing my job themselves. The officer who wrote me up told me, "Fifteen people came to me to say they'd get the ice." Yes, their gift to me, freely offered, was to do my share of our common work. What I offered in return, my gift to them, was precisely my noncooperation, my willingness to say on behalf of all of us that the prison authority was not legitimate.

The incident report was delivered by a lieutenant whom I knew pretty well and liked.

"How did you manage to stay out there so long?" he asked.

"I have friends."

"I thought it must be something like that."

An affirmation of his respect for me. He was *sure* that I couldn't have been signing out.

The clarity that I gained through this incident gave me great strength. I had a sense of having stepped past masks and veils to stand firmly face to face with reality, which left me feeling remarkably self-sufficient, in no way dependent on the prison's relationship to me, and truly free of anyone's opinion or expectations. I felt very whole, solid, connected, fully myself. Still grounded in my earlier prayer experiences, I saw God everywhere in the situation, pervasively, at the heart of all of it. The prison was nowhere, nothing, of no importance. It was irrelevant that my door was locked. I had already left.

Two days after my return to Davis Hall, I lost my centeredness temporarily, feeling like a hurting little kid again. What restored my freedom and self-sufficiency–really, God's sufficiency sustaining me–was recognizing how small and weak and prone to temptation I am. How prideful it is to take things personally, to consider myself so important that the world should notice me! How silly! How could I feel slighted by the failings of others when my own weakness was so overwhelming? Little by little, I was coming to understand how redemptive was my contrite awareness of my sinfulness, especially the sin of pride.

My spirits were beginning to soar again. God really did seem, by some miracle, to be getting my act together.

— ✂ —

December 6. Maybe personal painful experience is necessary for contrition, for compassion, for entering deeply into the presence of anyone, including God. The pain is okay. What isn't okay is feeling sorry for myself, or looking for comfort in anything less than God, or feeling personal injury (which implies a grudge and an ego defense).

I remember ages and ages ago articulating the concept that one can't be a healer without being a sufferer–that one heals precisely by taking on the other's suffering–as Jesus did. Great saints seem to live with a tremendous amount of physical pain. Pain refines us spiritually, if we let it unite us to God–and it seems to be the gift given to those God draws especially close. . . . And then there's its strange relationship with joy. I've been recognizing that I seem to go through alternating seasons of intense joy and intense pain–the joy of my spring and summer that started with the Palm Sunday action and the pain of the fall following, the joy of the first half of this sentence and the pain of the second–and guessing that the seasons will eventually merge, probably are merging, seeing that joy and pain go together, as the two faces of love.

— ✂ —

On December 6, I finally saw the IDC, which simply sentenced me to DS until my departure from prison. The captain was quite cordial and wished me well. His calculations put my out date at December 16. I mentioned that I had been told it would be the ninth. I didn't find out until the ninth that the final word was December 13.

Walking *out* of captivity is almost as strange as walking into it. I was a detention prisoner when awakened in the small hours on the thirteenth. Then I was an ordinary prisoner, among others, being processed out through R & D. Then I was an almost ordinary person waiting under the watchful eye of my case manager at the Greyhound station for the 5:10 A.M. bus. Then I was a free agent. I kept being amazed that first day by the expansive friendliness of the most ordinary strangers in the most ordinary situations. There was something different about the world out here.

6

Commissioning

When I returned in early 1986 to the Sunday afternoon prayer vigil at Rocky Flats, I met Alex, who had joined the group in my absence. Alex had created, in the rocky soil of the state highway right-of-way, directly across from the plant's west access road, a garden of flowers. He named it the peace garden.

— �֎ —

What can I say about the next three years? I prayed at Rocky Flats. I prayed in jail. I prayed in the inner city. I struggled with my soul. I gradually grew with God.

A religious vocation is never easy. You're always called beyond yourself, challenged to surrender your strengths and embrace your weakness, to unlearn what you think you know and to learn anew what you can't comprehend, to stretch and to empty, to risk and to trust. Always, I feel inadequate. Always, I'm amazed at God's eternal patience with me, guiding me step by step through a lesson plan I can't see. Every few years I'll come to some major new insight or integration and say, "Ah, now I believe that I've made it to the threshold. *Now* I'm ready to begin!"

Much of the inner journey is necessarily solitary, and mine has been strikingly so. My whole vocation has developed largely outside of the established structures and patterns. Without blueprint or guide book, I've relied heavily on God for day-by-day discernment. And God has somehow molded my life and work into those of a nun. Apparently, I even *look* like a nun. Strangers on buses, or jail guards, or people I run into on the street often ask if I am one. I'm honored.

But the journey never takes place in a vacuum. Its community is the church, the whole family of believers who are struggling together to know and serve God. The true church is not an institution or a body of doctrine; it's a fellowship of people, the body of Christ. And each of us who has made a commitment to Christ is nourished and supported in living that commitment through the ongoing life of a local family of faith. It took me two years to find my church home in Denver.

I didn't know what I was looking for until my retreat at the monastery. Then I didn't know how to find it in Denver. I worshiped at first with the people who had become community for me in other ways: the Arvada Mennonite Church, the Catholic Worker folks who joined me at the house of prayer, the Sunday afternoon vigil group at Rocky Flats. But my soul wasn't satisfied. In the fall of 1984, I embarked on a deliberate search. I had visited the Quaker meetings for worship. I visited the charismatic fellowship whose ministry I had appreciated at the Denver County Jail. And I asked Anna to introduce me to Catholic churches. At the fourth or fifth one we visited, a Hispanic parish within walking distance of the Worker, I was instantly and certainly at home. I still am. I love the sense of community and of celebration. I love the congregation full of babies and great-grandparents and everybody in between. I love the participation of ordinary people offering love and service to God in the midst of ordinary life.

It didn't exactly feed my hunger for monasticism, though. So Anna asked a Capuchin community (an order of Franciscan priests and brothers) who lived nearby if we could join them in their daily Mass. That, too, was perfect. One day a week, a priest says Mass at the Worker house. Without my deliberately choosing it, Catholicism had drawn me in and become family for me.

So had the Catholic Worker community. For a long time, I didn't consider myself an ongoing part of its life. My reason for remaining in Denver was Rocky Flats. I kept looking for ways to center my physical existence more closely around the bomb factory, perhaps by finding a place to stay within walking distance of it, or perhaps by camping nearby. But those scenarios quickly stumbled over practical obstacles; the folks at the Worker house kept offering me temporary shelter and prayer space in the apartment; and I gradually came to feel more and more at home in it.

— ✂ —

The first months following my release from prison were emotionally tumultuous. That isn't uncommon, especially after the longer sentences. You'd think that I'd just revel in the sudden expansion of my physical world when I first get out, and I do. I also delight in people—and treasure the delight, because I have so many friends that I often feel torn between the time I want to give to them and the time I yearn to spend in solitude.

But the transition is also confusing. The expansion of potential available choices adds layers of complexity to everything from daily details to major vocational issues. In prison, you know that you're doing what you have to do just by being there, and you are (at least, I am) prevented from doing most of the things that you'd otherwise choose anyway. So you try to pray. You try to love people. You cope with whatever comes up. You work on yourself. You're satisfied that there's nothing more you can do.

On the outside, I rarely feel as if I'm doing enough. I'm rarely satisfied with my choices. I question and question them, wondering what I could or should change. I *know* that prayer is my full-time work, and yet my prayer feels so inadequate that I keep wishing for some more observable criterion by which to justify my existence—which is silly, of course, since *God* isn't asking for any such justification. My prayer is further undermined by all the little activities and projects that can easily fill my time.

I also continually struggle with questions of meaning. In prison, the issues are fairly clear and straightforward. Reality is unmasked. You know what you're dealing with. Then you emerge into the larger society, where all the same dynamics are operating—the same selfishness, thoughtlessness, dishonesty, and manipulation, the same prejudice, coercion, and violence—but more or less subtly disguised. You feel the same oppression by negative values and institutionalized evil but have more difficulty in pinpointing the problems and confronting them directly. I agonize over how to relate to it all.

I was still too emotionally shaky and unresolved by Easter of 1986 to be able to consider celebrating on the Rocky Flats property. Instead, I decided to continue my weekday prayer vigil at the west gate, which had, as usual, carried me through Lent.

In another two weeks, I began to find some answers. After an evening of tears, which seemed pretty contentless—mostly hopelessness, meaninglessness—nothing seemed to make any sense, nothing seemed to matter, my life especially didn't seem to matter—it occurred to me in the morning that I might be grieving for the death of the world. For years I hadn't had any pragmatic hope for the world. I'd lived on theological hope, hope in the impossible. But now I seemed to have stopped believing that God *would* save the world—souls, yes; spiritual realities, yes; but not this material, historical planet, with all of its life, that humankind is inevitably, in quick ways and slow ways, destroying.

I knew that I could be wrong. Was I yielding to a temptation to despair? Had I stopped trusting God? Had I stopped believing in miracles? I reaffirmed for myself that I do truly believe that God intervenes in history. God does perform miracles. The resurrection of Jesus is the keystone in that faith for me. I found myself thankful in a new way for Christianity, because it shows us not only that God suffers and dies for us, but also that God intervenes in history. I needed that reaffirmation.

But I also needed to accept that God might not do it. God might let us destroy the world. We might be facing the death of the world, the death of billions of human beings, and animals, and plants. I seem to be able to accept my own death, and I needed to accept this mammoth death, too. And to choose to go on living—to be who I am the best that I can, not because it will make a difference, not because *anything* will make a difference, not because anything can be saved, not because of hope for a future, not for any reason at all except that life is to be lived, fully, in God, in the present, the best we can.

My spirits entered into another resurrection. By Pentecost I was ready to celebrate.

Prayer on the property at Rocky Flats was truly a religious celebration for me, never a political protest. It illuminated–in some sense, even incarnated–the great mysteries of my faith. Christmas, in particular, took on new depths of meaning for me that I had never encountered in more traditional observances. The difficult discipline was to hold back from that prayer until the time was right. Then I felt release and freedom and joy in being able to go ahead.

— ✂ —

My Pentecost witness returned me to the Larimer County Jail. The windows in the corners of the day room there are big enough to sit in, with your feet drawn up on the sill. I love sitting in windows, because you can ignore the room behind you and feel almost entirely absorbed in the out-of-doors. It seemed such a harmless pleasure that I was very surprised when ordered by an officer to move.

"Why?"

"It's against the rules."

"Why?"

Something about security. Not my responsibility, I decided, after some thought. Not a reason that deserved my assent. I didn't move. Two officers grabbed me and dragged me out of the window. I went limp.

I had been thrown out of a courtroom earlier that year for failing, along with a large proportion of the spectators, to suppress my giggles at a particularly funny exchange between one of the defendants, testifying on her own behalf, and the prosecutor, cross-examining her. The judge had singled me out and ordered me to leave. I apologized for laughing, adding that I'd try not to do it again and would like to hear the rest of the testimony. The judge ordered a bailiff to remove me. More quickly than thought, the man placed his left hand around my neck from behind, grabbed my right wrist in his right, twisted that arm behind my back, and jerked me to my feet. I let my feet bear my weight and walked out with him. Afterward (*always*, this seems to be how I learn), I wondered why I had cooperated. "Next time," I told him, "I'll go limp." This was the next time. Going limp is now a practically automatic response in me to physical coercion; I don't resist; I simply let go of all voluntary control over my muscles.

I was dragged into my cell and sentenced to ten days in lockdown.

I was allowed out of the cell briefly for each meal, for a shower, and for an hour of exercise each day, and was expected to lock myself back in after each break. I would never do it. Most of the officers simply did it themselves, though one put so much energy into trying to coerce and threaten and belittle and punish me into cooperating that I thought a lot about why I make the choices I do. Eventually it occurred to me that I'm actually very respectful of rules. I believe that rules should be taken seriously and either followed or challenged. What's not respectful is to disregard them or sneak around them or break them lightly.

On June 16, the marshals booked me out of the jail on my way to court. I was facing the simple trespass charge before a judge who was new to me. The trial seemed, if anything, more perfunctory and sloppy than my last. I was convicted. A sentencing date was set for three weeks in the future. Having to wait that long for sentencing was normal for most defendants, but a bit of a shock for me, since other judges had generally tried to reduce my pre-sentence detention time as much as possible. The marshals may not have expected it either. They now had to book me *in* to jail again, and they took me to Denver County.

I was well known there. The officer who strip-searched me asked, "Would you rather be in max than in a dorm?" Hmm. The answer was yes, but it had never occurred to me that max was something you could, or would, choose. I left housing decisions to the system and lived with them as best I could. However, she had asked. So I said, "Yes." She wanted me to sign a form.

I had already this summer made some discoveries about signing things for a jail or prison. Having reached a point of readiness to refuse in general, I found as I responded to concrete situations that that simple, attractive position was not fair to the system. If a jail gave me something, it had a right to my acknowledgment that I had received it. My signature on a receipt was a reasonable and appropriate return, which I wanted to offer, for the item received. So I couldn't rest in simple solutions. I had to keep discerning on a case-by-case basis.

This form, too, was merely an acknowledgment: I agreed to my placement in max. I wasn't entirely clear, and continued to wonder afterward, about the degree of assent to the system that my signature might imply, but the statement was true, and I signed it.

Soon, I was having to remind myself that the general population really was worse. There, you were locked into a big room with twenty-five other women, a television, and a radio. Here, you were locked into a little room with yourself and precious little else.

Except God.

Being with God was just what this empty time was for. But I still wasn't very good at it. I'd sometimes rather have distractions. It was gift indeed when I woke up feeling thankful for my four walls and locked door, the seclusion of this little space and expanse of time that was all mine to share with God. Filled with God. Surrounded by God. Gifted by God.

Mine was one of five cells that opened onto a common area. There were four of us here now, mostly women who were mentally or socially incompetent to handle dorm life. Only one was allowed out of her cell at a time. There was no schedule; the officers locked someone up and let someone else out when they happened to think of it, which didn't seem to be often. On my third day I had expected them to get to me by evening, but finally gave up on a shower and took a sponge-bath at my sink. I knew that I was fine. But I felt forgotten.

Then it hit me like a thunderbolt that *this* was what I was here for. To share the lot of the forgotten. This is how you're treated in this jail when you're *not* being punished. Always before, I'd been being punished. Now I was thankful that I'd agreed to come back here, because it entered me into the experience of those, not only here but in all sorts of institutions, who didn't do anything to deserve this. They're simply old or feeble or not up to some sort of mental or social or hygiene standard that our society worships. So they're shunted to the back rooms and forgotten. Society isn't trying to be unkind. But it doesn't care. It doesn't notice. So the forgotten ones end up hurting not only because they're restricted and deprived, but also because they're obviously considered so unimportant that no one even notices they're hurting. I was plunged into prayer and a sense of purpose.

The next morning another prisoner whom I'd met in the jail some years earlier was able to yell to me from outside the grille. She said that she'd been framed on her current charge and was facing a life sentence as a "habitual criminal": "They're determined to keep me off the streets." She'd been open about her criminal activity in the past, and I believed her story now. It filled me with a rather common state of agony over the cruelty and mercilessness of our world–beginning with the greed for power and control that's willing to use any means to drive any perceived threat into the ground, regardless of life, justice, or God.

I found myself entering into prayer with an image of the whole world as one open, ulcerous sore–holding that seething mass of woundedness up to God; asking God, "Is it always this bad?"; touching God's pain in the badness of it; and feeling God's love surrounding it, bathing it, enfolding it in warmth and light. Powerful depth of prayer, of meeting God.

Revelation: Intercession! *Intercession* is my vocation! I've always known it was in there, but it's the core, the essence. I don't know about contemplation. I keep not quite getting there, not getting beyond self to God. Maybe someday. But I'm there now in intercession. I'm still not sure what it means to love God, but I'm meeting God in loving people. I'm forgetting self in caring about the broken world. I've known that that's what all this journeying in pain is for. I'm being called and taught to cry with the pain of those who suffer and to hold it up to the healing love of God.

Some days later I was feeling dragged down by the dinginess of my cell, the restriction, the barrenness of the whole environment, so I said to myself, "Okay, Jennifer, this is your life. Imagine that it will never change, that you'll never get out of here, that this is the entirety of what you'll have to live with forever." Instantly, everything brightened and lightened and wasn't so oppressive after all! Can you believe it? The problem was that I had been needing for my surroundings to be other than they were, projecting myself into a future time that heightened their bleakness by contrast. Eliminating the fantasy placed me solidly back into the present, which simply is. And you go with it.

I was still somewhat in the valley of the shadow–living among the poor and oppressed, feeling directly the institutionalized sinfulness of the system that was oppressing us, and at the same time experiencing that same sinfulness within us. It was everywhere, practically unconfronted by alternative values. Our society hardly seemed to have values any more. And yet I knew that the answer was to go on living and believing in something better in spite of everything. What the current journey seemed to be all about for me was the destruction of things like optimism and idealism, the stripping away of everything but naked faith. There's absolutely no reason to believe, no evidence for hope, in my experience, except God. And there's no evidence for God either. I *know* God directly, in relationship, but am never very trustful of my end of that and don't always experience it. I have to be okay with walking blind.

July 7. Sentencing. I was facing a maximum of a $1,000 fine. The court knew that I would not pay a fine. I had said so, and I had not paid previous ones. It also knew that I had no financial resources; one judge had specifically instructed the probation department to find out. I sensed that this judge wanted to punish me, and the statute did not offer him a very effective tool. He sentenced me to the maximum. Then he added, "You are remanded to the custody of the marshals until you agree to sign the release paperwork."

Hoo-boy! He wanted to punish me. Or, at least, he wanted to force me to acknowledge the court's authority by cooperating. Which I knew that I wouldn't do. I had visions of months more in that dingy, restricted, barren jail cell. How long might such a stand-off drag on, neither one of us giving in?

On the other hand, I wasn't aware of any release paperwork that required my signature. All that I had ever been asked to sign in the past was a receipt for my property. One of the marshals said, " *We* sign your release paperwork." Did the judge know something that I didn't? Or vice versa? All day long, I sat in the marshals' holding cell, not knowing.

In the evening, I was released.

— ✣ —

July 18. I'm coming to the conclusion that one can choose joy only out of real pain. It's the God-choice when the alternative is despair, a "yes" to life in the face of death, the resurrection that comes only on the other side of the cross. As long as our lives and our suffering are relatively superficial, we don't even know what the choice is. I have to have acknowledged and accepted the suffering, the suffering of our whole poor, broken and wounded world, before my celebration of God in the midst of it really acknowledges and reverences God.

—— ✂ ——

Christmas fell on a Thursday. A large group of us gathered at the west gate at noon to sing Christmas carols. The symbolic little gates were closed when I carried my worship across the property line into the plant.

I was held eight days in the city jail before being transferred to Denver County, where I was assigned to max again, administratively, without my active consent or signature. Immediately I had to deal with my growing discomfort over the prisoner number on the ID bracelet. I had never had to relate to the number in any way in this jail, and had so far been able to ignore it, but now I was keenly aware of its being physically attached to my person. I allowed it to be attached one more time, but soon realized that I couldn't live with it any longer. I tore the plastic off with my teeth and threw it away. I knew that removing the bracelet was, in itself, against the rules, but I had no idea what the practical consequences might be.

The primary one turned out to be the denial of my visits. I wrote in February for the Denver Catholic Worker newsletter:

I don't even feel like a prisoner this time. I'm only locked in and ordered around and denied things. I'm content, and so I have everything I need. I like the officers, and so I'm surrounded by friends. I make my own choices according to my conscience, and so I'm free. . . .

A visitor was announced for me, and an officer I've known for years came back to maximum security to talk with me through the bars.

"Where's your ID bracelet?"

"I threw it away."

"Jennifer, why do you do this to us poor officers who have to follow the rules?"

"I'm sorry it's hard on you. That's not my intention. I'm just not willing to be identified by a number."

There followed a long and revealing conversation about the distinction I insist on making between numbers and persons. I won't use a social security number either, and the far-reaching implications of *that* boggled the officer's mind. She asked a lot of good questions, which I tried to answer.

Then an announcement came down the hall that I was to go to the captain's office.

"There," I reassured my friend, "now you don't have to worry about it. *He* can deal with it."

He did, or someone did. I'm now allowed my official visits [lawyers, news reporters, clergy, and representatives of prisoner support organizations] though not my personal ones. But what matters is that I'm free regardless of what the system does, free both to dissent and to love those who don't. There's ultimately no way the system can hurt or dehumanize or change me.

No one can hurt or dehumanize me because only my own choices can do damage to my soul. Lesser wounds heal. Those who do dehumanizing things to others damage their own souls. And I've gradually learned that the whole message of my life for those in power is contained in that combination of love and dissent. I resist the inhumanness that's built into the system at the same time that I love the people who are its instruments. I insist on both my own humanness and theirs. My love keeps me from rebelliousness, while my resistance keeps me from complicity. My personal caring for the officers is never misunderstood as flattery or manipulation, because I'm simultaneously being punished for noncooperation, so the love is received as love and automatically says something about God. And my resistance is not misinterpreted as being retaliatory or obstructionist, because of the simultaneous caring, so it has to be received on its own terms, too, and says something about values. My life ends up speaking powerfully of both faith and values, without my deliberately intending anything but moment-by-moment obedience to God. Aren't God's ways wonderful? Whenever I come to understand something like this, I'm awed.

The daily living of it, though, isn't exactly simple, requiring continuing discernment of the most godly response to one new and often complex challenge after another.

I was tried by a jury on February 23, before the judge whom I had first met in early 1983. I was convicted, and sentenced the same day. Though I was again facing a year in prison, I was sure that this judge would not act punitively, and even a sentence as light as "time served" would not have surprised me. He gave me ninety days, which was not much more, since I had already served about sixty. It seemed likely that the marshals would leave me in the county jail for the month remaining.

I was still in a wonderful spiritual place, serene and joyful and free. Looking at this spiritual high and remembering liking myself at Fort Worth, I wondered how I was feeling about myself now. One might expect it to be good. But I couldn't *find* myself. There was only my experience, and the larger reality it expressed. A positive perception of my nothingness.

I recognized something about injustice at the heart of the tension in my vocation—that tension between action and contemplation that Ted said I might be called to live in forever. It's the tension between injustice and the peace of God. They're irreconcilable, and you can't live at one pole or the other, so you have to live the tension. You have to be satisfied with whatever your circumstances are in order to be in the peace of God, but you *can't* be satisfied with injustice—at least, toward others. I found myself hurting with the pain of perfect strangers, and guessed that such vulnerability to the pain of the world is somehow the sacrifice of the cross—and perhaps is the answer to *how* one lives the tension between injustice and the peace of God. (Argh!)

On March 11, I was preparing to mop the floor when an officer appeared to announce that I was leaving; the marshals were here to pick me up. Now what did *that* mean? I had two weeks remaining on my sentence. I surely wasn't heading for prison for two weeks, was I? But I could hardly be being released to the streets. Of course, the officer didn't know. I packed hurriedly and said my good-byes. It wasn't until I reached Receiving that I learned from the marshals that the judge had simply ordered my immediate release. What an unexpected gift!

For a good year, my mind had been playing with the possibility of praying on the Rocky Flats property "continuously"—that is, returning to pray there whenever I was free to. The idea was attractive, because prayer there drew me so strongly, but hadn't become compelling, and this experience showed me why: My proper response to the gift of an early release was to receive it with gratitude and enjoy it. A light sentence left me *wanting* to stay off the property for a while—as a personal affirmation of the judge's human choice—whereas a heavy one had the opposite effect.

I had seen the compassionate magistrate early in this case. He had told me that he had orders not to make any pre-trial releases in the absence of a promise to return to court. But he had urged me to contact him at the conclusion of the case—he was scrupulous about maintaining the objectivity of his judicial position—and let him introduce me to a layperson who might be able to convince me to pursue my convictions within the law. So I wrote to him, thanking him for his concern, repeating my clarity about my vocation and calling—I needed to be on that property in the name of God, offering my prayer both as a testimony to my faith in God and as the most effective work there is for world peace—and affirming my openness to dialogue.

Since I usually walk my mail to the post office anyway, which was then just across the street from the federal courthouse, I hand-delivered the letter. A secretary took it in to him, and, much to my surprise, he immediately appeared at the door to invite me into his office. He gave me the name and number of a Christian friend whom he encouraged me to see, and suggested that I use his telephone to call her. She and I eventually enjoyed a friendly chat over hot chocolate.

—— ✕ ——

Even the gift of an early release couldn't keep me out of Rocky Flats over Easter. I did not cross a "barrier." My case was assigned to the same judge whom I had just seen. He came up with a new kind of gift. Just as my refusal to make choices within the system's parameters automatically gave me a jury trial, it also automatically saddled me with the "Speedy Trial Act," which requires a thirty-day wait before the trial can commence. I had no use for that preparation period, which merely extended my pre-trial detention. This time, the judge quietly ignored the "Speedy Trial Act," knowing, I'm sure, that I wouldn't object; set the trial for ten days after my arrest; and sentenced me to time served.

—— ✄ ——

July 19. The answer is: never to be against anything, only for. To live the kingdom of God. To think and dream and breathe the kingdom of God. To respond to everything positive with love and thanksgiving, and to respond to everything negative with forgiveness and love. No fighting against evil. No judging evil. No attending to evil at all. Forgiving injury and building good. Living as God would live–did live–on earth.

At Rocky Flats, I stand for God and love everybody. In the courts and jails and prisons, I stand for God and love everybody. And everywhere else, it should be the same–in the midst of the city, in the midst of the nation, in the midst of the world, even inside myself.

—— ✄ ——

My spiritual director had left Denver in May of 1984 for the mission field in Africa, where his spiritual life and service were flourishing and fulfilling for him. He continued to offer me guidance by correspondence. In May of 1987, we were shocked to hear that he had contracted hepatitis and died very suddenly. I felt abandoned by God–though I knew, of course, that I hadn't been.

I was already looking toward a commitment I had made for July at the invitation of Ted's superior, Hugh, who was the provincial of the order. It was an eight-day, silent retreat for Vincentians and their sister order, Daughters of Charity, on the "spirituality of justice," which Hugh was co-directing. He had asked me to attend as a prayer presence. I was deeply touched, both by the affirmation for the importance of pure and "useless" prayer in a retreat concerned with justice and by the personal affirmation for my own prayer vocation. The invitation was so clearly of God that I had accepted, in spite of my obvious inadequacy, trusting God to use me.

I gave myself as best I could to praying through and for the retreat. Truly filling eight solid days with nothing but prayer is an exacting discipline. I am rarely graced with such tender and enduring centeredness in God as blessed me there.

One day, praying with open hands, I suddenly knew that God had put a gift into them. I asked what the gift was, and didn't get an immediate answer. But soon, again suddenly, looking into my hands, I knew. The gift was emptiness.

The retreat itself was a blessing to me. How wonderful to be entirely surrounded by good, loving, dedicated lives, all pouring themselves out in God's service! Something of a corrective to what I more commonly see of the world. And I was tremendously impressed by Hugh's conferences. What a wise and humble and holy man! Here was the spiritual director for whom I was newly yearning. But how could I ask him? He's a busy, important person to whom many look for help, and I am nobody. But how could I not ask him? I needed what he had to offer. He could always say no.

He said yes, simply and without hesitation.

We met for spiritual direction, there at the retreat, and I shared my hunger for the sacrament of confession. I knew very little about it, having grown up without sacraments outside of the Catholic church, but I knew that I needed help in receiving God's forgiveness. Part of the importance of spiritual direction for me is the relationship with a confessor. I feel terribly burdened by my sinfulness, by things like self-centeredness and pride and falling short in my service to God, and, though I *know* that God utterly forgives every sin I confess, I fail miserably at forgiving myself. I continue to feel dragged down by past sins that I should have left behind. I hoped that the church might be able to help me.

Hugh said, "What you need is baptism."

Flashbulbs–and floodlights, too. Baptism! He was absolutely right. I had thought about baptism many times over the years, and not felt drawn to it. I had received the spiritual experience. But it was precisely the official, public proclamation of that experience that I saw my need for now: to ask the church to confirm for me God's assurance that my past sins are washed away and I stand a new creature in God's grace, ready to begin again.

Baptism involves church membership. I had not been an officially recorded member of any church or denomination since the Quaker congregation of my childhood had dropped me from its rolls after I had become inactive. But there was no doubt about which church had already received me into its spiritual family. So I went to my parish priest and inquired. We discussed doctrinal questions, and he gave me a catechetical book to study. I had studied such a book two years earlier, when the Catholic priest who served the Alderson prison had suggested that I might want to consider joining the church, but then I had become bogged down in doctrinal difficulties. Now my difficulties seemed to have evaporated. It was as if I had grown beyond them. It didn't matter that there were mysteries I didn't understand. It didn't matter that church teaching didn't always match my own perception of reality. God had obviously given this family to me and me to it, and I was glad to give myself to loving and serving and growing with God within it.

I was quickly ready and eager for baptism and glad, after some years of intense participation in the life of the church, not to be required to wait for the Easter vigil. On October 3, in a quiet and beautiful ceremony, I was formally received into the Catholic church.

—— ✂ ——

On October 4, I celebrated the Feast of St. Francis with prayer on the Rocky Flats property.

The symbolic little gates across the access road had been replaced with slightly higher symbolic little gates that were easier to duck under than to step over. So I ducked under them.

I was placed directly into maximum security at the Denver County Jail. I remember asking if I could attend Mass, being told yes, and then being forgotten. I remember writing a letter to my spiritual director at the table in the common area with the television on (for those in their cells who were watching it–a relatively recent arrangement in max, which was, as you can imagine, highly oppressive for me) and thinking, "*This* is what it means to be called to prayer in the midst of the world." I remember glancing up from the telephone to nod at the officer's instruction that I not unlatch the food slot cover of someone else's door, and then suffering such paroxysms of remorse when I realized what I'd agreed to that I called her back to retract it; she locked me into my cell. I remember watching the other women in the yard through my window. Sometimes, even maximum security was allowed to go outside.

My case had been assigned to the same judge before whom I had just appeared twice in a row. A jury convicted me on November 16, and sentencing was held three days later. Following are excerpts from the official transcript:

Mr. Black: This case involves Miss Haines, as I understand, her eleventh conviction for Rocky Flats protesting and for violating the trespass statute out there. I recall, I think I even prosecuted her a number of years ago, and virtually everyone in our office has.

               Because of her repeated violations out there at Rocky Flats, we feel that we have to ask for a significant penalty in this case involving incarceration for a significant period of time. . . .

The Court: She has already spent 47 days in jail for walking on this sacred ground in order to pray, you want more than that?

Mr. Black: Yes.

The Court: How much do you think it's cost the United States government to have 11—you said this is the eleventh case, how much do you think it's cost the taxpayers to have prosecuted this lady 11 times for walking on this hallowed ground of Rocky Flats?

Mr. Black: Well, Judge, I don't particularly call it hallowed ground, but I think it's cost a substantial amount of money, if you include the—

The Court: What's the point? Why do you—why can't you just pick her up and carry her to the other side of the fence and set her down again? Wouldn't it be a lot cheaper than involving the Court and the staff and all these jurors' time and making such a big deal of this every time it happens.

Mr. Black: That's really the problem, Judge, that doesn't seem to result in anything other than her walking back across and having to repeatedly pick her up and set her down.

The Court: I haven't seen any great rash and huge numbers of other people following her to do this, have you?

Mr. Black: Not recently. . . .

. . . .

The Court: My point is that with the federal budget on the point of bankruptcy, considerably beyond bankruptcy, at least insolvency, there must be better and more significant criminal acts and worse criminals that you can spend your energy on than this kind of conduct, which could be solved just as well by just having somebody block her way when she tries to go across the fence or through the gate. One person could do that instead of having 12 jurors, a Judge, a courtroom, with a prosecutor or two, we have two public defenders on this case, I have had clerks, we got three probation officers, got the U.S. Marshals tied up all the time defending—guarding against the great danger of this lady, whose whole life is dedicated to peace, it just seems to me preposterous that we keep on wasting federal resources prosecuting people who aren't of any danger to anybody. How much danger is going to be caused for somebody to go in there and pray? You must have great faith in the power of prayer, Mr. Black.

Mr. Black: No, I don't really care to express any view on the power of prayer with regard to this issue. . . .

It is the people who show no respect whatsoever for the law and for the property out there and who seek to use the Court as a vehicle for expressing their views by causing themselves to be prosecuted that have forced the government to draw the line, because—

The Court: Well, if you don't bring them into court they wouldn't be able to use the courts as a vehicle to express their views.

Mr. Black: And, on the other hand, if—

The Court: It's like a seminar in here each time for 12 jurors.

Mr. Black: Yes, it is—on the other hand, if they weren't prosecuted the security of that facility, whether that's a desirable goal or not, is something that I don't have any opinion on or input on, but the security of that facility would be at risk, and I think that's—

The Court: In what way?

Mr. Black: Well, that facility has a number of different perimeters, as I recall, and at some point these perimeters start having fences and higher and higher levels of security because certainly no one in this courtroom knows what really goes on in there. But as we understand it, it is a facility for the production of materials within the nuclear weapons realm. And at some point there is—has got to be an exercise of security on the part of the government and the people operating out there.

The Court: Nobody questions that. The only question is whether this is the kind of conduct that really fits in a criminal prosecution setting or whether it's something that ought to be dealt with in a common sense manner instead of making a mountain out of it. It seems to me you have taken what amounts to a minor trespass in the quality of a jaywalking offense and made it into each time a major federal trial, and I just think it is a waste of government resources and simply place into the hands of those who want publicity and want to be martyrs, and I just don't see much point to it.

Mr. Black: I respect that view, Your Honor.

The Court: But if we had nothing else to do, of course, you know, it's always fun and entertaining to try these cases, it's interesting, they are interesting people, but I just can't see that with all the case problems we have got why we ought to be trying these minor trespass cases in Federal

Court. If someone trespasses in the courthouse here I don't think they would get prosecuted, I think we would just take them to the door and kick them out. I don't see why it wouldn't be a lot cheaper and a lot more sensible to do that at Rocky Flats. . . . It seems to me that we have become the yo-yo on the string here and it's all being paid for by the taxpayers.

I just wish your office would take another look at their policy. . . .

Mr. Black: We will take another look at it, Judge.

. . . .

The Court: Very well.

It's ordered that the defendant is hereby committed to the custody of the Attorney General, or his authorized representative, for imprisonment for a period of 47 days.

It's further ordered that the defendant shall receive credit for the 47 days she has already spent in confinement. . . .

It seems to me that that 47 days in County Jail for crawling under a fence on somebody's property is enough. . . .

Court is in recess.

Thank you, Mr. Black. . . .

I started out with your point of view in the first seven cases I had. The first seven defendants I had I gave substantial prison terms, and I have come around after eight years now to the view that we are all just wasting our time on these matters because they are not the classic criminals, they don't fit into the criminal system. By and large these are very good people who are expressing their views about what they consider to be a great danger to the survival of the human race on this planet. Whether they are right or wrong is not for me to decide, but I do have to decide how much I can possibly do as one Judge with more than twice as many cases as I had when I started this job, and a limited amount of time and resources and people to do them, and I wish you would take a look at that aspect of the problem.

Thank you very much.

Defendant Haines, having served her full sentence, is discharged.

I hope I don't see you in court again, Miss Haines.

—— ✄ ——

Carol-singing at Rocky Flats on Christmas Day had become a tradition for several of us from the Sunday vigil group. I carolled with the group, smiled and waved to the security guards, and returned home. The ordinary felt oddly unusual.

That winter, the winter of 1988, was dry and full of struggle. I had no sense, though of course I had a knowledge, of the presence of God. I felt completely out of touch. I couldn't attend to God. I couldn't focus. I couldn't pray. Sometimes I couldn't even sit still. Nothing was working. I felt like a failure, unable to do what I'm called to do, or to be what I'm called to be. I felt bombarded by all the unmet needs around me that I was deliberately choosing not to address directly, knowing all the time that the prayer work I was supposed to be doing instead I wasn't doing either. I couldn't stand myself. I was depressed, and the knowledge that the love of God should fill us with joy made me feel even more like a failure. I knew that it was wrong to be so focused on myself, on my own inadequacy, and yet I didn't know how to get out of it. I'd been ardently yearning for a long time to be more focused on God, to *love* God, and I couldn't do that either. I was stuck and frustrated every way I turned.

So what I added, at the point when it became obvious that even sitting still was a failure, was reading. It was Thomas Merton who finally began to bail me out. What spoke to me this time wasn't so much his words as his being. In an early morning meditation, I gradually found myself realizing that a key to the way out for me is: I take myself too seriously. I need to stop thinking that any of this matters so much. I need to stop agonizing over my failure. I need not even to care about it. I'd realized this before: It's *okay* that I'm a failure. It's *okay* that I'm useless and not capable of anything I'm called to. I needed to remember it.

When I first began to understand that, because the light of God illuminates my darkness, getting closer to God was going to mean becoming more and more aware of my sinfulness—rather than less, rather than seeing it disappear—I couldn't hope to see it disappear—what a hard thing that was to accept! Now I was beginning to understand that the emptiness and poverty of contemplation don't mean achieving some sort of spiritual progress but simply *discovering* that one *is* empty and impoverished, that I don't have, and never will have, anything to offer spiritually. The purpose of this long journey into the desert isn't to purify oneself or prepare oneself; it isn't to grow or to learn; it's simply to stop kidding oneself that one has anything to offer. That's what I had to accept now.

I'd always felt that discernment of God's will for me, moment by moment, was crucial, because I wanted passionately to do God's will, to be faithful. I was always afraid that, because I'm obviously the weak link in the chain, I'd blow it—I'd get it wrong or do it wrong, I'd hurt someone or fail God, and I'd feel terrible about it. But I was beginning to suspect that God's will for me probably isn't that specific: there are a lot of "right" things I could be doing, and God will make use of even the "wrong" things if I'm open to God. And, more important, it's crazy to worry about blowing it because I can be sure that I *will* blow it, because I'm human and limited and fallible, and the thing to do is to ask forgiveness, get up, dust myself off, and try again. It's really pride–though I may want to call it compassion or something–that gets me all uptight in the effort to make as close to a perfect score as I can in the love or prayer or faithfulness department, and it's pride that so agonizes over mistakes. I could see that I really wasn't anywhere near humility.

I resumed my Lenten prayer vigil at Rocky Flats, where I was graced to find that, even in inner dryness, I was able to be quiet and present. I was touched by accumulating indications of the meaning that my presence had for others. Sometimes a passer-by would stop to sit with me for a few minutes, or to leave me a little gift. There was a period when Anna stood vigil with me one day a week, and there were other periods when Alex did.

It felt as if my relationships there had come to include not only the individual ones which developed through personal interaction, but also some kind of a friendship between me and the plant as a whole. I was known to workers whom I couldn't recall ever having seen before. They knew my face and my name, what I stood for, and that I was gentle and friendly. They tended to be gentle and friendly in response. I remember during my vigil once feeling a powerful urge just to walk over to the plant (looking so small in the distance there!) and give it a big hug. In a sense, I did that with my presence over and over again.

My new spiritual director had been in St. Louis, completing his term as provincial, when I'd asked him to help me, and had since been in various parts of the world on sabbatical. We'd been corresponding. In March, I heard that he would be living and working in *Denver* as of August! The ways of the Lord are truly marvelous.

—— ✖ ——

By Good Friday, April 1, I was ready to celebrate again at Rocky Flats. Alex had joined my regular afternoon vigil at the west gate. I felt a wonderful, relaxed freedom that day, very quiet and centered, and prayed for a long time without any sense of compulsion either to enter the property or not. Then the quiet, holiday emptiness of the access road began to invite me: I could probably really pray at least as far as the guard station, which had been erected across the road some years earlier not far in from the state highway–and maybe I could pray all the way across the property to the east gate and keep on walking to the local bus. Suddenly, without being aware of when or how or on what grounds I had decided, I was walking down the road.

I was arrested and transported downtown. But in spite of the fact that it was already after 5:00, the magistrate arranged for a hearing, at which the government announced that it wasn't going to file any charges. Amazing! So I walked home.

Easter was even more celebrative. Having attended the Vigil Mass the night before, I had no plans for the day. I decided that what I really wanted to do was to walk to the regular Sunday afternoon Rocky Flats vigil from Golden, nine miles to the south, which was the nearest bus stop on a weekend. Feeling light and happy, I took a big, yellow balloon with me. Alex greeted me with a white rose when I got there. I knew very quickly that I was going to walk in, gave the balloon to Shirley, and ducked under the little gate with the rose. Shirley released the balloon, which danced in beside me, and I gave it to the security officers who arrested me.

City jail. Someone who doesn't know me is booking me in, and she calls down the hall to ask someone else how many fingerprint cards she needs. "What's the charge?" "Trespassing on federal property." "Trespassing on federal property? That's not Jennifer Haines, is it?" And she's absolutely delighted to see me. She's effusive—to me about how great I look, to the other officer about what an impressive person I am. She explains to me that the city jail doesn't allow free phone calls any more except to attorneys or bondsmen, but she lets me make a free phone call to the Catholic Worker house anyway. She tells me to go into cell #6, and I ask if that's one where you have to shut your own door. When she realizes that it is, I say, "You know, I won't shut it," and she replies, "Yes, of course. What *was* I thinking of?" But she assigns me to it anyway, and comes back with me to close the door. Before closing it, she offers me a sack lunch, which is unheard of in my experience at that place; if you miss a meal, unless you were in court, forget it. Isn't it something the way relationships evolve?

At Denver County, I refused the ID bracelet from the officer in Receiving, who promised me max as punishment and escorted me herself to the women's building so that she could tell the officers there. Of course, I had rather expected to end up in max anyway. But I'd had no idea what I was getting into.

The jail had just completed construction of a brand-new women's building. And the new, modern maximum-security section is *much* worse than the old one—except for the absence of television, which may be appreciated only by me. There's no common area; the cells face each other across a corridor, with a shower at one end. And there are no windows—at least in the cell where they put me. I was incredulous. Human beings are expected to live without *windows*?! I might be here two months or more! You couldn't adjust the lights, which were too bright, or the temperature, which was too warm. In addition, there was a new kind of mat with a big, built-in hump at one end, which made it impossible to lie flat unless you were a great deal shorter than the bed—which I'm not. I asked, and was told that there was no alternative.

So I had a bit of a cry, grieving for the lost window, and then I adjusted. I was in a very good inner space for coping, and I'd learned that the key is to choose to be okay with whatever you're stuck with, never imagining that it might change. The cells *do* have skylights, so I could tell night from day and even watch the sunlight move in gradually shifting patterns across the walls. I put the mat on the floor with the hump at the bottom, letting my feet hang off the side. I used the solid metal bed frame for a writing table, sitting on the floor.

I reflected on how incredibly much easier everything is if I don't want *anything*, even the things I have a right to, if I'm content just to stare at the walls until someone offers me something, and then to be very grateful for whatever it is, to receive it as a gift.

I reminded myself that I could ignore everything outside my locked door. My world inside was not only complete, but very full and rich, pervaded and blessed by God. *That* was what I needed to keep attending to. It wasn't a matter of being content with not having, but of being thankful for having.

On April 12, I recognized further that, though it's good to keep trying to get free of needing things (the big benefit of living without a window was that I was going to discover that I could live without a window), it's even better to embrace the pain of whatever I feel deprived about and offer it to God as prayer for others. I don't know how our own personal suffering can be redemptive for others, but I do know that it can. I determined to keep trying to be thankful for everything that hurt me and offer it to help those who needed prayer.

That same day, I was offered a window! An officer who'd known me for a long time was distressed at how long I was expecting to be locked down pending trial and suggested that I could move to one of the two end cells, which do have windows. The windows are small and rather high but still expand your visual space and sense of being human, and they can be opened for some cool, fresh air. It was a great improvement. I even had a wildflower growing in the bare dirt beyond mine!

I had been reading the autobiography of St. Teresa of Avila, slowly and devotionally, for years. I was allowed to have the book in jail. Her all-consuming love for God and the depth of her prayer had been nurturing and inspiring me all along. Now I was struck by her insistence on staying close to the *humanity* of Jesus. Who are we to think that we can soar in realms of divine mystery? But we can surely understand and appreciate the entirely human suffering of our God, who loves us so much as to have become human and lived among us. Yes. It was a particularly helpful direction for me, who's always trying to stretch between earth and heaven. God has already spanned that gap in God's own person and provided the bridge for us.

—— ✄ ——

May 7. The answer is: to find the joy in the suffering, that is, in the acceptance of suffering; to embrace suffering with joy; to be glad to be allowed to participate in Christ's redemption of the world.

—— ✄ ——

I was again facing a year in prison. But my case had again been assigned, providentially (the world would say "luckily," but I no longer believe in happenstance), to the judge whom I had already seen three times in a row and who I was sure would not sentence me to it. He moved the trial date, originally set for mid-June, up to mid-May. I was, predictably, convicted by a jury. At sentencing, two weeks later, the judge directed his lecture at me. He was *not* happy to see me back in his courtroom. My choices, as much as the prosecutor's, contributed to what he considered to be a misdirection of judicial resources and of the taxpayers' money. Then he sentenced me to time served and released me.

Anticipating the likelihood of such a sentence from this judge had catalyzed an important decision for me about my witness at Rocky Flats. It was my third reprieve since 1985 from a potentially long stretch in prison. The time that I was not required to spend praying in prison, it seemed right to be spending in prayer at the Rocky Flats gate. It had made sense to me for a long time to continue my weekday vigil there throughout the year, but I kept stumbling against the cost of the commute. *Why* was I letting money stand in my way? If it was right for me to be there, the money would be available. The bus would cost about $42 a month, or about $500 a year. I mentioned the need to a few people, and almost immediately had $700 in hand for it.

So, following some visiting time with family and friends on the east coast, I began the year-round vigil in early August.

The regular schedule gave my days and my prayer a healthy rhythm. My persistent presence at the Flats spoke powerfully of my beliefs and values. My relationships with people whom I saw regularly at the gate, along the highway, and on the buses grew. The most obvious challenge was the weather. Summer heat is particularly oppressive for me, and inescapable. There's no shelter or shade anywhere near the west gate. I walked in the sun, and I sat in the sun. I avoided the asphalt of the traffic island on hot days and sat across the highway by the peace garden.

Cold is generally less of a problem, because you can prepare for it, at which I became *very* proficient. I learned to expect Rocky Flats to be a good deal colder than Denver and to travel with many layers to accommodate the huge temperature difference between walking in the warmest part of the day and waiting for buses after dark. I didn't mind snow, standing in my blue poncho, gradually being transformed into a white mountain. There was little rain. My one experience of hail came after I had, thankfully, already been offered a ride. Rides were common in inclement weather. I have a lovely memory of one snowy day when I saw, on turning to leave my vigil, that one of the people who often picked me up had parked on the shoulder behind me and was patiently waiting for me.

Wind was ordinarily the greatest challenge. It would pour over the exposed stretch of highway that runs north from the bus stop past the Flats, gusty and sometimes so strong that I could barely walk against it. If I could get to the gate, I could *sit* against it. Once, I was saved by a ride when it was all I could do to stay upright against the gusts, only occasionally recovering enough to take a step. Only under practically impossible conditions like that did I accept rides *to* the plant. And there was just one time when I didn't make it. I had stepped off the bus into a tempestuous wind full of blowing snow that totally obscured the road to the north in a thick, white cloud, and I decided that, whether or not I could walk in it, the danger of being hit by a car was too great to risk. Even as I was retreating to the bus shelter, the highway department arrived to close that section of the road.

One extraordinary challenge topped the wind. That was the day when the temperature hit eighteen degrees below zero in Denver; I don't know what it was at the Flats, and I don't know a thing about wind chill factors. I just took everything imaginable to try to stay warm, figuring that if I couldn't stand it, I could leave. It was sort of an adventure. And it's always a thrill to discover that you can do something difficult.

—— ✖ ——

The most dramatic event of that winter, though, was a very quiet, internal one. God was preparing me for my next ordeal by giving me a new understanding of my own ego—whom I had so far experienced as a perennial adversary in my attempt to be faithful to God. I perceived her as a domineering tyrant, who was forever blocking my spiritual path at one point or another, needing to be resisted, overcome, or gotten beyond.

My spiritual director had suggested, a year earlier, that I should try loving her, so she'd feel free to go away. That sounded right. I love everybody else, and so have no enemies. I've learned that all sorts of walls simply aren't there when I stop fighting them. I should be able to relate to myself in the same way. But I couldn't. I couldn't even imagine how. How do you love that part of yourself that you particularly don't like? I'd felt stuck at that point for a long time.

The answer came to me one morning in Mass when I was feeling vulnerable. I overreacted to something insignificant in an inappropriate and childish way, reminding myself of how I'd spoken once about "my little ego getting huffy without provocation." And then, in prayer, it suddenly hit me that my ego actually *is* this little girl in me who feels hurt and unreceived and needs to be loved. So Hugh's advice to love my ego suddenly made sense. I *can* love a vulnerable little girl. If I just allow and receive those inappropriate feelings instead of putting them down, they *will* go away.

It was an earth-shattering insight–blowing open a huge door in a long-standing, massive wall across my path and making the whole spiritual journey suddenly look *possible* again. I knew that I had been handed the key to a personal revolution, and, in fact, I soon found out that I had been handed the revolution itself.

7

Trial . . .

Wouldn't it be splendid to sail a hot-air balloon into Rocky Flats? That fantasy occurred to me, I don't remember why, during my first prison term, in 1982, and it continued to intrigue me. I had never even seen a hot-air balloon at that time–though many since–and I have never ridden in one. But my imagination was caught by the symbolism: freedom and lightness and beauty and letting the wind carry you, not even knowing if you'd end up where you thought you wanted to go. What an exercise in trust! Of course, I couldn't actually do it without a hot-air balloon, which is an expensive and rather uncommon item, and I couldn't just *borrow* one, since it might be damaged or confiscated. So I figured that if God wanted me to do it, God would provide the balloon.

Meanwhile, balloons became my symbol. I often left ordinary, little ones on Rocky Flats fences where I stood vigil. And I carried a beautiful, big, blue one with me on Christmas Day of 1988, when I ducked under that little gate again to carry my celebration of the Incarnation, of light arising in darkness, into Rocky Flats. I had no idea what an intense season of testing and discernment I was entering into. It began with lightness and grace.

At the city jail, one of the officers welcomed me with a big hug. At Denver County, a sergeant who saw me in the hall offered me his hand to wish me a happy New Year. I was booked directly into max. One of the regular officers came back to my cell just to talk, and to cry a little, about the mess our society is in and how oppressed she feels by it. It was tremendously affirming to see even the *relational* walls–the barriers that are established by roles and structures and categories–disappearing! As I made friends across them, the walls gradually dissolved in the warmth of the friendships, and we all walked through them with ease.

On January 3, I was called back to court. My case had been assigned to the judge whom I had seen most often during my early years in Denver. This was my fifth case before her. We had come to know one another rather well in the course of all those interactions. She didn't want me spending pre-trial time in jail. I reiterated my unwillingness to promise to return to court and added, "I'm not willing to appear in court because the court orders me to appear."

She answered, "I'm not ordering you. I'm asking you." Nothing could have carried more weight with me than such a human invitation. Of course, I wanted to honor and affirm it. I told her that I would like to be able to respond to her request and would come unless prevented by an unforeseen impediment. She released me.

I resumed my daily vigil at Rocky Flats. I finished quilting a quilt. The trial date was moved up from Friday to Monday, February 13, and I returned to court. It was delightful, for a change, to be able to move freely about the courtroom and to mingle with my friends in the spectators' section during breaks.

I had already discovered that not being concerned with goals or effectiveness includes the freedom of not needing to be heard or understood. I don't have to change anything, *and* I don't have to convince anyone of anything. The most wonderful consequence of that attitude, I find, is that I never lose my freedom to love. No one is ever an enemy or an obstacle for me. No one becomes the object of my need to make something or other happen. I can continue to appreciate each one as the unique and precious child of God he or she is, while standing clearly for who I am and what I believe.

I was in such an inner place of grace that day that practically my whole experience of the trial and sentencing was of loving people: all my friends who came to support me, all the Rocky Flats people who came to testify against me, the jury, the court personnel. I was sort of dancing around in a flood of good will. How freeing it is to have no stake at all in either the process or the outcome! I was able to be very wholly me.

The jury brought in a "guilty" verdict just before the noon recess. The judge wanted to know if I would return for sentencing. I said no, but that I was willing to return to discuss it further after the break. We agreed to that. A friend treated me to lunch and some quiet time in a lovely downtown church. The judge somehow managed to be ready for sentencing—which included the compilation by the probation department of a rather complicated PSI (Pre-Sentence Investigation)—by the time we had regathered to discuss it. I wasn't surprised. I understood and respected her as well as she understood and respected me, and each of us was doing her best to give the other human space within the confines of the system.

Sentencing presented a difficult situation for her. A new "Comprehensive Crime Control Act," which had become federal law in 1987, mandated sentencing "guidelines" that severely restricted a judge's discretion. Arithmetical calculations, based on many "offense severity" factors plus many "criminal history" factors, produced a sentencing range within which a judge was forced to act. This judge, among others in Denver, had declared the law unconstitutional and refused to be bound by it until the Supreme Court, just recently, had ruled in its favor. So now her hands were tied.

In my case, there was an aggravating factor under "offense severity," specifically covering nuclear facilities, but what really drove the guidelines up was my "criminal history"–exclusively petty and misdemeanor "trespass" at Rocky Flats, but a long list. The guidelines demanded a sentence of at least nine months in prison.

The judge could see no legitimate way within the law to depart from the guidelines. Her only option would have been to give me half of my time in a halfway house; she asked me about that, and I responded that I didn't see how I could last long in such a place, given my level of noncooperation. So, though clearly not at ease with it, she felt compelled to sentence me to nine months. I expected as much, and was prepared, too, to be taken directly into custody.

The U.S. marshal on duty, whom I'll call Max, had joined the marshals' office while I was in prison in 1985. Of course, I made friends among the marshals. I saw a good deal of them. But Max was one of those who tended to retreat into his macho power role and not reveal himself. He would tease me when I received a light sentence, saying, "You should do a year in prison." "I did," I would smile. "You just missed it." Now he had to take me into custody to serve a sentence that was not light. He wasn't at all happy about it. Our relationship had grown a lot in three years. He let me hug my friends good-bye, and he didn't even handcuff me for the short walk from the courtroom to the holding cell.

The judge had been concerned for me to do as little of my time as possible in county jails, but I was still surprised when the Bureau of Prisons was ready to transport me in less than three full days. The marshals told me on the way to the airlift that I was going to Arizona. Arizona? *What* was in Arizona?

It turned out to be a brand-new, low-security federal prison camp for women that had opened less than a month before. I lasted one day there. I was written up the first morning for refusing to work, and then, when I wouldn't stand up for the 4:00 P.M. count (the daily national Bureau of Prisons count), the prison gave up on me. So I spent the next three weeks in a county jail after all, which was what the prison camp used for detention.

The Phoenix jail was huge and regimented. My refusal to use an inmate ID (a plastic clip-on card) and an inmate registration number led to a lot of quiet deprivation. Confrontations over the ID and head count led to write-ups, denial of privileges, and eventually administrative lockdown in a small, dingy solitary cell with no outside window. I was thankful that the prison sentenced me to a transfer and moved me on relatively quickly.

Thankfully, too, the airlift happened to cover the stretch from Phoenix to Sacramento in a single day. From Sacramento, a prison van drove several of us directly to Pleasanton. Arriving on a Friday evening, I expected to have a weekend in the general population before being confronted by the work issue, but the prison had other plans for me. I had barely been assigned to a dorm before being told to report to "the top of the yard," where an officer ordered me to clean the staff lounge on the spot. I refused, knowing that I had been deliberately set up, and resigned myself to immediate immersion in detention.

It was quite an immersion! The crowding had become extreme. All but one of the eight cells, each designed for two people, were now quadruple-bunked. In addition, security had been tightened beyond anything I'd seen anywhere before. The way handcuffs had been used when I was at Alderson had been enough to move me into noncooperation. Here now, in order to leave your cell, you had to walk to the door, turn around, and put your hands through the food tray slot behind you. The officer cuffed you, then unlocked the door. You walked to where you were going, say the shower, which happened to be directly across the hall from my door about four feet away, and you were locked in there before being uncuffed through another slot. The already small recreation yard had been divided into two totally enclosed, wire-mesh cages with slots in the doors. When you went to a "disciplinary" hearing, the cuffs weren't taken off.

My heart sort of sank when I first began to see how the system worked, and realized that I might lose all my showers and rec, but I adjusted to the idea. I was willing to walk to the door and turn around. If the officer was willing to reach in, pick up my hands, and put them in the cuffs, then I got to go wherever-it-was. If not, I didn't. I could bathe and exercise in my cell, if necessary, as long as I was alone, though it was much more difficult when I had even one cellmate. Cellmates also increased the likelihood that you could be ordered to "cuff up" even when not leaving the cell. In order for the door to be opened for any reason, a stickler of an officer could require everyone in the cell to be handcuffed first. I flatly refused to approach the door *just* to be handcuffed.

Before I'd been locked down a week, I'd been forcibly moved twice. I refused to cooperate with a move into a freshly painted and unaired cell, and was simply picked up by four officers, who cuffed and shackled me, carried me into the cell, set me down on the floor, and removed the restraints.

Three days later, when I refused to "cuff up" for some inmate workers to come into the cell to do a quick repair job, the prison's response was much less gentle. About six officers charged in like a riot squad, dragged me off the top bunk by my arms—at which I went limp, and fell—jerked my hands behind my back to cuff them, and shackled my legs. I felt like part of a training exercise. They carried me into the empty two-person cell, laid me on my face on the bottom mattress, held me down tightly while someone removed the shackles, then jumped up, rushed out, and locked the door.

There followed a long siege in handcuffs. Occasionally, one of the officers would unlock the flap over the food tray slot and invite me to uncuff through the door. I wouldn't respond. They were clearly determined to make me come to the door, and I was just as determined not to. I would *not* have anything to do with handcuffs; they had insisted on putting them on me, and it was up to them to take them off.

My second refusal was recorded as a refusal of lunch. The lieutenant who, some hours later, delivered my incident report told me that the cuffs could be removed only through the locked door. I waited. I was quite sure that I could outwait them, thankful that I have a lot of patience, and beginning to suspect that I could probably suffer being punished longer than any compassionate person could suffer punishing me. The worst of the ordeal was that I needed badly to use the toilet, which I probably could have managed, but I couldn't reach to cover the window in the door, and the unit was swarming with inmate workers, in addition to the staff who were paying rather a lot of attention to me, so I continued to wait. I was very quiet.

After four or five hours, shortly before the end of the day shift, another riot squad arrived and simply stood in the hall. One person came in, knelt by the bed, and unlocked the handcuffs, gently massaging the wrist whose cuff had been tight and left deep ridges in the skin. I said, "Thank you." He answered, "My pleasure." Ordinary life resumed.

I reflected afterward on how incidents like this tend to test me and confirm the grace of God in my life: by calling on all my God-given resources—on faith and discernment, freedom, peace, and love—they show me how available and dependable those gifts are. The fact that I don't get angry is especially significant, really the crowning glory of God's action in my life. I never stop loving the people who are doing whatever-it-is to me. I don't blame them. I don't feel put upon. I *expect* the system to react coercively toward me when I resist it. So this kind of experience is basically positive, and the biggest danger is that my ego may try to grab onto the good things God is doing in me and claim credit for them.

Two days later one of the officers who had charged me and dragged me off the bunk—a particularly nice guy whom I'd liked from the beginning—came back to talk to me in the rec yard. I was very glad to see him, because I wanted him to know that I wasn't mad at him. He told me that he'd "read up" on me and understood now that I was peaceful and just standing by my word. "You're a good woman," he said. "I hope I wasn't too forceful with you the other day." I answered, "I know you have your job to do. I never hold that against anybody." He seemed to be relieved. And I felt that he had made my day; relationship comes out on top again!

That rec period was the last time I got out of my cell for a while. The quarterly shift change for prison staff gave us a regular day officer—I'll call him Hal—who insisted on full cooperation with the handcuffs. It was decidedly an asset that the most recent incident had left me in a cell by myself. It had lots of natural light, though not much view. And I still had a chance of getting out on Thursdays, when the regular officer was off and the relief officer was flexible.

With Hal, I gradually developed a relationship. He was required to offer me showers and rec, which I never refused, so we had many little conversations around the handcuff issue. I could tell that he was personally engaged when he responded to one of my handcuff refusals with, "You're frustrating the hell out of me."

I asked to see the Catholic chaplain, who gave me a rosary. There was something very comforting about having a crucifix in my cell, in my hand.

It was comforting, too, to know that people were praying for me. My own prayer seemed sort of oddly unfocused these days. I had loads of empty, solitary time, and it didn't feel as if I actually spent much of it praying. I didn't have a clear sense of being present to God or of God's presence to me or of an explicit faith basis to my choices. But there was a quality to my whole life—to my choices and feelings and perhaps even my being—that seemed not only grounded in something as solid as prayer, but that maybe somehow *was* prayer. I felt sort of whole and secure—able to be myself, to trust my intuition, to meet what I had to meet. I still wanted to *love* God, to listen to God, to attend to God-with-me; yet there was something about this dark and incoherent solidness that surely had to do with God-with-me, too.

— ✖ —

March 24, Good Friday. Good morning, new day!
    "Are you going to cuff up?"
    "I would like to take a shower."
    "Are you going to cuff up?"
    "I'm not going to put my hands through that hole."
    So much for showers. They aren't offered on Thursdays. I would particularly like a shower today, because sponge-baths are a mess when you're bleeding and you don't have tampons. (Tampons are available in the commissary, but not for detention inmates. The detention list doesn't include vitamins or dental floss or emery boards either. As far as I can tell, there's absolutely no authorized way to trim your nails in here.) I thought of saying something about the blood, but I didn't. The system demands that I suffer for my nonconformity to its demands, and I realize that it doesn't matter whether it knows how much I suffer. From its point of view, what's going on is a sort of battle of wills: Can it punish me enough to make me give in? Or will I hold out long enough that it can't stand punishing me any longer? But really what's going on is much deeper. My suffering is the price of the system's redemption, whether it knows it or not. If there weren't a price that I willingly pay for my nonconformity, then it wouldn't have any particular meaning. It's okay—probably necessary—that I feel the

pain, but not grudgingly. I need to embrace it, to absorb it, and to give it to God. I need to be thankful that I've been chosen for this work, which is part of the crucifixion. (I didn't choose it. The chaplain said something yesterday about our not needing to go out looking for suffering, and I agree. Plenty comes our way without our choice. But it's a grace to be chosen, and it's a grace to accept the choice.) And I need to accept it in the hidden solitude of my prayer closet, because that's where God transforms it. It doesn't matter what the system sees of my pain and how it might be touched by that. What changes the world is God's action in the realm of the spirit. My true cross is probably this hidden, daily, ordinary deprivation—rather than the brief, dramatic public events—and my challenge is to carry it willingly and cheerfully. It would be gratifying for me to see this officer change, to see him decide that he doesn't want to punish me any longer—it would show me the goodness that I know is in him and affirm again the power of relationship and caring in the world—but it isn't necessary. The only necessary thing is my faithfulness. That's what allows God to work in the situation, and God's work doesn't have to be seen by anyone.

March 25, Holy Saturday. On his way to lunch yesterday, [Hal] told his relief that the next group going out for rec was segregation. He let the relief officer deal with it, and he let me go out. At the end of the hour, [Hal] was back. He told me that if I'd just put my hands through the slot to be cuffed to go in, he'd let me have a shower. (Showers were long over.) I smiled. "Is this a bribe?" "Yes." "I appreciate your offer. I'd love a shower. I won't put my hands through there. I didn't do it to come out." He cuffed me without my cooperation and didn't let me have a shower.

    Found myself reflecting at bedtime on the tremendous strength there is in the position that chooses to accept suffering. It isn't one's own strength. It isn't the power of will or stubbornness. What it is, really, is the power of weakness. It has patience in it, and endurance. If one can endure weakness (and the ultimate freedom is the willingness to endure one's own failure and inadequacy) and vulnerability and pain without giving in to despair or anger or hatred, if one can suffer with an undamaged spirit, with hope and love, then one is invincible. What can anyone do to you? The worst is torture and death. And if you choose to accept that, if you willingly embrace the cross, not only are you free—you can't be threatened or pushed around or coerced or compromised—but you come through alive and whole, with your spirit bright and shining. And it's not because of anything you've done or anything great in you. It has to do with accepting your littleness, having nothing to do with any kind of power, taking whatever is dished out, not complaining, not fighting, not asking for anything—and not for one moment giving up an iota of your faith, hope, and love. Which is the same thing as clinging to God, resting in God. "Father, forgive them; for they know not what they do" [Luke 23:34]. The

more I try to put this into words, the more I find myself describing Jesus
and the crucifixion—which is, of course, our perfect model. But the seed of
the reflection was my own insignificant little experience with handcuffs
and showers. I don't feel as if I'm doing anything in particular—I'm not
making any effort, not deliberately choosing, not struggling, not striving for
anything or resisting anything—I'm just responding simply and honestly to
whatever comes along—and yet I'm struck by the invincibility of my
position: either I can just keep on suffering indefinitely, or people can
change their minds and stop punishing me, and I'm okay with either one.

March 26, Easter Sunday. Alleluia!
        [Hal] just came to my door, announced, "Sunshine!," stuck the open
handcuffs in through the door slot, and said, "Come over here." So I got to
go out for rec—with sunshine. Happy Easter!

March 27. No shower. I was hopeful this morning, almost expectant, and
so I feel hurt, but I'm not really very surprised. It seemed to me yesterday
that [Hal's] letting me out was about as frustrating for him as his not
letting me out had been. [I understand his organized, efficient, competent
sort of personality and can appreciate the struggle in him.] I think he feels
pushed around by my "unpusharoundability," and he's used to being in
control. [Later, he wheeled his chair to my door and lounged in it,
smoking, for] a long talk about why I don't cooperate. I think maybe he
was more trying to talk me out of it than to understand, but I was still
glad for the chance to try to explain.

——— ✖ ———

By March 31, I had completed the disciplinary segregation time I'd
been given on March 16, but I was sure that more (twenty-one days, I
found out later) had been added on March 22 at a DHO hearing that I
hadn't been allowed to attend. So I wasn't even considering the possibility
of a return to the compound. Imagine my amazement when I was told that
afternoon that I was leaving detention. *Me*?! *Really*? Really. I was released
to the compound after dinner.
    For a whole glorious week I immersed myself in the natural environ-
ment, enjoying grass and flowers, trees silhouetted against the daily miracle
of the gradually lightening morning sky, fresh breezes, singing birds; and
the reverse daily miracle in the evening, as I walked around and around
the track on the rec field while the setting sun spread color across the sky
and the color gradually muted into darkness. The rec field closed before
full dark, but the compound was open until close to 9:00, and I stayed out
as long as I could.
    During working hours I stayed in the unit, because prisoners on Admis-
sion and Orientation status were officially responsible to the unit officer

for work assignments, but I never responded to calls for all A & O's to report, and no one came looking for me personally for a full week. I also never signed out and in, as A & O's were required to do. I didn't feel as if I were in prison at all, I think mainly because no one was telling me what to do. I was living my own life in my own way, accepting some place and time restrictions without feeling restricted by them, and interacting with the officers as I do with everybody, in a friendly and egalitarian way.

My friend Barbara, whom I'd first met on the airlift on my way to Phoenix and her way here, was wonderfully helpful, making sure that I had everything I needed and embracing me with her life and world. I met many of her friends and spent lots of time hanging out and talking with lots of people. I was having a great time, giving myself exuberantly to all the opportunities that the expanded horizons of life on the compound offer, knowing that it couldn't last long.

At the end of the week, on a Friday afternoon just before 4:00 P.M. count (which hadn't caught me here, because you didn't have to stand up for it; I was willing to be in my room), I was paged by name to come to the unit officer's station. She ordered me to sweep the common area. End of R & R.

Back in detention, I was immediately confronted with the overcrowding issue in an intense and personal way. I was assigned to a cell where three women had only just been able to spread out a little after a fourth had been transferred out, I think that same day. For more than two months, the four of them had been locked down together, which is a level of crowding that I consider inhuman. You were essentially restricted to a space the size of your bed, because only one person could be moving around at a time, and the only moving available was to go to the toilet or the door. Those women didn't deserve to be punished by the addition of me, whatever the intent may have been toward me. I refused to enter the cell. Of course, I was forced, the simple way: two men just grabbed me by the upper arms and dragged me in. After my second refusal the same evening, I was moved to a cell with only one cellmate.

Meanwhile, though, my simmering frustration over the vegetarian diet issue, which had been building since before my sojourn on the compound, had been brought to a head. It wasn't that I necessarily expected a vegetarian diet; I was used to eating what I could from the regular trays. But I'd asked about it because it had been available to me in prison before, and the more I inquired, the more upset I became over the unreasonableness of the responses.

I'd been given conflicting information at first, but finally concluded that a vegetarian diet must not be available in the "hole" (the common name for a prison's detention unit) here. So I'd written to food services, asking if they could at least leave the meat and gravy off my tray, and received an elaborate reply to the effect that BOP policy required that we get exactly the same meal as was served in the dining hall. On the compound I discovered that the dining hall offered enough vegetarian options for me to eat well there; the hole obviously did not receive the same meal, but only a part of it. When I pointed this out to the food services administrator, suggesting that he send me the part that I'd eat instead of the part that I'd throw away, he acknowledged that there wasn't room on the tray for everything, but continued to insist that we had to get "exactly the same meal."

I was also able to see the dietician, who turned out to be an equally solid and unreasoning wall. Her answer was, "Stay out of the hole then." Doesn't a person on lockdown have a right to adequate nutrition, too? I knew that there were at least three other vegetarians in the hole who had been struggling to get the meat off their trays for a long time.

So when I landed in the midst of all the legalized insanity of overcrowding, I could suddenly no longer tolerate the corresponding insanity in the prison's denial of our nutritional needs—not the denial itself so much as the senselessness of it. I could no longer accept massive and arbitrary and unyielding unreasonableness. I refused dinner and told the officer that I wouldn't eat until I got a vegetarian diet.

I was in too emotional a space for clear discernment, but the choice felt inevitable, like the only one left to me under the circumstances. Perhaps I needed to enter it through that rather suspect emotional door, because it was the only way past my own stubborn and deliberate caution. I had earlier talked myself out of refusing the regular trays on the grounds that my motivation might have been a childish kind of pouting, that any kind of "hunger strike" would be an attempt to force the prison's choices and therefore wrong for me, and that I knew my body couldn't handle fasting anyway. I'd gotten so sick many years earlier after just four days on water only that I'd steered clear of it ever since.

Now I was suddenly committed. I wasn't certain that it was the right choice. The risk to my health was very scary. Even my own stubbornness, whose limits I've never discovered, was scary. I had no expectation that I'd get a vegetarian diet. I actually expected the prison to force me. But I just couldn't not stand firm. The prison was insisting on giving me an inadequate diet that would make me sick gradually, with no one noticing, while an adequate diet was available and denied me arbitrarily. I was no longer willing to cooperate in the prison's victimization of me by accepting the inadequate diet. Refusing all my trays, I became sick quickly, and everybody noticed.

I knew that the prison would monitor my health and try to prevent me from doing anything life-threatening, which was very reassuring. On Monday, I mentioned to a PA that I was already concerned about my condition. The PAs started checking my weight, pulse, blood pressure, and urine that day, and a doctor took over the next. Her position on the diet issue was as rigid as that of the food services administrator. She, too, assured me that it was impossible for me to receive a selection from the dining hall options that would include what I ate instead of what I didn't eat.

The captain called me into his office on Tuesday. The detention officers routinely record any meal that any prisoner refuses, and if you refuse several in a row or declare a hunger strike, supervisors are alerted. He said that if I didn't start eating soon, he'd have me force-fed. He was graphic about it–told me that they'd grind up in a blender all that stuff I won't eat and force it into my stomach through a tube down my nose. I was prepared for the possibility of force-feeding, but it was appalling to think that I might be fed *meat*. The doctor, however, said that this institution didn't force-feed anybody and that, if I didn't eat soon, they'd have no alternative but to transfer me to an institution that did.

By Wednesday I was weak and shaky and inclined toward transient dizziness. I could walk, but not stand for long. A simple activity like combing my hair, especially first thing in the morning, was very hard work, and I'd have to stop for breaks in order to get through it. I was sleeping less and less, though I spent essentially all my time in bed. The doctor was so concerned about my condition that morning that I was prepared for the institution to make a move very soon.

So when I was told, shortly after I'd gotten back from the prison "hospital," that the doctor wanted to see me again, I refused. I'd already decided that I wouldn't undertake any more activity that day anyway, and I wasn't about to participate in anything coercive that the prison might do to me. A riot squad dragged me out of bed, not too roughly, cuffed me, *carried* me to the "hospital," which was, fortunately, next door, and set me down on a chair in the doctor's office.

She said, "Miss Haines, we've decided to offer you a special diet, which will be a selection from the meal served in the dining hall. There will be no meat on it. Would you be willing to look at your next tray and consider eating it?"

Amazing. I was actually being offered the minimum of what I had asked for. The whole ordeal was suddenly over. I wasn't going to be forced, and I could start eating again. It was the last thing I had expected and the best possible outcome. And I found that my feelings were utterly matter-of-fact, sort of along the lines of, "Oh, here we are." There was no elation or triumph. I had been flowing with the situation all along, here was where it had come out, and I was already flowing on beyond it–reminding me of Chögyam Trungpa talking about how much *space* there is when you get beyond ego. I hadn't accomplished anything. I had merely stood firm.

The good diet quickly restored my health. I told the inmate orderly about it, hoping that the other vegetarians in the hole would benefit as well. But the only result was that I received a "high severity" incident report for "encouraging a group demonstration." The prison continued flatly to deny to others the diet I was now receiving. Its position seemed to be: Unless you're willing to fight for it, forget it! I was prepared to support their struggle as vigorously as they wanted, but they apparently didn't want to struggle that badly–which struck me as rather sad. Was I really doing anything for anyone else? If my example offered something that others could follow, would there be anyone who would want to follow it?

The captain was remarkably amicable at my next routine review. I was soon living with two cellmates in the women's segregation cell and not feeling oppressively overcrowded. I was enjoying the simple things of daily life, glad to settle into a season of ordinariness.

Ordinariness, however, was not in the picture. Two days after the resolution of the diet issue, the overcrowding issue took over. I overheard an officer remarking that a new woman coming into the hole would have to be put in the seg cell, which had the only open bed for a woman. I announced that if they tried to put a fourth person in this cell, I'd protest the overcrowding by leaving it.

The officers reconsidered the situation, decided that there was no other option, and came back with reinforcements, including Hal, who was acting lieutenant that week. They cuffed up my cellmates, then opened the door, all standing in the doorway. I said, "I'm leaving"–which was patently impossible. I took one step, was grabbed, thrown on the floor on my face, cuffed, and held down, while someone stepped over me to bring in a mattress. The woman came in. They uncuffed my cellmates through the door and invited me to come to the door, too. Sound familiar? I decided that I just wasn't living in this cell any more. I sat on the floor in the corner until, after about two and a half hours, someone came in to uncuff me. The new woman, meanwhile, had been released back to the compound.

Four days later I was sitting quietly on my bed writing when suddenly, with no warning at all, the door opened and another woman was coming in with her mattress. I acted faster than I can think–tore off my glasses and jumped down from the bunk, yelling, "Oh, no you don't!" I made it to the door not quite in time to get through it before Hal began closing it again, but in time to impede it with the weight of my body and put all my fingers inside the jamb so he couldn't close it all the way without crushing them. He held it just short of my fingers, while I continued to push out against it, saying, "No, *no, no!*," and he radioed for reinforcements.

It was a good thing that it was Hal who was responding to all this, because he knew exactly what my bizarre behavior meant. Standing there with my legs shaking from the entirely unhelpful rush of adrenalin, I wondered how I'd ever gotten into such uncharacteristic and active resistance. I certainly couldn't have *thought* my way through this one.

Someone stuck a hand through the food tray slot from outside and held me against the door by grabbing the back of my clothing (the standard T-shirt and boxer shorts that detention prisoners wore in our cells) while Hal opened it. The person clutching my underwear turned out to be the captain. He had me handcuffed. I was willing to follow him to the staff restroom/strip-search room, where our brief conversation was so intense and passionate that I remember more of the feeling tone than the content.

We didn't raise our voices, but he was obviously increasingly furious, and I was charged with an emotion that had been common for me in these interactions over justice issues and that I couldn't quite identify—not exactly anger, but it had the heat of anger—maybe passion. It wasn't gentle or courteous, and it would sort of rise up and overpower me.

He was basically saying that it was my fault I was in the hole, and if I didn't like it, I should stay out of here. I was basically saying that the conditions in here were inhuman and unnecessary. There must be alternatives—such as transferring the people who'd been waiting two and three months to be transferred. We were both talking past and through each other. He finally stepped so close that his face was just inches from mine and grated out, "You *will* live in a cell with three other women, and if you make any trouble, I'll have you strapped to your bed, and you can piss and shit all over yourself with all those other people in the cell." I answered, "Feel free," but missed my usual casual tone and heard it coming out intense and assertive like all the rest of the conversation. He ordered me to go back to the cell, which I, of course, refused to do, so the officers carried me.

During the ensuing siege in handcuffs, Hal checked on me periodically, clearly concerned to know that I was all right physically, which I was, and his solicitude kept confirming my good feelings about our relationship. I enjoyed talking and laughing with my cellmates.

By the time, late in the shift, that a lieutenant came quietly in to unlock the handcuffs, I had figured out my response to being stuck in an overcrowded cell. Since someone else had moved in, I would "move out." I would not accept the situation by returning to my normal life and space but would just stay here on the floor, in the corner by the door. It would have been consistent to stop eating as well, but I was afraid the captain would perceive that as a power play on my part, inspired by my recent "success" and now employed as a weapon in a new pitched battle between him and myself, so it seemed clearer and more humble to eat.

That was Tuesday, April 18. On Wednesday I was called out to the "hospital" for a routine consultation with a doctor, refused to reenter the overcrowded cell when I returned, and was dragged in the simple way.

On Thursday I was allowed out for rec, even though I'd warned the officer, a guy whom I liked a lot, that I wouldn't come back in. At the end of my hour, he floored me by offering me a second hour, and at the end of that, he offered me a bribe: "You've had two hours of rec today, and though I'm not usually on, I could be on tomorrow, and if you don't give me any trouble today, I could do the same for you then." I said that the rec had been wonderful and I really appreciated it and I wasn't willing to walk back into that overcrowded cell. So he called for reinforcements.

The captain came out to talk to me. He was very quiet—rigidly controlled, I think—and I was quite restrained, but when I got onto my soapbox—"I assume that someone who's running this prison has decided that it's okay to put four people in these cells, and it's not. *Nobody* should be in

a four-person cell this small. Nobody. This hole can't hold thirty people"–
he just turned his back and walked away.

Another prisoner was moved out of the two-person cell. Several supervisors came out with the video camera and unlocked the cage. A riot squad
of four men charged across the yard at me. One grabbed each of my limbs,
and they rapidly straightened out my body, spun me over on my face, and
lowered me to the ground. My forehead banged the concrete as I went
down, and I later had quite a lump. They held me down hard while they
cuffed and shackled me, then quickly and efficiently picked me up in a
prone position and carried me into the two-person cell.

Someone ordered, "On the floor." It occurred to me later that the person must have been the captain, and the order must have been a code
signal for what happened next, which was surely illegal. They laid me on
my face and again held me down hard while someone stepped on the
back of my left knee, applied pressure, and held it. It hurt like crazy. I sort
of squealed with the pain, and when I couldn't bear just to endure it any
longer, I tried to move my leg, to at least shift it, and whoever-it-was pressed
harder. Someone else said, "Now just relax" (did he think *I* was causing
the problem?). And then it was over. It probably hadn't lasted more than
a minute or two. But how cruelly gratuitous! Never in my life before had
someone deliberately hurt me purely for the sake of hurting me–a little
introduction to the world as so many other people experience it.

They then lifted me onto the bed, still on my face, and again held me
down hard, which hurt, too, because the man holding my arms was leaning on my wrists so that the handcuffs cut edgewise into them. The captain
ordered that they remove my jumpsuit, so I was left lying there in my
underwear. They put leather straps on my wrists and ankles, and chained
the straps to the four corners of the bed. The strap on my right wrist was
too tight, but fortunately the PA who checked the restraints could tell that
it was too tight and had them loosen it a notch.

My friends in the cell next door were concerned about me, but I wasn't
ready to talk to anyone yet. I just lay there, absorbing the experience,
unwinding (these things always happened so fast that I needed some space
for catching up with myself), and working through my emotions–the most
powerful of which was a sort of horror at that gratuitous little torture ses-
sion, though the *pain* was already over. Remembering it made me shudder, and the shuddering helped to discharge it.

Other than that, my discomforts were petty. Mostly, I was cold. I was
sure I could live with it. And I was released after only about two hours. I
was struck again by how quiet and low-key the releases were, after all the
gestapo-like excess of the captures. A lieutenant simply unlocked the restraints from the bed; carried me, with the help of the detention officers,
back to the seg cell; and removed the straps.

I felt pretty shaky and was only gradually able to "come out" of myself
and be present to people. But I asked the inmate orderly for some ice for

my forehead and told her a little of what had happened. She brought my lunch, which the officer had saved for me. He came over to check on me, obviously concerned.

That evening two of my cellmates were moved out, so I returned to my space. The third was moved out the next day. By then, I was feeling *good*. I had the same sense of having gotten out of a box that an actual expansion of my physical space gives me. I enjoyed cleaning and organizing. My knee was bruised and sore but healing. And I was aware that my response to the captain, who had chosen to hurt me, had to be to absorb the pain, suffering it without complaint or withdrawal, not letting it change me or my relationship to him at all.

8

. . . by Fire

I was intrigued by how much more assertive and activist than ever before my response to general justice issues in prison had been these past months. Though I continued to affirm the spiritual benefit of accepting deprivation and embracing suffering, I also found myself objecting passionately to things that needed to change, not because of their effect on me and not in the spirit of sticking up for my rights, but just because they needed to change. I wouldn't consent by standing quietly by, which was exactly how I felt about Rocky Flats.

I had no expectation that they *would* change—was always tremendously surprised if they did—and I think the fact that I wasn't invested in results actually contributed to my confidence. My confidence was striking. I suspected that it came not only from the freedom of paying no attention to consequences, but also from a basic acceptance of my own powerlessness and insignificance. Nothing about me mattered. I had nothing to gain, nothing to lose, nothing to worry about. I wasn't engaged in a campaign and had no goals. I was just responding as clearly as possible out of whatever integrity I had to whatever situations I was presented with.

The absence of goals, all by itself, makes one "undefeatable." What is there to defeat? That's true of powerlessness, too, and of embracing suffering. How does one "win" over them? There's nothing to overcome. So, I concluded, if the system was determined to "break" me, or my resistance, it would have to wear down my ability to endure—which was very likely what it was trying to do—and my refuge had to be powerlessness, the absence of goals, and the embracing of suffering.

I learned that the punishment for my four most recent protests about overcrowding was a total of 123 days in segregation plus a recommended "disciplinary" transfer. The most serious charge, which Hal had written for "interfering with a staff member," had been changed to "encouraging others to riot" and earned me sixty days. I guessed that I'd earlier received thirty days for "encouraging a group demonstration." I was already prepared for an extended stretch in DS.

But I was badly unsettled by an extraordinarily invasive shakedown on April 28 and was feeling assaulted by the system in more and more ordinary, daily sorts of ways. I could see that resilience was going to be crucial to my endurance. Prison functioning is regularly arbitrary and unreasonable. The restriction of the almost constant lockdown was telling on me. I appreciated my solitude, but the unit in general was overcrowded, with either three or four people in almost every other cell, so my protest hadn't helped anyone else. And I was feeling sort of alienated from myself, because I was hardly able to pray at all. Who, me?–a person of prayer? There was nothing in me. The best that I usually could do was to cry out to God.

Then I was completely undone by a cellmate, who was moved in while I was outside for rec. In the short time she was alone, she rooted through my personal property and stole my best pair of underpants. Argggh! At first I couldn't believe she'd done it, because I don't think people are like that, but as I broke through her lies with my mounting certainty, my voice rose in that assertive kind of passion that probably *was* anger this time, and then I dissolved into tears. I totally lost it–so much so that she couldn't stand my pain and was telling me *anything* in an attempt to comfort me. She said that she was sorry, and I said that I forgave her. But then I climbed up onto my bed and cried and cried and cried.

I felt devastated by this further assault on my personal space. I *had* no space, no safety, no refuge. I couldn't build a little world around myself without someone violating it. And this intimately personal violation felt much worse than being tortured by the prison. I was stripped and torn down in a subtle, hidden way that didn't simultaneously call forth the resources for rebuilding, the way public confrontational situations seemed to do. I felt as if I couldn't stand it, as if I had to go to the officers, to the lieutenant, to beg and plead for them to take one of us out of here. But, of course, I couldn't do that without ratting on her, and I couldn't run to "Mommy" to solve my problems for me, so I was trapped. I *had* to stand it. I had no choice.

Two days later my cellmate was moved out, and three others moved in. I protested the overcrowding, as usual, but Hal responded in such a low-key way that I didn't feel as if I'd made much of a statement. He let me walk out to the common area and simply dragged me back in when the moves were completed. In the morning I told the officers that I'd leave the cell when they opened the door for any reason. They arranged, by mid-afternoon, to move me to a cell where I'd have only one cellmate. That was a good solution for everybody, so I cooperated–though it didn't seem right that I got preferential treatment for being difficult.

Argggggh! The arrangement didn't last ten hours. It was after we'd both gone to bed that we were ordered to get up and move again. Oh, no! Not this soon! I'd had it! Something in me fell right off the edge of a cliff. I wasn't moving, and I didn't care what they did with me or my property.

This was the cruelest inhumanity of this place: total disregard for our existence and needs as *persons*. The officers were counting slots and matching bodies to them as if we were logs of wood or sacks of potatoes that could be rearranged twice a day without trauma. I couldn't consent to it by cooperating any more at all.

I ended up, predictably, on somebody else's floor—where I now had three cellmates on "administrative detention" status—and two "detention" inmates were eventually moved into the cell where I'd been before, so my move had been utterly pointless. The emotional assault of it left me so tense and shaken that I managed to sleep for only a few hours. And here I was in an overcrowded cell again! I protested by keeping the flap over the food tray slot open.

The morning shift officer was controlling and contemptuous. My protest angered her, though she contented herself with writing me an incident report. But fireworks erupted when my cellmates got up, and the most vocal one started yelling at her, complaining about the noise throughout the night and about the prison's treatment of me. I added my two cents about overcrowding in general, and the officer and I both got very passionate, talking at each other without stopping to listen, until, absolutely furious, she turned and walked away.

I asked my cellmates' indulgence to take a sponge bath, closing the flap and covering the door window with a piece of toilet paper, which is allowable only for temporary bathroom privacy. In the midst of the bath, I heard the officer outside our door, and then a man, one of the lieutenants, suddenly opened the flap. My vocal cellmate screamed, "She's bathing! She's naked!"—which he could undoubtedly see, because the sink is right by the door. He reached up through the slot toward the window covering; couldn't reach it; and then ordered, "Take that thing off the window!" But I reclosed the flap and finished my bath first.

I was barely toweled and dressed in my T-shirt and boxer shorts when fireworks erupted again. The officer ordered me to cuff up, and I refused, routinely. The door opened. The lieutenant quickly stepped in, grabbed me by my nearest arm, and dragged me out of the cell. As I went limp in the doorway, my cellmate screamed, and someone else helped lay me on my face and cuff me. They left me there, wondering what was going on, while they cuffed up all my cellmates and took them out to one of the rec cages. Then they dragged me to the other one, two people holding me by the upper arms, which pulled my wrists painfully against the handcuffs, and a third holding the handcuff chain and forcing one of my hands into a doubled-over position that was painful in itself. My toes scraped across the concrete. They set me down gently, though, and I just lay there, trembling with emotion and close to tears.

My vocal cellmate was already crying and moving toward hysteria: "She didn't *do* anything. She was only taking a bath. Why are you treating her like that? I can't stand it." And then we finally heard what was going on:

someone was ordered to strip the cell of everything that could be used to cover the door window except blankets and clothes. My cellmate immediately responded, "You mean we can't have *tissue*?" I was sorry that they were getting fallout from the prison's excessive overreaction to me, but it had taken me as much by surprise as it had them.

Our deprivation was temporary. A lot of people were released to the compound, and "normalcy" was restored the same day. The next day I was returned to the seg cell, where I now had only one cellmate, with whom I laughed a lot. The evening officer came over for what turned out to be a good, long, passionate conversation about why I make the choices I do. He had helped to move me in the middle of the night and subsequently heard about the morning incident, and was sort of intrigued by me. He wasn't defensive or angry, but he seemed incapable of understanding either why I was willing to take so much punishment without a chance of accomplishing anything or what I was talking about when I said that this situation was inhuman. I kept trying to convince him of the basic fallacy in the prison's assumption that the hole had a capacity for thirty when in fact it had a capacity for sixteen. Just because someone put four beds in each cell, it apparently never occurred to the officers that four people really couldn't live in that space. I wished *they'd* try it.

The fact that I could bounce back emotionally as well as physically was encouraging. But I found myself more and more inclined toward resistance. All the ways in which the prison kept pushing us around left me feeling feisty and frustrated. As cellmates were moved in and out in quick succession during the next several days, I realized that having to adjust to a new personality every other day or so was as hard on me as the overcrowding and my own frequent moving. It was all a consequence of the assumption that four bodies could be stored in each of these boxes and rearranged whenever. It was inhuman! It was intolerable! I kept wanting to protest more forcibly at more points. And I wished that I could resist the oppression of *others*.

Now I had a cellmate who was my most difficult relational challenge yet. She was totally self-centered, dishonest, and manipulative, with the morality and emotional maturity of a two-year-old overlaid with lots of charm and street smarts. I got along with her well enough but hated to keep hearing her getting away with lies, was always in danger of benefiting from her con games, and didn't *like* having to be so careful not to trust someone. I spent an afternoon in tears when I found out that the yogurt she'd shared with me had been *stolen* by her boyfriend, who was the current inmate orderly, from the officer! Arggh! How could I accept anything from her without compromising myself, and how could I *not* accept anything from her without putting her down? The tension felt so irresolvable that I confess I prayed that she get out of seg soon. The next morning she was transferred.

That same day I was joined by a new cellmate, and then the two of us were ordered to move to a different cell together. The move was meaningless and felt like harassment. I was already past my tolerance level for cooperating with insanity, and in a sense this was a move that I had earlier refused. I refused again.

The men who forced me were gentle, and the evening officer brought over all my property, including extra blankets and food. I knew that he was being kind to me. But I was running out of resilience, and found that I was feeling resentful and angry. My property had been dumped on the dirty floor, and my cellmate was already established on the only top bunk in this cell. When I blurted out, "I *hate* the bottom bunk," she insisted on moving down to it, which made me feel terrible; she had more generosity than I did. And I snapped at the officer for having lost my comb. But by the time I'd done the most essential cleaning, I was feeling better and able to apologize to him. I was thankful that I could still recover my balance, but I didn't like myself until I did.

The following evening the officer came to my door to talk. He stood for most of the conversation, bending at the waist, with his head on his arm on the shelf made by my food slot flap, face down, eyes closed. It was all about the move: What had the system done with the incident report he had written? Why, why, why did I make the choices I did? I could tell that he had felt forced, caught between my choices and those of his superiors, and I gradually realized that he was hurting, hurting somehow over what he had done to me, over *his* choices. He had had to tell me to move and to write me up for refusing, and he had been the main actor in the move, one of those who had pulled me off the bunk and carried me. "You forced me," he said, and I said no, that he had chosen to obey an order from his superior. I hadn't expected otherwise. But I talked later, in reference to *my* choices, about the need to question authority, not to obey orders just because they're orders but to judge their morality.

I asked, "Did last night upset you?" He nodded. "I'm sorry." He nodded. I assured him that I was okay and that I wasn't worried about the incident report. He worried, "If you refuse something else, we'll be called in." He'd be working the yard when the shift changed the next day and so might have to move me again. He obviously didn't want to. I tried to reassure him about that, too, but of course it *could* happen. I'd never seen him so touched, so vulnerable. I told him that I appreciated his humanness and, later, that I was glad we'd had some chances to talk. I left him with "God bless you."

That conversation was an oasis in a desert. I was feeling assaulted by nonsense. I was still being caught off guard by how much the system lies. I could hardly believe it when it ignored its own rules. And the general incompetence was driving me up a wall.

On May 31, I refused to cooperate with another general shakedown. (The prison's answer to the inevitable clutter of forcing up to four people to live in a 7½' x 11½' space was to purge them periodically of possessions.) The lieutenant in charge this time apparently wanted to hurt me enough that I'd choose to walk. Two officers dragged me out to a rec cage by the upper arms, while a third put one of my hands into that doubled-over hold, which I was later told was intended to make you stand up. It didn't hurt much this time, but he also lifted on the handcuffs, pulling both my arms back, which hurt a lot, and the most painful thing was something about the way the whole weight of my body twisted against one of my upper arms, making it feel as if the arm would pull out of the socket. I try to stay mute when I've gone limp, but I didn't manage it. The pain forced squeals from me, and once I cried out.

On the way back in, they carried me the same way, but for some reason it wasn't hurting as much. The lieutenant ordered the person holding the handcuffs to hold them higher, which twisted my arms behind my back and forced a squeal from me, to which he responded, "That's better."

I was actually injured by a dragging handcuff as they hoisted me back onto a bed, but not seriously and probably by accident. What was much worse was that both my cellmate and I received incident reports for "possession, manufacture, or introduction of a weapon," one of the most serious possible charges and one that was an attack on my very identity. It hurt just to think that anyone might believe I could do such a thing. I was sure that those who knew me didn't believe it, and it hurt that they seemed prepared to prosecute it anyway. I hated to think of the slander that might end up in my permanent record.

Someone had apparently found a piece of broomstick hidden in the air vent. It was a total surprise to both of us. The thing could have been either planted or imagined for all we knew, though I also knew something of a prisoner who had lived in the cell before us. In any case, my cellmate and I were innocent, but what recourse did we have? All that we could do was to be honest, and I already knew how people here valued honesty. I felt framed. It was staggering to realize how much more vulnerable I was to the retribution of the system than I'd been aware of before. At the same time, I recognized the spiritual challenge to keep working on letting go of my identity.

It was a spiritual challenge, too, to remember all those men handling a gentle and defenseless woman in such a way as to deliberately hurt her, and then expressing satisfaction at the evidence of her pain. It left me deeply sad. I could hardly believe that human beings were still so small and barbaric, so far from self-respect, that they'd cling to power and control at such a cost, the cost of their own God-given humanness. How tragic! How wounded those little boys must have been inside!

I had already discovered that a major key to loving all people, no matter what they do, is to remember that their negative behavior is generated by their own inner woundedness. The more cruelly they behave, the more wounded I assume them to be, probably from childhood, certainly in that part of themselves that has not yet matured. Focusing my response on those hurting inner children frees up my compassion, often in spite of my own pain.

But so many people are so wounded! They need so much more love than all the wounded people around them can give. I couldn't imagine how we could ever get from the infantile state the human race is in to some sort of spiritual maturity and wholeness. The more I saw of the neediness of the world, the darker and more hopeless it all looked apart from prayer. I could see how urgently important it was for me to keep trying to pray, to get above being hurt myself, to live so fully in the spiritual world where I was called to live that the stuff of lesser worlds would roll right off my back, to uphold values and spirituality even if I seemed to be alone in a vacuum where no one understood. I should be thankful for all the challenges that kept pushing me to grow.

I could see that I *was* growing—was clearly beyond where I'd been in 1985. In spite of all my apparent prayerlessness, God was obviously with me in a powerful way. The insight that God had given me about accepting my own hurting inner child was a particularly great grace, which enabled me to keep bouncing back emotionally. I could say, "There, there, little girl. I know it hurts." And I'd get over it, usually in a matter of hours. I'd get up and go on, able to be friendly and sunny again, my inner freedom restored for principled response to the prison.

As the oppression of the system tightened around me—both through the cumulative weight of incident piled upon incident and through my growing understanding of the meanings and intentions behind them—the responses that integrity and faithfulness required of me became more radical. The sphere within which I could conscientiously cooperate with the expectations and demands of the system shrank. I stood firm at places of increasingly fundamental non-assent.

That Friday, June 2, I fell off the final cliff. My cellmate and I were ordered to move *again*, without explanation. It was my ninth cell move since the last week of April. I refused. Again, I was treated like an object, though without hoopla or physical injury, by the angry and contemptuous officer, now our regular evening officer. My cell was totally stripped. My clean clothes, including my jumpsuit, only just replaced after Wednesday's shakedown, were again all thrown into the laundry. My personal property was held in the officers' station. I was deposited, with my bedding, on the floor of the cell next door. I stayed there. I would not request anything of the officer. Eventually, she returned my personal property. After the shift change at midnight, I asked the morning officer for clean sheets so that I could go to bed.

But I knew that I would not rebuild again—not because I was withdrawing or pouting, but because I had come to a final clarity: I would not make the statement, by picking up the life of a human being, that a human being could be treated this way. I had done it over and over again, and I had reached my tolerance level for such complicity with the system's inhuman assumptions. I needed now to abdicate and let the responsibility for the consequences of the prison's choices fall back on the prison.

It was insisting on treating me as an object, and I would stop resisting it. I would stop claiming my humanness. No more attempting to provide for my needs. No more "moving in." No more eating. No more approaching the door to cuff up for anything. No more walking out of the cell. I would stay in relationship, though. I knew that the captain was responsible for Friday evening cell moves, and I wrote him a letter explaining my position.

I couldn't imagine any next steps that wouldn't be ugly and painful and frightening. But I still had the strange sense of being engaged in a long series of inevitable choices, doing the only possible, necessary thing–trusting myself to God's care. And I was finding a new kind of freedom in this extreme position. It felt like a retreat into strength, into something that I was pretty sure I could do, which was to endure suffering. Since what the prison might do to me was almost certain to be horrible, I could simply expect the worst and not think about it. I'd given permission for it to treat me as an object, so I could dispense with being outraged by that. And I finally felt that I was no longer complicit, that my stand was clear and simple and unambiguous.

I realized that I'd put the prison in a rather difficult position by not asking anything of it, so that it had no choice but to transfer me. There was nothing it could offer me that would enable me to eat. Then it struck me that if it chose to offer something, I *would* accept the permanent reduction of the detention population to sixteen or fewer. *That* would allow the benefit of my stand to reach everyone in the unit, which was precisely what I'd been longing for and hadn't been able to see a way toward.

On Monday my cellmate and I were moved back to the cell we'd been moved out of on Friday. On Tuesday she was moved back to the cell we'd been in the day before. Now I was alone, undoubtedly being isolated because I wasn't eating.

The "hospital" called for me in the afternoon. I explained that I was glad for the prison to monitor my health, but my withdrawal of cooperation left all choices up to it. Its choice–though the kind of monitoring involved could have been done anywhere–was, literally, to drag me over there. The riot squad included the lieutenant who seemed to want to hurt me, and it was rough. Two men cuffed me, pulled me off the end of the bed, grabbed me by the upper arms, while a third person held my hand doubled over, tried to make me stand, and then dragged me all the way to the doctor's office.

Argh! I hated to think of having to face that every day. Physical pain may be transient, but it sure hurts at the time. The asphalt outside tore up my socks. And something fairly major happened to my left shoulder, which I discovered afterward when I rolled over in bed and it hurt like crazy. I really hoped that the space between assaults would be enough for my body to heal.

That night the new inmate orderly told me that, in protest of the same abuses that I'd been protesting, the whole unit was going to start hunger-striking in the morning. And at least half of them did. After the second meal, a crew of extra staff descended on the unit and, skipping me, pulled everybody out of one cell after another, absolutely stripped the cells, and then reshuffled people in a lot of cell moves. Everyone was eventually issued bedding, and eaters were reissued their personal property. Every non-eater was called into the captain's office. I was undoubtedly instantly elevated to the status of ringleader in the eyes of the prison.

Two men dragged me over to see the doctor in the afternoon. They ignored somebody's pleading cry, "Pick up her feet! She's not going to walk." In the sally port, a third person stepped on my toes, which could have been an accident, but I didn't think so. Those dragging me were probably just trying to get me there, as if I were a sack of potatoes. Some-how, the way they were holding me was less hard on my shoulders than the day before, but much harder on my wrists. By the time we got out of the sally port, the outward pressure on my arms was dragging my wrists so hard against the handcuffs that they burned like fire and my hands were turning numb. Lying on them on the doctor's table while we waited for her was almost more painful than I could bear—and having the handcuffs removed when she came in was even worse. But then it was over. The trip back wasn't as bad. I made a point of enjoying the brief passage through the outside air. And the pain, as usual, didn't last, though my wrists were becoming more tender every day.

I still felt physically better than I'd expected. I'd never fasted on water only this long before. I was weak, but I had enough energy for simple tasks if I took it easy. I moved my bed down to the bottom bunk to con-serve energy, especially since people kept coming to talk to me at the door. I didn't get dizzy if I got up slowly. I was sleeping fairly normally. I spent most of the days just lying still, amazed at how content I was with long stretches of doing nothing. One morning, I'd awakened with a lovely sense of the goodness of life in God's world.

The next day six people, in addition to myself, were still refusing break-fast. The prison was coming down very hard on them, withholding things, like showers, that they had an absolute right to, probably more or less temporarily, undoubtedly hoping that they'd break. Some had. But I could still hear the friend with whom I'd laughed so much when we were cellmates—who was also a principled protester of injustice—laughing with her current cellmates at the far end of the unit.

The trip to the "hospital" that day was the worst yet. Of course, it didn't help that I had no physical resources. Whoever had stepped on my toes in the sally port, probably the captain, did it again, three times, obviously deliberately, and the third time he got a cry out of me. I shudder to think that that may have given him satisfaction. One of the men who was dragging me was holding my arm too high, probably unintentionally, pulling the wrist against the handcuff so that it burned unrelentingly. I cried out several times. Lying on the doctor's table, I needed some time just to recover a bit from the assault and the pain before I could give any attention to her. I tried reaching out to God, and that made me cry, which I didn't want to do. I felt very vulnerable.

The first two days the doctor had mostly tried to persuade and scare me into eating. She had told me that I should be drinking sixteen cups of water a day in order to flush the poisons produced by my body's eating itself up. Today she wanted to give me an IV. I had nothing to say about IVs. My response to coercion so far had been to go limp as soon as I was grabbed and remain limp until I was returned to a cell, so presumably I would remain passive in the face of whatever the doctor did to me. But she pushed for some indication that I didn't "object," and finally seemed satisfied with my neutral reply, "I don't fight anything."

The IV ran for about four hours. Sitting up afterward, I felt worse than before: lightheaded and headachy, and my vision was going blurry. The doctor wanted me to drink a potassium solution. She said that the lack of potassium in the IV had left my system badly unbalanced, and I could have all sorts of problems, including heart problems. (The prison had earlier diagnosed me as having mitral valve prolapse.) I felt trapped and cheated: my health was more at risk now than before, because of what I'd let her do to me, and I couldn't undo the damage without violating my clear choice to take nothing by mouth but water. I decided to accept the potassium now, and then refuse all other treatment. But would a verbal refusal be enough to keep her from giving it to me?

The next morning was suddenly refreshingly gentle. I was told that I was being transferred. Three men *carried* me to the "hospital," and didn't hurt me. One of them surprised me greatly by saying, "You're the toughest one we've ever had here"–I felt almost insubstantial in my fragility–and then, "We're going to miss you, Haines." I refused everything the doctor offered me, and she answered, "Okay." No one tried to force me. The lieutenants took me back to detention in a wheelchair, modestly covered with a blanket. The sort of treatment a human being might expect.

In the "hospital" corridor we had run into, of all people, my nuclear-resistance friend Helen, whom I'd gotten to know at Alderson. She called my name. I looked up, smiled, and greeted her. "Keep it up," she said, and I replied, "I probably will."

The prison staff who transferred me were prepared for my passivity. Two female officers carried me into the strip-search room, sat me in a wheelchair, conducted a fairly thorough strip-search, dressed me in my own underwear, prison khakis, canvas shoes, and the usual hardware, and wheeled me out to the waiting van. *All* of my property was left behind, including my glasses. How could I ask for them when I was nonparticipating so totally? The hunger-strikers yelled out farewells.

Two lieutenants and a PA escorted me all the way to San Diego, while a second van was taking three other prisoners to Los Angeles. One of the lieutenants commented, "You know, Haines, we'll never forget you. Ten years from now, we'll be saying, 'Remember when . . . ?'"

—— ✄ ——

MCC San Diego was rather a shock. Shoddy. As if it had slipped into the gutter since my last visit. Very little professionalism or initiative or evidence on the part of many staff people that they cared in the least about what they were responsible for. The officers on the medical floor seemed to spend practically all of their time watching television, and the inmate workers did little more. Things were falling apart, both physically and organizationally, and apparently no one knew anything to do about it. I was put in a cell without hot water and with a sink that didn't drain, and the only alternative seemed to be a cell with no running water at all. I was told that the proper people had been notified; what more could anyone do?

The most disturbing aspect of the situation was that I was receiving almost no medical attention, in spite of being directly in the care of medical staff. I had arrived already sick enough for Pleasanton to have intervened and too inexperienced myself to know how dangerous my condition might be; yet nothing more happened over the weekend than that my blood pressure was taken about twice a day. I had been placed, I discovered, in the psych ward on suicide watch, which seemed to mean only that someone looked in through the door window at me fairly frequently. No one asked me why I wasn't eating or what would encourage me to eat–except for a caring officer with uncommon initiative who dropped by to chat on Sunday afternoon.

I was no longer sure myself why I wasn't eating. Having left the oppressive situation from which I had withdrawn cooperation, I was prepared to reconsider my position; but the shoddiness and negligence here were oppressive, too. I wondered if I shouldn't wait for a vegetarian diet. What actually swayed me the most was how sad and unappealing the meals looked. They offered so little that appeared edible that I couldn't get interested in them. I was willing to drink milk at my first breakfast, but it was sour. Someone called down to the kitchen for some more, and it was sour, too. I gave up. I kept refusing the trays one at a time until I reached clarity that I *would* wait for a vegetarian diet.

The doctor told me on Monday that he couldn't order me one and that the dietician wouldn't be in until Thursday. Arggh! But I continued to resist all interim and compromise solutions–until, all of a sudden, the doctor was bringing me the food services administrator, who offered me essentially whatever diet I wanted as long as the "hospital" would order it. The psychiatrist, who was a consultant from outside the prison, ordered it, and the food services administrator himself presented me with the first tray, featuring a huge, beautiful salad. Succeeding diet meals were unspectacular, but a tremendous improvement over the regular trays, being not only meatless but also much more substantial.

There wasn't much protein, though. On Thursday I spoke with the dietician, who was distressed to hear it. Apparently, the protein was ordered–she'd seen my lunch tray leave the kitchen that day with both milk and cheese on it–and all the most essential stuff was being stolen by inmate workers before it reached me. No one seemed to know anything to do about *that* either.

Meanwhile, I had been moved from the psych ward to the "back"–which was clearly furnished as a medical ward, but appeared to be used for assorted misfits without major needs. We were locked into solitary cells and largely ignored. There was no officer and no TV; occasionally, a doctor or a PA came by. It was very quiet. My time was extremely empty. Without my glasses I couldn't read and could barely write. The window was too stained and clouded to provide any view. There was no exercise outside of the cell. I had neither deodorant nor shampoo and could shower only irregularly. But I was not anxious to return to the general population, which would lead right back to detention; here, at least, there was gentleness and freedom from handcuffs.

I was depressed, though, for no specific reason. There wasn't enough sunniness in me to try to cheer up the staff. I appreciated the value of feeling identified here with the innocent institutionalized, since the lonely and forgotten had become a special prayer concern. But I was wondering if I could be a person of prayer at all. There seemed to be nothing in me, and all that I could reach of God were the pain and tears of a loving parent for this sick and broken and dying world. I saw too much sickness, too much cruelty and perversion and evil, too much hopelessness and escape when my whole world consisted of inner cities and prisons. It was all too complex for me, too crazy. And I wondered if I were simple enough for God. I wanted just to fall on my knees somewhere and give myself over to God, but I wasn't *doing* it.

My inner child seemed to have become my voice of wisdom. When I asked how I could get past my prayerlessness, her response was, "You can sing." How could I shift my attention away from myself? "You can sing." One night, I did a lot of singing, remembering some of my favorite scripture songs, and after a while found myself tumbling into intercession, remembering some of my favorite people.

A few days after that, my spirits began to rise. I don't know why. By June 21, I was clearly coming out of myself, letting the world in, and opening up freely to spontaneous intercession again. It occurred to me, again, that intercession might really be my vocation. I may not be able to love God, but I *can* love the world.

Dinner that day was a good meal with plenty of protein and solicitous attention from the inmate worker who served it. I had barely finished eating when I was suddenly being told to hurry up and get my things together: I was leaving. *Leaving*?!?! The judge had decided to depart from the guidelines after all, arguing that they overstated the seriousness of my "criminal history" and failed to consider my sincere spiritual convictions. She reduced my sentence to time served. That same evening I was on a bus to Denver. Alleluia!!

——— ✄ ———

My protester friend from Pleasanton was transferred to Lexington, Kentucky. She wrote that a few of the hunger-strikers had held out for a conversation with the warden. My nuclear-resistance friend Helen was transferred to Marianna, Florida. She had spent some time in Pleasanton's hole before my arrival there and was engaged in a lawsuit against it. She wrote that the entire detention unit had been closed. Someone, somehow, had finally heard our message.

——— ✄ ———

Reimmersed in the ordinary life of the outside world, I was buying stamps one day in the downtown post office when, without warning, a man's hands encircled my neck from behind and a voice whispered in my ear, "You're supposed to be in jail."

Max! I had occasionally spoken with U.S. marshals on the streets of Denver, but never before had any of them stepped so thoroughly through the role barrier.

I turned to greet him with a delighted smile and explained why I wasn't in "jail." He was obviously as pleased to see me as I was to see him. We chatted happily on our way out of the building. He had left the marshals' office. He was engaged to be married. I congratulated him, truly rejoicing in the positive new directions for his life.

Isn't it beautiful the way relationship keeps coming out on top?

9

Submission

No one dropped a hot-air balloon on my doorstep. I continued my weekday prayer vigil at Rocky Flats. I was finally beginning to understand a big chunk of what God had me doing out there. Evangelists would call it evangelism, except that I wasn't pushing any particular program. I was simply standing for God. People were struck by my persistent presence at the Rocky Flats gate, and some knew the meaning of the gaps in it. "How can you endure so much?" they would ask. "How can you risk so much?" "God," I would answer, in essence. I would put lots of words around it, about faith and love and prayer. But the fundamental message, I could now see, amounted to this: "*This* is how central and directive God is for my life. This is how *real* and important God is to me." Perhaps others could feel a little of God's power and faithfulness through their obvious effect on me. That was undoubtedly God's intention.

On Christmas Day, 1989, the gates were open when I carried my worship onto the property. Two security guards tried to escort me off again, picked me up when I sat down, and carried me back to the traffic island. Then they closed the gates.

Hmm. What was I supposed to do now? I sat and prayed about it. Receiving no clear leading to walk back in, I finally concluded that I was free to go home. *That* was fun.

It left the question open, however, for the following days. Rocky Flats was on vacation between Christmas and New Year's Day, so there was little traffic, and I had long quiet stretches of holiday time for my vigil. Was I supposed to be praying on the property? Each day I sat with the question. And each day, at some point, I ended up walking in and being carried back out. I was told that I could expect to be arrested as soon as I crossed a "barrier."

On December 28 I walked in almost immediately, was carried out, and the gates were closed. I continued my prayer. Was I supposed to walk in again? I wanted to be clear. Clarity had become a major support for me in risking and enduring as much as I did. I felt ready to take on anything as long as I really was sure that it was God's will for me. At the same time, I recognized my own fallibility in the discernment process, so my most ardent prayer, and the one that I most frequently requested of others, was for grace for discernment.

I wasn't clear. What was God asking of me? I prayed for a long time outside the gate. And then I found myself moving, effectively about three steps forward, except that, instead of walking through the barbed wire, I went around it, ducking under the little gate and returning inside the fence to sit down again on the traffic island.

Afterward (if I figure things out at all, it's only afterward), I realized what an important freedom God had given me in enabling me to act *without* clarity, that is, without processing the choice through my mind, where I could easily grasp and control it, clinging to the security of knowing. Rather, I have to abandon myself blindly to God, who keeps nudging me at levels below thought. The more I reflected on it, the more certain I became that I *had* acted in obedience to God and that the great learning in it lay in the freedom from needing to *know* that I'm right *before* I act.

I was arrested immediately. On the way downtown to jail, the junior security person, with whom I'd had some friendly chats, asked, "How long will they keep you for this? A week?" I answered, "I think they'll keep me a year." She was shocked. Fellow prisoners, too, were frequently shocked by the severity of my sentences: "You're going to *prison*? For *trespassing*?"

When I heard which judge would try the case, I was *sure* that they'd keep me a year. It was the judge who had so obviously wanted to punish me when the charge hadn't given him an opportunity; I'd assumed since then that, if I ever saw him again, I'd receive the maximum.

Then the magistrate—a different magistrate from the two whom I've mentioned before, but an old hand in the system—doubled the jeopardy. He released me, in spite of my explicit refusal to promise to return to court or to sign anything, and he handed me a copy of a p.r. bond as if I were being released on personal recognizance. Of course, I wasn't. I had refused the conditions of bond, so my release was necessarily unconditional. But I was still ordered to return to court, which I wouldn't do, and I expected that I'd probably be given a second year in prison for contempt.

It could be even worse if I walked back into Rocky Flats and got arrested and released again. But I didn't anticipate a need to do that, not so much in the spirit of affirmation for the gift of unexpected time outside— since I strongly suspected that the magistrate was acting on orders from the judge, with the deliberate intention of setting me up for additional prison time—but more because it felt important to let the interaction with the court around the issue of my not returning develop independently of any other complicating issues. I simply continued my weekday vigil.

I wrote to the magistrate. I did not appear for a hearing. Then nothing happened for long enough that I began to wonder if the court was actually going to let me stay out until the trial. That seemed possible, because it would save a fair amount of trouble and expense, and the marshals could easily pick me up at any time. So when they *did* come for me, on a Thursday afternoon in late January, I was no longer particularly expecting it. I had gotten halfway through a thorough cleaning of the kitchen before leaving for the Flats that day. Anna was praying there with me. A car parked, two men walked toward us, and I knew what was coming next.

Denver County. Even though I refused the ID, now a clip-on badge, I was initially booked into the general population. But an officer who knew me well asked me in the morning what I was going to do about the ID and about working, and moved me back to max. I was not offered a window, and chose to decide that I could live without one. I lived in that cell until mid-April.

The captains (approximately equivalent to a federal prison's lieutenants) were not happy about it. Several of them had become acquainted with me over the years, and though they saw me as a "management problem," they generally liked me and had no desire to treat me punitively. Three or four of them discussed the max situation with me at a conference in their office. They felt that a way could be worked out for me to stay in a dorm. Because their intent was clearly to consider my best interests, I decided that I should let them know my preference: punitive as max was, the dorms were even worse for me, because of their almost total lack of both quiet and personal space. So I stayed in max.

As the weeks wore on, one of the captains became so concerned to give me an occasional break from the extreme restriction that he offered me a job in his office. I was touched and grateful, but I couldn't accept a job.

Theoretically, my refusal of the ID meant that I couldn't leave the women's building except for official visits. But most officers still let me go out to the yard—a significant expansion of both physical and visual space over my cell, though it was a huge step downward from the old yard, being a relatively small, paved courtyard with high building walls on three sides. I was also allowed two infirmary requests, one to the dentist to have a lost filling replaced with a temporary, and the other to talk to somebody about a vegetarian diet.

Food had suddenly become a serious problem for me with the institution of a new serving system. The inmate workers used to serve our trays from a steam table, and they were willing to leave the meat and gravy off of mine, often also compensating with larger portions of vegetables. Now individual, pre-served trays were sent from the kitchen. I wasn't willing to give up the freedom to keep dead animals out of my cell. My vegetarianism dated back to 1967, when, having known for a long time that I wouldn't kill an animal in order to eat it, I could no longer live with the inconsistency of allowing other people to kill the animals for me. I had made many compromises over the years, including eating around the meat on prison trays, but the compromises were becoming more intolerable to me than the deprivation of the alternatives. I refused to accept any tray with meat on it.

Now I was eating much too little, mostly the items that came separately from the trays, such as milk and cold cereal at breakfast. So I explored the special-diet option. I was surprised to be told that a vegetarian tray would be ordered for me, and not surprised that none ever arrived. I asked about it enough times to be convinced that the effort was futile. I was still functioning physically. And the inmate workers did their best to take care of me, even occasionally gifting me with commissary food—which I had no access to myself, since a prisoner number was now required on the commissary order form. One of the great blessings in being needy and helpless is that you see so much of the compassion of others!

Prisoners in max were routinely denied religious services now, so it was a treat when an officer would unexpectedly let us go. Once I was the only prisoner at Mass. The truly spectacular gift of that occasion was flowers—fresh flowers in a little paper cup on the communion table, which one person was allowed to take back with her at the end of each service. These were daisies. I kept them on my sink for close to two weeks, glorying in them every time I glanced in their direction. Natural, living beauty *in* my cell with me! A window on God.

I came up against an irresolvable relationship. I'm used to relationships growing increasingly friendly over time, but one officer seemed to have more trouble with me the more we interacted. I couldn't understand it. So I finally asked her what the problem was. She told me: "You're so high and mighty! You think you're so above everybody you don't have to use your ID." I explained: "I'm not asking for special treatment. I choose not to use the ID. The jail is free to choose how it responds. In fact, it takes away privileges." But I thought about it a lot. She felt offended by my position. I didn't want to offend her. So the next time I had an opportunity, I apologized for whatever offense she felt. That made it even worse. The more I tried to do the right thing, the more she resented me for being "holier-than-thou." I still wonder what would mend that relationship.

—— ✂ ——

And then there was court.

I had been charged, as expected, with misdemeanor trespass. But for my nonappearance at the hearing, instead of the expected "contempt of court," I was charged with something called "failure to appear," which is the title of a statute about violating bond conditions. The public defender who had been appointed as advisory counsel for me felt that I had a strong case against the second count and brought the statute book to a visit to explain the law to me.

Of course, I wasn't planning to present a defense. And, as usual, I had declined legal representation. But a public defender was usually appointed for me anyway, to be available in case I had questions. I had met several of them over the years and appreciated them as people, but I asked them to do nothing at all for me in court. They respected my wishes, though I know that it was frustrating for them to have to keep refraining from speaking up about an error or a technicality or a mitigating circumstance. On my last case, the public defender had been so upset about the inappropriate severity of the guidelines sentence that I had given him permission to make a statement about it on his own behalf.

The same public defender was prepared to advise me again, and now, for the first time, I actually had a legal defense. I was not guilty of the second charge. I had, indeed, not appeared for the hearing, but I was not bound to appear under the "failure to appear" statute, because I had not agreed to. The statute did not even apply to my case. It covered *only* the cases of people who had agreed to bond conditions. In fact, it's precisely because I'm determined *not* to violate any condition to which I've agreed that I refuse to agree.

Nonetheless, I still didn't intend to present a defense, because of my nonparticipation in the legal process. I was going to let the court do whatever it was going to do. I *was* in contempt of court for ignoring the magistrate's order to appear, and I was prepared to be punished for it.

The trial was set to commence first thing in the morning on a Monday. After the end of the business day the preceding Friday, I received in the mail a copy of the prosecution's proposed jury instructions. The jury instructions are read by the judge to the jury after the presentation of evidence in a trial, for the specific purpose of explaining the applicable law to them. One of my charges rested solely on the law. And the prosecutor's representation of it was so inaccurate as to amount to an out-and-out lie. The prosecutor claimed that the law had to do with my response to an order to appear, whereas no such thing is mentioned in the law at all; I knew; I had read the statute; the law is about failure to abide by bond agreements.

Now I *couldn't* let that go by, could I? That was an issue of *truth.* Surely the prosecutor didn't intend to have me imprisoned for a year on the basis of a *lie?* Surely the judge would want as badly as anybody to represent the law accurately to the jury. Surely all that would be required to get it corrected would be my bringing it to their attention. I had the courtroom rights of a lawyer, since I was representing myself, so I could talk with the prosecutor as soon as I arrived in court on Monday. If there were still a problem, we could both talk with the judge in the conference where we discussed and finalized the jury instructions. I was used to judges taking great care with that process.

I was brought to court on Monday, February 26, at the last minute before the trial began. The judge was already seated on the bench. There was no opportunity to talk to anybody, apart from whispered asides to the public defender. The jury instructions conference took place in the court-room, while the jury was out for a bathroom break, and there was no discussion. The judge's version of the instructions had corrected the bla-tant errors in the prosecutor's, but it was still imprecise and misleading. Why couldn't he straightforwardly explain what the law said? How else was the jury to know? I raised my concern; the judge declared, "Objection overruled"; and the conference was over.

I could hardly believe it. Everything was happening too fast for thought. The trial proceeded at breakneck pace, and I could now see that abso-lutely nothing would be done about the truth issue that seemed so impor-tant to me unless I did it myself. So, effectively, without any kind of prepa-ration, I offered a defense. I cross-examined the witness who presented the p.r. bond paper in order to establish that I hadn't signed it; she either couldn't or wouldn't confirm my statement to the magistrate that I wouldn't promise to return–though it's in the court record, which the public de-fender later ordered a transcript of. I read and explained the law to the jury as part of my closing statement, though it felt sort of schizophrenic to be giving my attention to legal issues at all. Only a few of them appeared to be listening. The prosecutor lied to them, again claiming that the law had to do with obeying court orders. The judge refused their request to see a copy of the actual statute. How could they possibly make a decision on the basis of it?

They must have made some effort, because they deliberated for a good hour and a half, which was quite a record for my cases. But they returned with a verdict of "guilty." And not only was I, in fact, *not* guilty on the second count, but all that would have been required to prevent a convic-tion was *one* juror out of twelve holding out for a "reasonable doubt" about it. I can only conclude that, in the absence of the necessary information for making an independent judgment, they simply opted for trusting the "authority" of the court.

I returned to the jail in a daze, so disoriented that I tripped over my shackles and fell, unable to break the fall because my hands were chained to my waist, and my mind couldn't catch up with its own sense percep-tions anyway. I watched it all happening impassively, as if from a distance. The marshals picked me up. I hardly knew where my own body was.

For the better part of two days, I plumbed the depths of my pain. I felt betrayed by the court. I already knew that the "justice" system is unjust. I had seen plenty of evidence of it in other people's cases. But until I was the victim of it myself, I was still somehow assuming that the system would at least play by its own rules, that there was something "professional" about it, and that respect for truth was built into its very structure.

More than that, I felt betrayed personally. I receive people openly and honestly, and I unconsciously assume that they'll respond in kind. It never occurred to me to doubt the integrity and good faith of the prosecutor and the judge. Their betrayal of my innocent trust in them was like a slap in the face.

And then I uncovered the heart of my woundedness. They had betrayed my trust in basic human goodness, which is an article of faith for me. God has created us good, and that goodness is in there somewhere, in everyone, no matter how little it may show or how many choices we may have made against it. I had believed in their goodness, and they had run roughshod over my belief.

Once I had identified the pain, the amazing grace was that I knew immediately what to do with it. I could not choose to stop believing in basic human goodness, including the goodness of those who had betrayed my faith. Faith does not rest on evidence. I could not choose to stop loving them, or to stop being open and vulnerable. The only choice available to me in God was to accept the pain, to embrace it, to suffer it—held in the healing and forgiving love of God.

The miracle was that, the instant I made that choice, God somehow transported me all the way through the crucifixion into the resurrection beyond. I wrote for the Denver Catholic Worker newsletter:

> Suddenly I was in a clear, strong, free, loving place, where I could see that my greatest gift and freedom, the freedom to love, had been preserved. (The freedom to suffer, I think, somehow complements the freedom to love, and the two of them together can, and do, redeem the world.) I hadn't been dragged down spiritually. I had no negative feelings. Even the pain was over. My essential self was intact, and stronger than before through having been tested by fire. I hadn't been hurt at all! Praise the Lord!

That was my Ash Wednesday. It catapulted me into an awesome spiritual awareness:

> It began when I saw that I'd been dragged through hell and gained rather than lost! . . . I don't know how it happened. . . . I find myself (in the wonderfully mysterious ways of God) in a whole new realm of spiritual experience that's so glorious I yearn to be able to share about it, and I can't find words. A metaphor is that it's like standing on a mountaintop where everything is beautiful and clear and fresh, noticing that one's material circumstances are tiny and insignificant in the distance.

But it's not as if one has stepped out of one's material circumstances, but rather that one sees *all* material reality as a vehicle for spiritual glory. There's nothing we go through materially, no matter how difficult or painful, that can't make us richer spiritually. . . .

I've known for some time that spiritual reality is more *real* than material reality–more immediate and tangible and vivid, more solid and dependable–and now it's as if that knowledge has moved from my head into my heart. I'm living and breathing it. I'm seeing it all around me. But even that isn't the whole story, and today in prayer I was given a glimpse of how to talk about the deeper meaning of this new level of awareness.

It's *in us*–in our behavior and choices and attitudes–that the reality of the spiritual is manifested. It's our calling and vocation to enflesh it, to bring it into the presence of the world, and there's nothing more important that we can do for God or for the world or for ourselves. The miracle and the triumph for us is that it's possible, that we never need to be dragged down by material reality because we can always choose to touch the spiritual through it and be lifted up. . . .

We actually end up transforming material reality into spiritual, thereby giving it meaning. The material doesn't have meaning in itself. It simply is what it is. Pain is pain. A stone is a stone. Whether we choose to stumble over it or to use it as a stepping-stone to the kingdom of God is entirely up to us. . . . Even hell itself can be used as a highway to heaven–and how much richer the whole world is for the transformation! . . .

The truly nonviolent reaction is simply to accept the pain, to not want or need to do anything at all with it. It's okay for it just to be there. Our responsibility to God and to ourselves is to stay loving, giving, and forgiving regardless–because our calling as Christians is to reflect God's love to the world and because every single human being, no matter what he or she may have done to us or to others, is precious in God's sight, is one of those whom Jesus died on the cross to save. And we participate in that redemptive work by our willingness to embrace our pain, which keeps us free to love unconditionally, which *is* God's work in the world. What a privilege to be allowed to share in it![1]

[1] A major portion of this article was quoted in an article that I wrote for the *Denver Catholic Register*, which was published on April 15, 1992. Reprinted with permission.

On April 2, I was sentenced to two years in prison.

The public defender visited me in the marshals' visiting room. He made me an impassioned plea to appeal the conviction. He felt that the honor of the court was at stake, that the illegal conviction would set a dangerous precedent. I learned much later from a friend who had taken the prosecutor to task for his conduct in my case that the prosecutor had shrugged it off with, "She can appeal it." I was not willing to appeal it. My position of not participating in the legal process had not been altered by my impromptu involvement in the trial, which had not extended beyond talking to people: asking questions, explaining, trying to represent truth. I was certainly not willing to seek vindication from the court. I was innocent, no matter what it said. I would not confer legitimacy on it by petitioning it for what was mine by right.

But I also felt the pain of the public defender. I wanted to do something for him if I could. And I realized that there was one thing I could do. I could talk to the appeals court. I could write a personal letter, such as I regularly wrote to judges. They might well not accept it in place of a legal motion, but in case they did, his concern would be addressed. For myself, I continued to trust that, since I was doing my best to do God's will, the consequences were in God's hands. God would make use of that prison time.

I arrived at FCI Lexington (Kentucky) on April 19, after nearly a week in Norman, Oklahoma, which was a decided improvement over the old Oklahoma County Jail. Lexington was then the closest thing in the federal prison system to a medical facility for women; it received FMC (Federal Medical Center) status before the end of my sentence. The physical plant was daunting: a huge complex of three- and four-story brick buildings, almost all connected to one another, with small courtyards and air shafts between them. You felt closed in and restricted. And it was very crowded, housing almost two thousand prisoners, with large newcomers' dorms and as many as sixteen people even in a long-term room. That's what I was told anyway. I never set foot on the compound.

I complied with some demands of R & D staff and not with others. One officer in particular grew increasingly irritated as I kept asking for reasons and making independent judgments. I don't think that he appreciated my smiling, easy confidence either. The last straw was my refusal to sign a receipt for bedding that I had not yet received. He called the lieutenant.

Another officer appeared, ordered me to stand up, put handcuffs on me, grabbed a corner of my clothing as if I might contaminate her, and led me off. She didn't tell me anything and seemed angry that I didn't know the way to wherever we were going. I wasn't surprised that it turned out to be the lieutenants' office. The lieutenant wasn't pleased with me either and typed out a detention order on the spot.

Lexington's hole (called "segregation") was larger than any I'd seen before. Most cells were double-, triple-, or quadruple-bunked, and if I'd thought that Pleasanton was rigid about handcuffs, I hadn't yet discovered the meaning of rigid. At least you were cuffed in the front here. The handcuffs were replaced *after* the entrance strip-search for the short walk down the corridor to your cell. Every person in the cell was routinely handcuffed before the door was opened for any reason. People were awakened and ordered out of bed to be handcuffed for a cellmate to be let in or out. I saw no reason for anybody in any prison I'd experienced to be handcuffed at all, and the grinding dehumanization of forcing everyone in the hole to undergo it many times a day screamed oppression at me.

I didn't know all of that yet, though. My immediate problem, now that I'd been locked into a cell with two other women, was whether to cooperate with having the handcuffs removed through the slot in the door. I never had cooperated with such a thing, but I was feeling appreciative of the segregation officer, who had been gentle and friendly with me, and it didn't feel absolutely necessary to make her deal with a new issue—particularly hard to explain with respect to *un*cuffing when it hadn't come up yet over cuffing—right off the bat. After some hesitation, I finally gave her my hands.

Never again! I was surprised that I could do it even once. I was surprised that I'd been able to live for as long as I had with the Pleasanton compromise of walking to the door and letting the officer choose whether to handcuff me or not. It might not even have been possible without my cooperation here, since the food tray slots were significantly lower. How bizarre to have felt *thankful* when I was handcuffed, so that I could go somewhere! No, I could do without going anywhere. I would not so much as walk to the door any more.

And it was demanded of me again almost immediately, because one of my cellmates was being released to the compound. I refused to "cuff up." I was sorry to delay her departure, but I knew that the officers would let her go. They had to call the lieutenant, who came in with several staff to handcuff me. They left me cuffed in the cell while they released her. Then they moved me to a cell by myself. I cooperated. They removed the handcuffs before leaving. Yes, I could see how this would be the only workable solution for them under the circumstances—and it was an improvement for me as well.

I asked an officer the first evening about a vegetarian diet and was told that there wasn't one; I would have to eat around the meat on a regular tray. Well, I could try it one more time. I tried it for about four meals and gave up. For some reason, the dead animals bothered me more than ever before. I couldn't stand the smell or the sight of them. I would rush through the meal to get them out of my cell as quickly as possible. It wasn't worth it. I stopped accepting the trays.

About another four meals later, an officer finally asked me why I wasn't eating. I explained. "Oh, that's no problem," he answered. "I'll order you a no-meat diet." I didn't believe that he'd be able to and was stunned to begin receiving no-meat trays regularly from then on. I could live with that.

But the nutrition was far from adequate. Since there was no attempt to provide alternative protein in place of the meat, I was receiving almost no protein—or whole grains or fresh fruit—except at breakfast. Even beans were uncommon. I wasn't willing to compromise by filling up on empty starch and sugar—a much wiser choice than I knew at the time, since sugar rushes cause my overactive insulin to depress my blood sugar level too far—so sometimes I ate very little. A couple of the officers encouraged me to talk with the dietician. In mid-May I wrote her a "cop-out" (the common name for an "inmate request to staff member"). She wrote back:

> The Bureau of Prisons does not recognize vegetarian diets. No substitute is provided to those who choose to avoid meat. I suggest that you purchase the peanut butter, nuts or cheese in commissary to replace the meat. Keep in mind that eggs and legumes may also substitute for meat when they are served.

I couldn't buy anything at all from the commissary, because of my refusal to use an inmate registration number, and was beginning to feel discriminated against. The BOP recognizes an adequate diet as a *right* of all prisoners, even on punishment status. Didn't that right extend to indigent vegetarians?

Meanwhile, I had learned a lot about the parameters of my situation. Three days a week, I was asked if I wanted a shower, and five days a week if I wanted to come out for exercise. I always said, "Yes." "Are you going to cuff up?" "No." I never got out of the cell.

There was one exception: shakedowns. About a week after my arrival I was quietly attending to my own business when I was ordered to come to the door to cuff up. I refused. The lieutenant came in with the segregation staff and cuffed me. No hoopla. Holding the handcuff chain, he led me out into the corridor. Not clear that I needed to refuse, I walked. He ordered the female officer to pat-search me. She was very thorough. The male officer searched the cell. He didn't tear it apart. I was led back into the cell, and the handcuffs were removed. No big deal.

But I felt invaded and assaulted. I hadn't been doing anything. I hadn't been hiding anything. And prison officials feel free to break into my space at any time without warning or provocation and treat me utterly like an object. I needed to withhold the assent of my cooperation. The next time, about two weeks later, I did. I went limp when they tried to lead me from the cell. They handled me gently, taking care to avoid hurting me. After that, they came prepared with an office chair on wheels.

The scenario became routine. I received an incident report each time for refusing to cuff up, specifically, "refusing to obey an order of any staff member." You generally waited a while for DHO hearings here. My first was on May 9. I was sentenced to seven days in disciplinary segregation, and before I'd completed the punishment time, I was awaiting a hearing on a new incident report. By the time I was sentenced to seven more days on that, I had another one pending. It looked as if the prison could, and perhaps intended to, keep me in segregation indefinitely simply by writing me up every week or so for refusing the handcuffs.

I was in a centered and flexible inner space during these early weeks, trusting that things would work out somehow and discovering either that what I needed somehow came my way or that I didn't really need it after all. I'd never been so relaxed before about the way I smell without deodorant. At one point it looked as if I might not be able to realize my *only* agenda item—which was to make a phone call to assure my friends on the outside that I was fine—so I simply, quietly let go even of that, trusting that they would be able to trust me to God. And then I was unexpectedly able to call after all.

I had decided not to ask about an inmate registration number on my mail, and simply to try sending letters without it. The first four, including two to the public defender, were mailed. The fifth was returned to me, with the assertion, later confirmed by superiors, that I would be denied written communication even to an *attorney* if I didn't use that number. Thankfully, though, I'd been assigned to a very human and caring counselor, who made a point of offering me the phone as often as he could. I was apparently officially allowed to use it only once a month, but never had to wait that long.

The public defender was being actively supportive, especially in trying to encourage the appeals court judges to initiate judicial action in response to my letter to them. As it turned out, they didn't. He also became involved in an effort to influence my sentence computation. The judge's official record of my sentencing gave me sixty-eight days of pre-sentence jail credit on *each* of the two sentences; the prison's computation gave me the sixty-eight days only once. Sincerely wanting to help, the public defender became sort of overeager, and there was an exchange with the prison's records office that was aggressive, perhaps even threatening, and certainly fell short of the love and understanding that I'm always reaching for myself in response to the people in the system. I requested gently that he desist. I wrote an apology to the head of the records office. And I found myself knowing, with absolute certainty, that I would rather spend sixty-eight days in this cell than have anyone receive a nasty letter from anyone on my behalf.

I received a spectacular gift from my sister Debby. We had visited on the phone when I was in Denver County, and she'd asked me what I wanted for my birthday. "A song," I'd replied. So she'd written me a song. But songs depend on inspiration, and it was a month or more late by the time it reached me in Lexington—which was perfect timing, because that was when I needed it.

1. The Lord is my shepherd, wherever I go
   The blessings of heaven are there;
   I walk in green fields where the sweet waters flow,
   And joy lifts the wings of my prayer.

   Joy is the song that I sing each day,
   For God's love is patient and strong;
   It washes the cares of the world away;
   Joy is my song.

2. Yea, though I journey the vale of despair,
   No sorrow will darken my sight;
   God's love enfolds me as close as the air,
   More real than the fears of the night.

   Joy is the song that I sing each day;
   Though the road be winding and long,
   I trust in a guide who will never stray;
   Joy is my song.

3. How can I number the gifts I receive
   When bounty around me is poured?
   My cup overflows; I have all that I need;
   I'll dwell in the house of the Lord.

   Joy is the song that I sing each day;
   I know I am where I belong;
   Goodness and mercy adorn my way;
   Joy is my song.[2]

The words were so perfect that they made me cry, but the real miracle was in the tune. She had sent me a copy of it. I can read music. I could have played it on a piano or other instrument. But I can't sight-read with my voice. I can't reproduce the intervals. Yet I wanted so badly to hear the song that I tried. I can hold a bass note in my memory, and I can sing a

---

[2] ©Deborah L. Haines, 1997. Used by permission.

chromatic scale. So I sang the chromatic scale from note to note, trying to remember each new note that I'd located as I went on to the next, going over and over and over it, until the whole melody had emerged. I knew that I'd gotten it right. I could *hear* the rightness of it. I gloried in it. I sang it and sang it, and it drew me into prayer.

Suddenly, the bottom fell out of my universe. An ordinary evening was shattered by wild laughter in a cell a few doors down the corridor and the exclamation, "I can't believe it! They've just turned off my *water!*" I couldn't believe it either. It wasn't funny. It was insane. Surreal. Impossible. I couldn't imagine anything more cruel than deliberately denying water to a prisoner who was locked down.

I found out what was going on. She had declared a hunger strike—I never did know over what—and after seventy-two hours (nine meals), one's water was shut off. The officer explained that it was policy. I had never seen or heard of such a thing before. It was unconscionable. I couldn't stand it. There was no alternative but to do something about it, which was terrifying. The pain of *her* situation was already more than I could absorb, and the consequences to me would be even worse; she, at least, was still allowed to take showers. I cried out some of my anguish into my mattress, and then I told the officer that there was no way I was willing to eat as long as her water was shut off. I even put it into writing for him. I was absolutely certain of the necessity of that choice.

I have never gotten sick so fast in my life. That was scary in itself. By the second or third day, I felt sort of nauseated and crampy even when I was lying still. My whole body was complaining. I didn't remember it being this bad at Pleasanton. In fact, it hadn't been. Only much, much later did I finally realize that I'd entered into this fast so woefully undermined by months of terribly inadequate nutrition that my body had no resources at all. That was undoubtedly the reason that my hair had been falling out at an alarming rate, too. I clung to my birthday song, and endured.

After three days, the prison shut off my water. It was bad enough to be deprived of essentially all personal hygiene, most basically the ability to wash my hands after using the toilet. But the critical issue was drinking water. One officer told me, "No problem. Just ask us for it. We'll give it to you." But another added, "Sure, I can give it to you. But if you accept it, it means the same thing as accepting your tray." The lieutenants confirmed his interpretation: If I was serious about this refusal to eat, I was required to refuse to drink, too. And I was committed to the *statement* that was being made by my choices. They were a declaration of non-assent to cruel and inhuman punishment, and I would not retreat an iota from the meaning that they had for the prison.

But I was terrified. I carry in my head the rough rule of thumb that a person can live for three days without water. This was already the second day, and it was the Friday before the Memorial Day weekend. Would they let me die over the long weekend? I actually asked the officer, and he responded, "They'll continue to monitor your health."

What "monitoring" I was receiving from the PAs, who made daily rounds, was not reassuring. One of them had told me, "Of course you shouldn't drink water when you're fasting. Do you want to get deathly ill?" Statements like that quickly convinced me that I was taking my life in my hands to trust myself to prison medical care. But I had no choice.

By now, I was weak and dizzy. Standing for more than a minute or two gave me tight abdominal cramps. I could feel the pressure on my heart from almost any activity. The constant thirst raged at me. On Friday night a caring officer tried to talk to me, but I couldn't stand at the door for it. So he said that he was coming in to shake down the cell, put handcuffs on me, and let me sit at my desk, with my whole upper body lying on it, while he did. It was an excuse to talk. He couldn't change my mind, but maybe he learned something relevant about my condition.

When I woke up on Saturday morning, I could still urinate a little. But when a PA asked for a urine sample some time later, I couldn't produce a drop. I tried again in the early afternoon and still couldn't. An officer relayed that information to somebody, and shortly my cell was full of people, including the head doctor. I didn't want to move, but somebody coaxed me off the bed. The doctor was gentle and polite. He asked me some questions and did a simple examination while I sat at my desk. Then he told me to stand up. I could hardly imagine the effort of it. He ordered me sharply, and I obeyed, sort of dazedly. He said, "We're taking you to F4 [the prison hospital]." I answered, "I can't walk." But they already had a wheelchair waiting for me.

Simply sitting up was exhausting. I was thankful to reach a hospital bed and crawl into it. The doctor explained that I could drink measured quantities of something-or-other or they could give me an IV. Even if I had been drinking water, I would have become dehydrated from fasting, because the salts that enable the body tissues to *retain* water are flushed out through the urine and not replaced, so my body needed salts as well as water for rehydration. I was clear about refusing to take anything by mouth, and I had decided after my Pleasanton experience that I would refuse another IV. But I wanted those fluids so desperately! Wouldn't it be hypocritical to claim that I didn't? I don't remember how I said it, but I passively allowed them to give me an IV. A very competent nurse started the needle in the side of my right wrist, and let a whole liter of fluid pour into me as quickly as my vein would take it. Then he set a second liter to drip, monitored by a computer-controlled pump.

Though my door was locked, there were occasions for conversation with many people, all asking me why I wasn't eating. I was absolutely appalled by the matter-of-fact way in which even *medical* people defended that water shut-off policy. *No* one within the institution seemed to think that it was a big deal, in contrast to the universal horror that it generated in people whom I later told about it outside. I was carefully advised that the purpose of the policy was medical and was directed toward monitoring one's fluid intake and output. However, I hadn't seen any monitoring in the hole, and here in the hospital, where the nurses charted every milliliter of it, my water was *not* turned off, so I was drinking it, and they found out how much by asking me.

My original position had been that I wouldn't eat as long as anyone's water, including mine, was shut off. The other woman had started eating and had hers turned on before I left segregation, and now I had running water, too. But my position had shifted at the point when I'd found out that you couldn't get even drinking water from an officer without renouncing your principled protest. I couldn't cooperate with the *existence*, much less the implementation, of a policy like *that*. So I was still refusing to eat– and prepared within myself for the likelihood of being force-fed for the entire remainder of my sentence.

I learned only gradually what a long-term arrangement the IV was. When a nurse, rather to my dismay, brought in a third bag of fluid, I asked how long I was going to be stuck with it, and gathered that it would be at least overnight. It wasn't too difficult to sleep with, and its pole was on wheels, so I could get to the toilet and the sink as needed. But I had to be very careful with my right hand. I couldn't get the IV site wet. I couldn't bend it. The next time I asked, I was told, "Until you start eating." Argh. But I kept hanging in there with it. I was trying to cooperate with medical care in general, and it *was* supporting my health. I had a bit more energy now and less cramping and nausea.

I was still concerned, though, about my heart. The pressure on it felt practically constant. Even a simple activity like washing my underwear would push it to hard, painful pounding, and sometimes it would just hurt, suddenly and inexplicably. I felt increasingly fragile physically, didn't know how dangerous my condition might be, and prayed that I could trust the medical staff not to let me deteriorate too far before they intervened further. The head doctor seemed competent. Still, I was scared and vulnerable, and I remember crying through the wonderfully comforting second verse of my birthday song.

By my fourth day on the IV, the needle was working its way out of its dressing, so the evening nurse redressed it. She must have poked it through the vein in the process, though, because it infiltrated (the fluid, missing the vein, entered the surrounding tissues, causing immediate swelling) and had to be replaced. The only vein that she felt confident of hitting with the new needle was in the crook of my elbow. She bound my whole arm to a board to keep the elbow immobilized, which seemed necessary to me under the circumstances, but I soon discovered that there was only one sleeping position in which it didn't hurt. It was grace to notice, as I made it fitfully through the night, that I could thank God for the one position.

The board was slipping by morning, and I asked the competent day nurse if he could adjust it. He looked askance at the needle in my elbow and offered to move it for me, which I gratefully accepted. It was while he was doing that that a conversation about the water shut-off policy finally got off the ground. The lieutenants' interpretation of the drinking water issue didn't sound right to him. Surely that wasn't the intention of the policy! He set right off to discuss it with the doctor.

The doctor came to see me. No, he said, the policy did not intend to tie drinking water to the message of a hunger strike like that. The lieutenants were misinterpreting it. How about the addition of a clarifying statement? He'd have to discuss it with the warden, but would I be willing to eat if a sentence were inserted in the policy to make it clear that the acceptance of drinking water did not alter the stand being made by a hunger strike? Yes, that sounded acceptable to me. He left to consult with the warden.

Amazing! It had never occurred to me that anything might change as a result of my protest, and it was exciting to begin to imagine the possibility of eating again. Since the doctor's workday was already over, I assumed that nothing more would happen before morning. But he returned the same evening, just to assure me that the warden was in agreement with his proposed policy amendment. He must have been *very* anxious for me to eat. I decided that I should trust him actually to effect the change he'd promised, and broke my fast with dinner. It had been ten days.

I would accept only trays without meat, which the hospital was glad to provide, and I must have talked about vegetarian diets with the nurses. I think that it was the same, competent one who arranged for the dietician to come visit me. How wonderful to have an opportunity to avoid the handcuff barrier, which would prevent me from going to see her! She explained the policy constraints that limited her, and I explained what would be workable and helpful for me. She agreed to try to work something out. Alleluia!

The hospital released me back to the hole on June 5. The segregation lieutenant came in and handcuffed me. An uptight female officer conducted a very thorough pat search. Returning me to my old cell in segregation, she was so affronted by my refusal to uncuff through the door that she tried to force me, leading me to the door, locking it between us, and then reaching in through the slot. But she couldn't get at my wrists in that position, and I resisted her attempts to drag them down. Eventually, she gave up and uncuffed me in the cell.

The cell had been stripped, and probably used by others, in my absence. I had to wait hours for bedding and other standard prison issue, and it wasn't until late at night that an officer finally located my personal property, which had been stored. My bra had been tossed into the laundry—where it was later found by a *very* helpful orderly—and my devotional books, which the Denver marshals had agreed to send home when I left the jail but which had ended up here anyway, had been thrown onto the book cart. I never recovered two of them.

At lunch the next day I was served a regular tray by the regular officer, who knew me well. "That isn't my diet," I said. "They don't have those no-meat diets any more," he answered. Oh, no! My heart sank. My response was clear: "I don't want it." But the prospect of another fast just now, in my fragile physical condition, was horrifying. How quickly might I end up accidentally killing myself this time? Fortunately, I didn't have to wonder for long. The officer returned with my no-meat tray. The other had been a threat, gruesomely calculated to force a compromise from me by taking advantage of my recent ordeal and current weakness.

The DHO, now that I was back from the hospital, picked up my latest pending incident report and sentenced me to another seven days in DS. For a while, it looked as if I might be allowed to finish the punishment time without incident and make it to the general population. But no. There was another shakedown and another write-up. It kept happening every week or two. Soon the DHO was increasing the sanctions: fourteen days and then twenty-one days and then thirty days with a recommended "disciplinary" transfer. I knew that I would never see the compound.

The hearings took place in my absence, because of the handcuffs, but the DHO often stopped at my door to chat. We disagreed about practically everything, but cordially. I remarked, "We can still like each other."

"I never like a convicted felon," he retorted.

I recoiled inwardly from the attack, but I didn't stop smiling. "Well, that needn't stand in your way with me, because I'm not a convicted felon."

"What?" He was very surprised. "Are you saying you're not convicted?"

"Oh, I'm convicted. But it's misdemeanors."

"*Misdemeanors*? They're keeping you in *prison* for *misdemeanors*? What a waste of government resources!"

Soon after my return from the hospital, I was moved into the unit's most indestructible cell, usually used for people who were out of control. I didn't see a need to refuse, but it felt punishing. The bed frame was a single concrete block, instead of a metal bunk, so it wasn't high enough to give me a view out the window; and there was no locker for my property, which had to be kept on the floor. But I can make almost any place livable if I can clean it thoroughly. And the major advantage grew on me: the cell was very spacious. My soul expands into space and light.

I'll never forget the day when I was sitting on my bed, looking across at the large, empty wall opposite me and thinking, "That's an ideal wall for a mural." And the mural began to emerge. How can I describe this? I knew what a portion of the mural was, not actually seeing it on the wall, but seeing it in my mind. Not creating it. Recognizing it. And only part of it. The background. The background, especially toward the top, was full of angels.

I looked at those angels often, feeling both a sense of companionship from having them there in the cell with me and a sense of protection, not materially, but symbolically. They reminded me of the spiritual reality that surrounded and sustained me. And I brought my intercession to them. Whenever I was trying to pray for someone with whom I had difficulty, I imagined him or her among the angels, reminding myself of how very precious to God and able to be used by God for my good even this difficult person was.

My life was rich in intercession these days. The inspiration had come to me during my first weeks at Lexington—quietly, clearly, without thought or preamble—that one of the uses I might make of this empty prison time would be to fold 1,000 prayer cranes for peace. The 1,000 origami cranes have an ancient history as a symbol of good fortune; when a child who was dying of leukemia from the atomic bombing of Hiroshima tried to fold 1,000 cranes against her death, they became a peace symbol. I wanted each one that I folded also to be a prayer, a prayer for an individual or a specific concern. Through a phone call, I invited any of my friends who wished to participate to send me prayer requests and/or squares of colored paper. And I used whatever I had at hand, much of it white, including the backs of some court papers.

The tremendous, unexpected gift of the project was the depth and breadth that it gave to my intercession. I would spend perhaps fifteen minutes on each crane, completing five to ten of them in a day, and all of that time was deliberately focused on prayer for individuals. I had never before been able to attend so well for so long to intercession. I found that I could pray through the cranes even when I hardly felt prayerful at all. If any of my prayers had seemed too distracted, I would spend more time with those people on my knees, visualizing each of them as a point of light in our world. I prayed on my knees a lot, including prayer for my own needs and for those of the people around me.

I also started praying the rosary. This helped me through prayerless times, too. I figured that, if there were nothing in me to offer, I could still offer a prayer of the church. The Catholic chaplain—a priest who was warmly personal and blessed me with Communion on Sundays—had given me the rosary, and a flier I'd received in Denver County taught me how to pray it. Praying to Mary made me very aware that I didn't really know her personally, so I sent a message to my spiritual director asking him to introduce her to me. He gifted me with a copy of a French icon (a sacred painting) entitled "Our Lady of Intercession." Of course, I could also meet her in the scriptures. I would pray a decade of the rosary in the presence of Mary at the annunciation (Luke 1:26-38), or the visitation (Luke 1:39-45), or the nativity (Luke 2:1-7). I prayed before Mary crowned with stars in the stained glass of St. Benedict's Monastery, Mary appearing to Juan Diego in Mexico as Our Lady of Guadalupe, Mary in heaven receiving the prayers of our whole nation on its knees, Mary as a young mother enduring the nuclear contamination of Chernobyl, Mary crying over the incarnated evil of Rocky Flats.

I suddenly recognized the rest of the mural on my blank wall: it was a painting of the annunciation, of Mary kneeling before the angel Gabriel. "Let it be to me according to your word" (Luke 1:38). The model of faithful obedience for all of us.

And I received a vision. In the visitation—an image that I brought consciously to mind—Mary was usually running to meet Elizabeth, young, joyful, full of expectation. Now I saw her at Rocky Flats, running, laughing, her hair flying in the wind, running through a meadow bright with wildflowers over the place where the whole nuclear weapons plant had been shut down and bulldozed into the ground. Yes, I thought. Not a bad use for that contaminated soil. It could grow wildflowers. I shared the vision with the director of the weapons complex in a letter. I had long ago given up on mailing letters, but I tried to mail that one, and it went out.

—— ✂ ——

I had not heard anything more from the dietician. After two or three weeks, I'd written her a cop-out. I still didn't hear anything. I was trying very consciously to offer my bodily hunger to God as a spiritual sacrifice for the benefit of others, and so to be thankful for whatever came on my tray, whether it gave me enough to eat or not. It was a good discipline, though I wasn't always successful at it. But the nagging sense that I was cooperating with the system's choice to discriminate against me grew more and more insistent.

My emotional resources, in general, were being worn down by the daily, relentless oppressions and restrictions of prison life. There were perpetual challenges to submit to indignity and deprivation, to embrace pain. Much of my spiritual journey seems to have consisted of lesson after lesson in stretching to embrace more and more pain, ever-widening spheres of the world's pain and my own as well, staying vulnerable, caring deeply, letting it in. I wasn't always equal to the challenge, even with the support of prayer.

I had a special friend on the unit by now. She's a woman with both physical and emotional problems who's such a charming, delightful, innocent little kid in her good times that you can't help loving her. In her bad times she's assaultive and suicidal and sometimes totally out of touch with reality, and you can't help loving her then either. It breaks your heart that she's in prison at all. With a twenty-year history of residential mental health care, she was locked up for writing a threatening letter to the U.S. president. We visited in her good times, calling from cell to cell, and sometimes I could help to talk her clear of a bad spell. A lot of the officers were caring and helpful with her, too. But sometimes one would respond inappropriately and hurtfully, and the pain of her woundedness was excruciating for me. I was *so* helpless!

The most persistent personal oppression for me was the refusal on the part of the prison in general to call me by my name, Jennifer, the only name that I've ever been identified with or called myself by. The Quaker tradition in which I grew up doesn't use titles; formal address would add my last name to my first. Even when I taught school, I was Jennifer. And in all my previous experience of the prison system, people would automatically come to call me Jennifer as they got to know me. It had never been an issue before. I didn't notice the difference here at first, because the familiarity grows with time. Most people here called me Haines. Some added a title. I found the first terribly offensive, and the latter less so only because of the intention behind it. It still wasn't me. And the practice didn't change. I eventually discovered that my first name wasn't even written on my door, so a stranger wouldn't know it without my saying something. Each of us was identified by a last name and a number. It was dehumanizing. The worst thing about it was that, I gradually learned, it was policy. It was apparently required of the officers. It was, one of them explained to me, specifically intended to create distance between "them" and "us." It was *intentionally* dehumanizing. I could hardly stand it.

Shakedowns, too, left me feeling assaulted and helpless, though they were quite low-key and not destructive. The worst was when the officers tore down the mobile I'd received in the mail, which I'd been delighting in. They didn't damage it or confiscate it, but the pain was in being denied the delight. I wasn't allowed to hang it up. Why do they take such simple joys away from you? They take almost everything away from you. You're stripped and left lying in the dust. My little girl cried over that one for almost a full day, knowing that it was a little thing, but there was no refuge even from the little things.

My safety valve was a kind of innocent craziness. Sometimes I felt a little crazy, and sometimes I let it show. It was a relief from the constant demand to be strong when I wasn't strong. If my little girl needed comfort, I could pull my mattress and bedding onto the floor in the space between the bed and the door, which was cozy. It was a good deal shorter than I and had two corners I could retreat to. Sometimes I would sleep there. Sooner or later I would become relaxed enough to be able to take up again the full, adult burden of "ordinary" life as a prisoner on punishment status in the hole.

It kept getting harder to carry that burden, though. One day I reached my limit on the diet issue. A concerned officer had arranged for a supply of peanut butter and crackers that I could keep in my cell, which was a big help nutritionally, but I was still chafing over the broader discrimination question and the lack of response from the dietician. I was trying, at least, to do what I could about vitamins through the medical people, especially since I tend toward anemia if I don't take iron. Somebody ordered a blood test, for which I was called out to the lab, and the officers refused to let me go because I wouldn't cuff up through the door. That was the last straw. One coil too many of the whole impossible situation had tightened around me, and I suddenly could no longer breathe. I stopped eating.

I knew that my choice was essentially emotional, but I wasn't distressed that it was, because my emotions were in trouble, and the choice helped. It gave me enough internal space to be able to breathe again, to move a little, to cope. I found myself gradually feeling freer and sunnier. The lieutenant came in at the beginning, when I was still in tears, and heard all about it. I wanted a nutritionally adequate diet. I had had it with being discriminated against as a vegetarian. I wasn't *demanding* a vegetarian diet. I was always open to the possibility that they might choose to force-feed me. But *I* couldn't stand to assent to the discrimination by accepting it any longer.

In three days I had a vegetarian diet. The dietician came to see me to work out the details, and she came *back* after the first meal to ask how it had been. It was wonderful. I was getting peanut butter. I was getting whole wheat bread. I was getting fresh fruit instead of cooked desserts. I indulged in a favorite treat: apples with peanut butter. I was getting milk at every meal. I was eating well. I started gaining weight right away. Why had I cooperated with being deprived for so long?

Then, in the second week of August, I made a terrible mistake. I was flossing my teeth. I rarely had access to dental floss in prison any more, but the woman whose water shut-off I'd protested had, naturally, become an instant friend, and she'd insisted on helping me out with some commissary items. One of the orderlies had been helpful, too. What I didn't have was a mirror. I misjudged the location of that temporary filling, which the county jail dentist had simply rammed in between two teeth, and accidentally dislodged it. Oh, *no!* I stood there for the longest time just staring at the thing in horror.

I didn't dare eat on the cavity. It had already been sensitive in the county jail. If I tried to eat around it, it seemed inevitable that I'd have to keep on trying for another year and a half, living with the pain and fear of losing the tooth. When would I ever be allowed to see a dentist? Somehow, it felt as if I had to intervene right away, to get it taken care of before I ate again. But how could I do *that*? I almost certainly wouldn't be allowed to see a dentist here as long as I refused to cooperate with the handcuffs. And I *couldn't* assent to handcuffs. I could see no way out at all, except for the possibility of compassion on the part of the prison. Perhaps something deep within me trusted that I could count on that compassion.

I stopped eating–how sad to pass up those beautiful diet trays!–but continued to accept my milk, both to show the prison that I wasn't trying to force it with a "hunger strike" and to protect my health as much as I could. But the milk seemed to do a lot less for me than I'd expected. I probably had no idea how depleted I was. I began to feel sick quite quickly. By the third week I was experiencing some alarming new sensations, including quirky spasms in my legs, tightness all across my chest and upper back after activity, and a pervasive sort of nausea that seemed to invade every cell of my body.

As usual, I didn't know how serious my condition might be, and I didn't know if the prison knew. How dangerously ill might both of us let me become before someone gave a little on the handcuffs? *I* couldn't seem to, but I was becoming scared enough to feel desperate for medical monitoring. When I was called out for an EKG, the segregation lieutenant came in and cuffed me—and I made the huge mistake of walking to the lab, feeling sicker than ever as a result. But when a doctor called for me, on the nineteenth day of the fast, a different lieutenant was on, and I wasn't allowed to go. I fell apart emotionally. It wasn't that I blamed the prison. I just felt trapped and helpless and scared. I asked to see a chaplain. A psychologist arrived first and was very helpful in walking me through my feelings.

Then all of a sudden, everything happened. The doctor came to see me. The captain avoided the handcuff issue by sending a dentist to me. She came first for an examination and soon returned to give me a new temporary filling right there in my cell. (*Very* temporary, I was told. But it hung in there for all the many months left in my sentence, until I was finally able to call my own dentist back in Denver, and in the few days between the call and the appointment, it fell out. "Mission accomplished," you could almost hear it remarking.) I felt so gifted and grateful to everybody!—feeling as if the prison had done me a big favor and wondering if I ever did favors for it.

That was on Wednesday, August 29. Exactly one week later, I was transferred.

10

Submersion

I leave Lexington in the late afternoon, in handcuffs through the entirety of the R & D processing except for the strip search. I'm struck by the incongruity of being so carefully restrained and guarded, as if I were a violent and dangerous criminal.

Two of the airlift marshals recognize me. "Didn't you come through last spring? From Denver?"

"Yes." I smile. "You have awfully good memories."

One of them checks my restraints and orders me to stand "over there"– the spot is pointed out precisely–"and face the airplane." I stand there, but I see no need to turn my back to them, and say so. The supervising marshal is furious. "She wants to be uncooperative; she can travel in a black box."

A black box is a high-security device that attaches to your waist chain and locks over your handcuffs, immobilizing them. Someone fastens it onto me. The whole trip I keep glancing down at that piece of hardware, unable to relate its identity to mine. How do I get myself into these things? It's not that I had some principled objection to looking at the airplane. It's not that I was trying to be difficult. I wasn't even consciously choosing to disobey an order. I just keep making independent judgments, based on reasonableness, to which coercive authority is irrelevant. And it seems common that I end up being treated as if I were a violent and dangerous criminal.

— ✂ —

It's late by the time we reach the county jail in Norman, and later still by the time we're processed upstairs, well past my bedtime. But the toilet paper situation has suddenly become unconscionable. The officers are declaring that no more will be issued before tomorrow. There's very little in the whole living unit, very little in the crowded cell where I've been assigned floor space. The officers accuse us of wasting it, of putting it in our hair.

Now wait a minute! I wasn't even here. Whether or not anybody wasted it before, how can you punish those of us who've just arrived? I say as much to the officer over the intercom in the cell. Her answer amounts to, "Tough." I know that there's no way I'll passively allow myself to be locked into a cell without an adequate supply of toilet paper. I return to the day room.

The officers are running very late. The evening count is usually accomplished by 11:00, and we haven't seen a sign of it yet at close to midnight. The sally port door opens. I enter the sally port, a step for which one ordinarily waits for permission, to talk to whichever staff person must be out there in the corridor. It turns out to be one of the sergeants.

Shades of my conversations with the Pleasanton captain. He's insisting that we can't have toilet paper because there isn't any, isn't any in the whole jail. I'm responding that no one can run a jail like that; if there isn't any toilet paper, someone had better go out to the store for some. He's growing practically apoplectic with rage, ordering me to step back into the unit, and I'm refusing, quietly, saying that I'll wait for toilet paper, thank you. Other prisoners, afraid of what will happen to me, are begging me to obey, and I know that the jail will force me, but I can live with that. I will *not* accede to this insanity voluntarily.

He radios for reinforcements. Another staff person arrives. "What's the matter?" she asks. I explain. "Oh, that's no problem," she assures me. "Just step back into the day room, and I'll get you some."

Okay. I do. If she's lying, I can still refuse to walk into my cell. She's not lying. She returns with eight or ten rolls of toilet paper and distributes them.

Amazing. I'm perennially amazed by the solutions that turn out to be possible after all.

—— ✶ ——

The second night is truly lovely. All the prisoners agree to turn off the television so that one who is known to have professional skills can entertain the rest of us with her singing. I'm delighted by the sense of community and stay up way past my bedtime again to enjoy it (the community, that is, more than the singing).

—— ✶ ——

Back at the airlift, the marshals ask one another if I should be restrained with a black box again, but no one's angry at me yet today. The supervisor shakes his head.

The incident occurs at the end of the trip. The marshals "ID" you at every point where you change jurisdictions. Someone who's holding your paperwork calls your name, and you're usually expected to respond with your number. I respond personally instead. Some marshals shrug it off. They have my picture; I'm easily identified. Some pursue it a bit and give up. Some engage the issue of my unsubmissiveness to their authority with heavy-duty threats. On my way off the airplane this time, the marshal is determined to pry a number out of me.

When demand and threat fail—and what more can he do?—in a few more minutes, I'll have left his jurisdiction—he hisses at me, "Get off of this airplane!," grabs the back of my waist chain, and *pushes* me down the steep steps as rapidly as he can negotiate them. I thank God that I don't lose my balance in spite of the shackles, and it's over in seconds.

A memo about my uncooperativeness travels with me all the way to MCC San Diego.

—— ✂ ——

Yes, MCC San Diego. I found out before I left Lexington that this was where I was headed. Bad news. I wasn't expecting anything so awful this early in my sentence. And I might have to do the entire remainder of it here. I'm on a "six-month disciplinary" transfer, which means that I'm supposed to stay in the place of punishment until I've completed six months of "clear conduct"—six months without incident reports. I'm wondering how I'll survive it.

My Lexington experience convinced me that I should wait to eat at any new institution until I'm offered a vegetarian diet. Here, though the Lexington diet is in my medical records, my mentioning it to the PA in R & D has no noticeable effect. I'm placed in the general population, where my health is particularly at risk because no one monitors anything. I won't be able to see the dietician for almost a week. I agonize over what to do in the meantime and decide to accept any individual tray that happens to be meatless. There are a few.

After five days I'm moved to detention for refusing three nights in a row to report for work on a graveyard-shift cleaning crew. I stop eating altogether. I receive essentially no medical attention. By my fourth day on water only, I'm weak and shaky. I stand to reach for a sanitary napkin from the top bunk, black out, and fall. I've never blacked out before. On the fifth day, having stated my need for a vegetarian diet all along, I'm simply, suddenly granted one. I resume eating.

Two days later an officer demands that I move my mattress off the floor. When I demur—because the top bunk is too close to the ceiling for me to be able to sit up on it and is full of my cellmate's property—the officer grabs me by one wrist like a piece of trash, drags me aside, and removes my whole bed from the cell. Demonstrating to the captain that I can't sit up straight on the top bunk suffices to have my bed returned. But I'm concerned about my inner state. This place seems to be a degree more barbaric than any other federal prison I've experienced, and I find myself reacting with more sharpness and defiance than I'm used to or comfortable with. Instead of simple firmness, which can be very gentle and friendly, my response to escalating authoritarian unreasonableness here seems to be an equally escalating insistence on my position.

I can tell that I'm uncentered. It's hard to focus, hard to pray. I'm interiorly dry and scattered. I can't fold prayer cranes. I feel as if I'm camping out in my cellmate's space, perennially in transition, perennially expecting to be moved again when I see the DHO, which keeps not happening. When my cellmate is suddenly transferred, I revel in having a cell to myself, hopeful that I can pull myself together and reestablish some sort of a prayer discipline. And then I'm ordered to move in with the woman next door. Sigh!

I cooperate, not discovering until the last minute that her water doesn't work. No way am I going to accept *that*! I stand in the doorway, preventing the officer from closing the door, and refuse to be locked into a cell without functional plumbing. I refuse to accept his excuses and evasions. He appears about to explode in fury at my intransigence by the time I finally step back in deference to my cellmate, who adds her quiet, gracious explanations about how she's been asking for three days if she could please have the water adjusted. And the other officer unlocks the little plumbing-access door outside the cell and turns up the flow. Why, why, *why* are these simple things so difficult?

My new cellmate is a vegetarian. She'd given up any hope for a vegetarian diet in prison, but now that she knows it's possible, she wants to fight for it. I tell her that I'll support her, well aware that I may lose my own diet in the process. She stops eating. Two days later, she's moved down to the medical floor. I suspect that the primary reason is to separate her from me.

A smoker is moved in with me. I object, fruitlessly. But I'm no longer willing to accept passively being locked in with cigarette smoke. I refuse to reenter the cell after rec in the caged common area the next morning. I'm assured that there's no space for separating us, that nothing can be done before Monday. Of course, I expect to be forced anyway, but I will not consent. A supervisor arrives. He promises to separate us today, and I decide to risk trusting him. Trust is one of the things I stand for. I return to the cell. After some hours, my cellmate is moved out.

During my few days alone, I'm not quite able to pray, but I'm able to fold cranes while focusing on scripture verses.

My former cellmate is returned from the "hospital." On the sixth day of her hunger strike–if she hadn't eaten by the end of that day, policy would have required that it be reported to the national BOP office—she was offered a vegetarian tray. Thinking that it meant she would receive a vegetarian diet, she ate. That broke her "strike," and it broke her resistance. She accepted the regular trays she was served from then on.

The next day, October 3, a doctor comes to see me. He asks if there's a medical reason for my diet. I reply that there isn't. He stops the diet. I stop eating.

Two days later, after less than a month at MCC, I'm transferred! Alleluia!! I'm certain that it's because the prison views me as an organizer and a troublemaker and is eager to get rid of me. There's no greater gift it could give me.

— �֎ —

My first stop is the federal MDC (Metropolitan Detention Center) in Los Angeles. It's newer than MCC San Diego but exudes the same air of shoddiness, sloppiness, and unprofessionalism. What a surprise to discover that Pleasanton's former captain is now the captain here! He calls me into his office before I've even completed the R & D processing. I explain that I'm not willing to eat in the absence of a vegetarian diet. He offers, "We could just put you in the general population and let you die."

Where he actually has me put, though, is the hole. I hear later that he told the lieutenant to "drag her up there," but she arranges for a wheelchair. I'm thankful to be spared more walking and standing, as I sit around in the wheelchair, with my hands cuffed behind my back, for about two hours before the segregation officers arrange a solitary cell for me.

Before dawn I'm awakened and prepared for transport again. The captain himself, accompanied by an officer, drives me, and no one else, all the way to Pleasanton.

A lieutenant whom I recognize meets us. The captain asks him, "Do you still have those vegetarian diets?" "Yes." Doesn't sound very believable to me, so I ask the receiving officer about it. "Oh, those vegetarian diets are standard," he answers. "Seven or eight people have them now. You just tell the PA at intake screening that you want one, and he'll prescribe it." I'm not convinced. Another lieutenant escorts me to the "hospital," where he conducts a hush-hush conference with the PA and calls food services. I tell the PA that I'm not eating because of my need for a vegetarian diet, and he doesn't respond.

I'm locked into a solitary cell in the hole and served brunch. It's a substantial, appealing vegetarian meal. I refuse it. The lieutenant returns and asks, "Why didn't you eat lunch?"

"I don't want a vegetarian *tray*. I need a vegetarian *diet*."

"The BOP doesn't have any vegetarian diets."

"I know."

Oh, do I ever know! And what a lot of trouble they went to to try to deceive me about it!

—— ⌘ ——

This is the same old detention unit, but the overcrowding has been eliminated by removing the extra beds, so that no more than two people are being locked down in a two-person cell. Precisely what I was advocating last year. The atmosphere feels much more sane. I'm in solitary both because I'm not eating and because the L.A. captain forgot to bring my paperwork with me, so I'm "pending classification."

The PAs are monitoring my health over the long holiday weekend, which isn't entirely reassuring, since they obviously know less about what they're doing even than I do. But at least I have enough experience by now to guess that my condition isn't too serious yet. I'm taking it very easy, and a wheelchair is available for my trips to the "hospital."

On the seventh day of my fast, October 9, I'm relieved to see a doctor. This doctor hasn't treated me here before, but I know her to have an excellent reputation among the prisoners, and I instinctively trust her, finding her human and caring. She examines me, says that she'll recommend my return to Lexington for medical reasons, and offers to see what she can do about a diet. I'm very grateful.

I haven't really been expecting a diet, because I think that I'm about to be transferred again, but I start receiving one the same day. It's wonderful: a weight-gain diet, with not only vegetarian protein but vegetarian cooking. I wish that I could thank the cooks. As soon as eating has restored my energy level, I find that I'm feeling expansive and happy. The oppression of MCC is gone. I seem to have space for being myself.

I soon learn that there's another vegetarian in the hole. (There must be a lot of vegetarians in the world.) She complains to the officer that she's been trying to get a vegetarian diet for a year; she is indignant that I now have the diet she's been denied. She's very vocal about it, yelling things like, "Are starvation cases the only ones who get vegetarian diets?"–and declares a hunger strike. The next day, the captain calls her into his office. She returns with a "no meat/fish only" diet. I'm so glad! At last my protest has helped someone else!

I like this captain. He's human, down-to-earth, hands-on. He treats us, unaffectedly, like human beings. He doesn't mince words, telling people off freely, but is right there with whatever the situation or problem is. He works hard. He cares. He's responsive. He puts judgment and good sense–and *people*–ahead of protocol.

But the regular day officer is difficult for me, because he's egotistical and capricious and uses very poor judgment. He seems to be extremely insecure, which he covers with a macho facade of posturing, lies, blaming others, and clutching control to himself. You feel unsafe just knowing that someone so unstable is in charge of the unit five days a week.

The handcuff situation is becoming confusing. Because I refuse to "cuff up" through the door, the officers have been denying me showers and rec, but have been coming into the cell to handcuff me for "hospital" trips, even routine, non-emergency ones. Now they start letting me out for showers and rec as well. It feels very human but leaves me unsure about where I stand.

October 17. I'm washing up at the sink in my cell after the last early morning count and before breakfast—because I can expect to be uninterrupted then and the dark gives me lots of privacy—when the officer suddenly takes it into his head to "check" on me, turns on my light, and stands *staring* at me, nearly naked. I freeze, because any move would be even more exposing, until he finally turns the light off again. I feel utterly violated, partly because I thought I was safe from precisely that sort of intrusion, and partly because I could see absolutely nothing human in the way he treated me—no announcement of his presence, no sign of embarrassment, no apology, no hasty withdrawal, no word at all—as if I were an inanimate object. I'm devastated—discovering how completely later, when I try to tell him that he had no call to treat me that way and I don't want any breakfast from him. I hear myself screaming at him through heavy tears to "please go away!" and I cry for the rest of the morning.

I work through enough of my feelings by dinnertime to be able to return to eating in general. (I'm trying to keep myself from opting out altogether, so that I don't fall into it accidentally. I want to be sure, if I ever do reach that point, that it will be because it's the only right, faithful choice, whose consequences I can safely trust to God.) But I just can't deal with the morning officer and refuse breakfast for many days.

Life in the hole suddenly becomes crazy. Someone gets herself locked up with the deliberate intention of making the prison transfer her. She starts fires, each of which requires the evacuation of the whole unit to the rec cages. Other new arrivals are supposed to be separated from each other, and the officers are having a hard time figuring out who can room with whom. My "unclassified" status means officially that I can't have a cellmate, which is a protection of my solitude that I'm tempted to cling to.

October 19. The day officer is preparing to move someone in with me, and I object. I particularly object to a cellmate who smokes. He claims that she doesn't smoke. I know her from Lexington; she does. He tries to maneuver me out of the way by telling me that I have a medical appointment and coming in to handcuff me for it. I say that I'm not going anywhere if he's planning to put someone in the cell while I'm gone. He asks if I'm refusing to go to the "hospital." I will not let him camouflage the issue: I want to know if he's planning to put someone in the cell. He ignores my question and turns to leave.

I'm feeling so pushed around by the lying and manipulation that I can't passively watch him go without responding to me. I follow him to the door. He orders me to step back so that he can close it. I'm not willing to step back without an answer. I don't know how I got into this. Somehow my refusal to accept his dismissal of my personhood has become embodied in the physical confrontation. He tries to push me physically. I resist being pushed. I'm not fighting, and I'm not trying to leave the cell, but I'm determined to stand my ground.

This is the sort of situation in which an officer calls a supervisor. But he doesn't even call the other officer already in the unit. He's suddenly behind me, picking me up, pinning my arms as he wraps both of his around my body and lifts me from the floor. As soon as he grabs me, I go limp. The ground I was standing on is gone. I'm no longer resisting anything.

He throws me bodily, head first, into the cell. It flashes through my mind that this is likely to hurt. But it never occurs to me to do anything to save myself. I've gone limp. I've surrendered all control. My eyes are closed.

I crash into the edge of the metal toilet bowl with my forehead, and roll over onto the floor against the foot of the bed. I moan once and lie still. After a moment, I touch a hand to my forehead. It comes away wet and sticky. I'm not surprised.

Soon I'm receiving a great deal of attention. A lieutenant comes in with a camera to record the scene. A PA arrives. Someone brings a wheelchair. I sit in the wheelchair with my head back, handcuffed in front, for the short trip to the prison "hospital." I insist on being treated by the doctor. She cleans the wound and closes it with six stitches. I've never needed stitches before. She tells me that the cut is about an inch long, in the middle of my forehead, ending at the hairline. She tapes a piece of gauze over it and says that I'll have to wash the blood out of my hair. I'm returned to detention and locked back into my cell.

I lie down for a while but discover that I'm actually fairly functional. I clean up the puddle of blood from the floor. But how can I wash my hair? It has to be done from behind, without getting the dressing wet. I ask the evening officer if someone can help me. He finds another prisoner who's willing and locks her in with me. I lean back over my sink while she washes it. Gentle hands. A good deal of blood. She gets most of it out.

The officer who injured me writes an incident report in which he lies about the assault, saying that I "fell." The lie upsets me, but I'm allowed to see my unit team, so I'm able at least to explain what really happened. Eventually, I'm sentenced by the DHO to thirty days in disciplinary segregation, half of it for refusing an order and half, as if it were a separate incident, for refusing a "program assignment"–the putative "hospital" trip. An extremely heavy punishment, it seems to me.

Now there's another regular officer with whom I can't deal. I'm no longer willing to accept anything from him, or to have the cell door open between us for any reason, not because I think that he'll hurt me again, but because I need some distance or something. Maybe I'm partly wary of whatever in my reaction to him may have contributed to the incident. The feeling is incoherent and irrational. Trying to articulate it to others leaves me in tears. I can't talk to him. He thunders my last name at me–knowing that I'm insulted by it, which most people here respect–several times a day, and I refuse whatever-it-is with a "no" or a shake of my head: no, I don't want lunch or rec or a shower or to come out of the cell for anything at all.

A second person starts fires, and then a third jumps on the bandwagon. The unit is racked with negative energy, verbal abuse, and waves of chaos. I wonder, in a new way, what my protest means, when the behavior of the system I'm protesting is, on the whole, more sensible than that of these difficult children, for whom some level of control is obviously necessary.

October 24. I hear the relief officers who are on today planning a shake-down just for me, most likely because there hasn't been an opportunity for a routine cell search in all the days that I haven't been out of the cell. It makes me very tense to know that I'm going to be assaulted again. They come in with the riot squad and the video camera, though they don't hurt me physically. They cuff me, carry me out to a rec cage, and leave me on the cold concrete in my summer nightgown, while they literally tear the cell apart. I'm really rocked when I see what they've done to my space. It's outright vandalism. Almost everything, especially bedding, has been thrown on the floor. This is the final straw. I'm no longer eating. I need to withdraw my consent from "business as usual" here.

In the course of the afternoon an alarming new problem overtakes me: an unfamiliar pain spreads across my entire lower abdomen, becoming intense. The officer refuses to let me out of the cell for medical attention unless I cuff up through the door. I'm terrified, and pray desperately to God to please protect me. The pain gradually subsides. I thank the Lord. I'm confirmed in my decision, finally, to withdraw cooperation from daily life in this prison.

The next day the captain comes to see me. He's been away. I'm glad to talk with him. He wants to know why I'm not eating. I tell him the stories that upset me the most. He listens. He points out that, if he'd been here, he would have dealt with things as they came up–which I suspect is true. I realize that I should give him a chance. I agree to start eating again, really as a personal favor to him, because I respect and trust him.

October 28. I decide that I really must stop simply avoiding the officers who have been the most difficult for me. I'm a Christian, no matter how wounded I'm feeling, and believe that relationship is foundational to life with God here on earth. The morning officer is, I suspect, basically a nice guy who is hurt by my repeated avoidance of him and would like to be reconciled. So I accept breakfast. Can hardly believe how painful it is for me! I have to force myself to take the things from his hands and then sit down and cry before I can eat. I'm reminded of Simone Weil's insight about the pain and suffering having to get to someone who refuses to pass them on. I probably *was* passing them on every time I refused breakfast, and now am accepting them, *experiencing* them, and hopefully somehow releasing them. I thank the Lord for the grace of stretching my littleness enough to embrace and pass on the forgiveness of Christ.

I can't do it for the day officer yet, though. I try to remember what an insecure little boy he is, desperate to be liked, and needing to be enfolded in God's love. But I still feel so attacked by his repeated verbal assaults and so repulsed by his macho posturing that the best I can manage is silence.

I'm told that the prison is planning to keep me here, so I try to settle into that. But I'm altogether unsettled interiorly. I've lost all of my prayer disciplines from Lexington, and most of my capacity for experiencing life spiritually. I have no centeredness. I can't fold prayer cranes.

The heat is oppressive. The sun pours into the cells on this side, and now that it's cool enough outside for the heat to be on as well, there's no relief from it. I live in a little summer nightgown, sleep with no more than a sheet, and ask the officers to keep my food slot flap open as much as they're willing to for a little ventilation. I refrain from opening it myself, allowing them their control. The regular evening officer, who's unaffectedly human and whose genuineness is a breath of fresh air in itself, is always willing, and I'm thankful when she comes on. I've moved my mattress to the floor. I keep the light off as much as possible. I'm trying just to expand my tolerance.

But I'm beginning to feel desperate for something–almost anything–to change. Would welcome a clear reason to withdraw cooperation altogether, because I sense that it would lift me up out of my muddle. I wonder if it wouldn't actually free me up inside. But I keep telling myself that if that's what God wants me to do, God will make it obvious. I keep forcing myself to cooperate minimally.

By November 4, I feel as if I'm drowning in insanity–the insanity of the world as concentrated in the crucible of prison, the craziness of the system, the craziness of the prisoners. It pours through my locked door and drums through my consciousness. I can't separate myself from it, but keep responding interiorly, drawn tight, like a bowstring, between the way things should be and the way things are. Incompetence. Ignorance. Lack of communication. Lies. Manipulation. Anger and violence, which ricochet around the unit like gunshot, mostly in the form of unprovoked verbal abuse on the part of prisoners. It's more than I can absorb, and I feel ready to burst.

I haven't been able to release the pain of it to God, and I have no other legitimate channel for getting rid of it. The pressure has been so great that I've even experienced some of that strange alchemy that transforms pain into anger, embarrassing myself by tightness and sharpness in my response to something unpleasant. I'm determined not to become angry, but I feel helpless in my incapacity to pray. Prayer is crucial. Without it, I'm just a very weak and vulnerable little girl who's easily overwhelmed. I'm overwhelmed. I see that I'm inadequate and have been acknowledging that I need help, but what can anyone do?

I know that I need to change my internal reality, to somehow reconnect with God, but can't find any way to do it. The only choice available that could change my external reality would be to stop eating, and I can't see any legitimate reason to do that. The things that are driving me crazy at this point are mostly in the realm of general human frailty, not the sort of thing one protests. I've managed to absorb incident after incident that I *could* have protested, and now the prison is really trying to give me some space.

So the only thing left that can give is my sanity. I feel as if I *am* going crazy, am literally being driven closer and closer to it. And it dawns on me that I have one other option: I could stop eating for no other reason than as a last-ditch effort to halt the tide of insanity. If I have no other choices, not eating seems better than going crazy. I don't know if it's a right choice. It feels like grasping at straws. But it's a wonderfully reversible choice. I can try it. I find some peace just in seeing that there's *something* I can do.

In the morning I'm finally able to pray—quiet, more or less centered prayer, with images of the crucified Christ drifting into it. What do you know? The choice to stop eating *has* freed me up inside. It's changed my *internal* reality. I realize that the key is that I've separated the need to stop eating from the idea of protest. This is not a protest. It's not a complaint. It's not against the prison. It's merely a statement of my own need—my need to step back and let go of some of the responsibility for dealing with this impossible situation, for staying strong and Christlike beyond my capabilities. And so, of course, it's opened a new door for the grace of God.

I'm confirmed in the rightness of the choice and grow increasingly certain of it. It's freed me again to slip into that gentle, accepting, welcoming space that I recognize as my best spiritual self. I feel better every day, both emotionally and spiritually, more relaxed, happier, more prayerful, more open and loving toward everyone around me. I have a strong sense of the hand of God sustaining me and am feeling in touch again. What a remarkably fruitful spiritual fast this is turning out to be!

The doctor tells me that she's going to get me transferred in a hurry, before I get too sick. On Friday, November 9, I leave.

11

Emergence

Very early in the morning, two other women and I are processed out of Pleasanton. I'm weak and shaky, with little energy for walking or standing, but the prison is gentle with me and provides a wheelchair as far as the van. It's while waiting in the van to board our tiny chartered plane that the first signs of my period hit me. I'm totally unprepared. Climbing the few steps into the plane leaves me feeling nauseated and wishing that I could lie down. I don't even consider walking to a bathroom when we stop for fuel in Wyoming, but the lieutenant locates a wheelchair for me. No one is able to locate a sanitary napkin. I do what I can with toilet paper. I don't think to take a drink of water, not realizing until later that there's no water on the plane.

My traveling companions are on their way to Lexington, but I have reason to guess, correctly, that my destination is FMC Rochester (Minnesota). I'm excited to be heading north and looking forward to winter. Rochester is the top medical facility for men in the federal prison system. Occasionally it takes a woman whose medical needs can't be met at Lexington. It agreed to take me, I gather, at least partly because Lexington doesn't want me back.

Rochester staff people drive me from the airport to the prison, parking at a distance from the front door that rather daunts me, but I accept their urging to try to walk it. It exhausts me. In R & D, all I want is a sanitary napkin—I keep asking—and a place to lie down. But I keep being ordered to walk from room to room—to be strip-searched, to stand, to squat; to be interviewed, to be fingerprinted, to be photographed. I say, "No more walking," and am told, "It's not very far; you can hold onto the wall." I'm close to tears from the tension and fatigue. Finally the sanitary napkins arrive, and a wheelchair takes me up to a hospital floor, where I've been told that I'll be on detention status until I'm "evaluated."

Thankful to make it to a room at last, I use the toilet, and it doesn't flush. Oh, no! I have no water! In a *hospital*! I can't believe it. It suddenly crashes in on me that my water has been turned off because the prison considers me to be on a "hunger strike." That's why I'm locked down, too, of course. I fall apart, just lie down and cry.

But I'm clear about what I have to do. This fast wasn't a protest. It's been very beneficial for me spiritually, and I was expecting that, as soon as I had a sense of myself in my new environment, I'd be ready to discern the endpoint of it–though I'd have to wait for a vegetarian diet as well. Now it instantly becomes a protest. I'm very vocal about it. That water shut-off policy is the epitome of cruel and inhuman punishment. No way will I cooperate with it! I refuse all compromises to help me clean up from my trip and my period. I refuse drinking water. I won't accept anything short of having the water turned on in my room.

At the same time, I'm struck by how very caring and concerned for me everyone is. At least two nurses spend a lot of time with me. A doctor examines me immediately, and a resident is a little more thorough later on. An AW (associate warden) and hospital administrator drop by for no clear reason. A psychologist visits pleasantly with me for a long time.

In the morning I wake up fully recovered from the effort and trauma of transition, feeling better than ever spiritually and emotionally. My prayer is flowing spontaneously into intercession. What better evidence that I'm not all tied up in my own pain any more? I feel gentle and happy and receptive. The little girl in me wants to skip in delight at just a glimpse of the brisk fall morning outside.

A resident comes in to check my condition. I'm fairly seriously dehy-drated–one of the earliest signals of distress from fasting, exacerbated this time by my having had no water for more than twenty-four hours. Dehy-dration makes your heart work harder and is the cause of dizziness and blackouts. It's easily measured by the change in your blood pressure and pulse between resting and standing: the more dehydrated you are, the greater the change when you stand up. The resident can't hear my blood pressure at all when I stand up. As he tries it two or three times, the effort of standing becomes too much for me, my vision dissolves into stars, and I collapse heavily onto the bed. He tells me that I need an IV if I won't drink anything. I reply that I won't cooperate.

I've already accepted that I'm again facing the horrendous possibility of indefinite force-feeding, and I know that I'm going to get an IV whether I cooperate or not. A lieutenant appears to make it explicit: "It looks as if we're going to be seeing quite a bit of each other." When I respond to something with, "All I need is to have my water turned on," he retorts, "We don't play compromises!" I don't expect anyone to "play compro-mises." All morning, I expect to be strapped down.

The psychologist visits me several times. We talk about how good I'm feeling spiritually. Eventually, she asks what I would do if my water were turned on. I say that I'd drink water and monitor it for the staff, and I'd be ready to talk about diet, since I'm now satisfied that the spiritual fast is complete. She asks if I'd cooperate with an IV. I don't know, but my initial reaction is that I probably would. After leaving to consult with others, she brings back the proposal that they turn on the water in return for my accepting an IV. I consider it, and conclude that I can't even make promises as long as the water is off. The water would have to be turned on first.

"I don't think they'll do that," she answers.

"I don't think they will either."

"There are always four-point restraints . . . "

"I've already been expecting them all morning."

The doctor comes in. When I acknowledge that I'd accept an IV if the water were turned on first, he agrees to it. An officer turns on the water. The doctor starts an IV in the back of my left hand, one liter of balanced salts flows in rapidly, and then the IV is removed.

Now I'm eager to use my shower. A nurse makes it easy for me, bringing in towels and clean clothes and a shower chair, which helps a lot, staying with me in case I fall, and helping me to dry off afterward. I feel so cared for! The medical people here are wonderful. There's an entirely different atmosphere around them than there is in a typical prison. This prison doesn't seem to be typical at all. Nonmedical people here seem to be caring, too, and human, treating problems as resolvable rather than needing to be stamped out coercively.

The doctor discusses diet with me, and orders a no-meat diet with protein substitutes for seventy-two hours; nothing permanent can be approved until the dietician returns on Tuesday. I'm not willing to eat until I know that I have something permanent.

The warden and two more AWs stop in to meet me in the course of the holiday weekend. Two chaplains drop by just after it. I'm very favorably impressed with the Catholic chaplain, whom I find receiving, positive, and forthright. She and I have a long talk.

On Tuesday the prison resumes normal weekday functioning. The doctor comes to discuss my diet again, and ends up suggesting that I simply write down a list of the foods I want to eat. He takes it to the dietician. The dietician and the food services administrator show up almost immediately, are warm and accommodating, and give me everything that I've asked for and then some. The trays are superb. More good food than I can eat. Milk, cheese, *and* peanut butter at almost every meal. Fresh fruit. Homemade bread. Homemade yogurt. I feel a bit spoiled. Do I deserve all this?

Almost as soon as I've started eating, my door is unlocked. Now, once my energy is up to the walk, I have access to a telephone and a pencil sharpener. As the only woman in the prison, I'm housed on the hospital floor for the most seriously ill and am allowed to leave it only with a staff escort. Sometimes a nurse is free to take me outside for exercise, though usually rather briefly. In any case, the room is wonderfully commodious. Designed for isolating someone with an infectious disease, it's large, clean, private, and self-contained. Even relatively cool. Very quiet. I have not

only a window, but a view, encompassing a chunk of the prison compound with trees and sky beyond it. I absorb sunrises and weather changes
and the daily human drama. I thrill to flocks of wild geese streaming over-
head every morning.

Wednesday is my first full day out of bed. On Thursday, the warden
pays me a visit because it's come to his attention that I refused to sign
forms in R & D. This place locks people up who refuse to sign forms. He
was willing to give me the diet I wanted–a selection from what's available
in the dining hall–but now it looks as if I'm not willing to meet the prison
halfway. He's not sure that they can keep me here if I won't work with
them.

Arggh! All the pleasant possibilities of the place crash down around my
ears. Maybe I *can't* stay. I can accept being locked up or transferred. But
what really bothers me is that I'm afraid he's right, that I may not be able
to meet the prison halfway. I want to. I'm so appreciative of all they've
done for me and given to me! I want to be as generous myself in response,
and I particularly want to affirm all the caring, human, relational things
they're doing, which are so much what I believe in and so uncommon to
find in a prison. But what can I offer in return? Just my usual friendliness
and attempt to be undemanding. I can't compromise my principles; I *can't*
sign a fingerprint card. I share all this with the warden, spilling over into
tears. I say that I'll cooperate as much as possible, but I can't say ahead of
time what will be possible, and it might not be enough for the prison.

On Sunday I'm able to attend Mass. It's wonderful to be physically
present in a worshiping community again. I like the chapel, the sense of
community, and the priest–who comes in from outside the prison. Everything he says and does expresses a simple, fraternal equality with all the
rest of us. I thank him afterward. Warm handshake. He thanks me for my
presence and my "radiance." I guess I was feeling pretty radiant.

On Friday I'm ordered to move out of my room. Argggh! Of course,
I've known all along that it might happen. I cooperate. But the new room
is so much worse than the old one that I can't seem to adjust to it. I can't
even begin to move in for hours. I sit on the floor in the hall and cry,
grieving, again, the loss of a space in which I could be myself. This room
is small, cluttered, and much too hot. I've lost the view. I've lost the quiet
and privacy of having two solid doors. I don't even have bathroom privacy from inmate workers, who don't expect a woman and often walk in
without knocking. I've lost my own shower and space for exercise.

I finally force myself to move in, but can't relax enough to sleep until a
caring nurse finds me a fan around 2:00 A.M. I sleep little and am a mess for
days. I'm trying very hard to adjust and failing utterly. Over and over again
I feel as if I can't stand it. I develop a headache, which is so unusual for me
that it scares me. By lunchtime on Monday I'm too depressed to eat.

One of the nurses is responsive. She receives permission from her supervisor for me to move into one of the double rooms across the hall. I'm

leery about the potential temporariness of a room that I'll have to leave again if the floor becomes crowded, but it's such a great improvement over where I am that I decide to try it. It restores the northern exposure and view, the coolness and spaciousness, and some of the privacy that I had before. And my spirits soar. It's hard to imagine how *just* moving across the hall could change me from an extraordinarily fragile, minimally functional, withdrawn, depressed, and easily upset little girl, struggling for survival, into a relatively normal, happy, and warmly relational adult. But maybe my emotions needed just that much help. Of course, the willingness of the prison to give me options helped in itself.

I continue to be impressed by all the ways in which the prison chooses to be more human than coercive. I wonder if it isn't living my values toward me more fully than I'm living them in response. I'm doing my best, but I feel uncomfortably limited between those aspects of the system that I can't conscientiously cooperate with and those fragilities within myself that still can't handle everything.

I settle in now in a lot of ways. The institution is apparently planning to keep me for a while. The room is working. I can fold prayer cranes. Rochester allows me to receive whole packages of brightly colored paper in the mail. I can exercise. I'm always eager for more time outside but try to be satisfied with what the nurses can offer. An inmate vegetarian who works in the kitchen is allowed to talk with me about my diet, and my dinner trays become fantastic. No vegetarian cooking, but fabulous fresh salads and loads of protein. I find out that I'm "medically unassigned," which takes care of the work issue. I expect to be able to use the visiting room (at Lexington the handcuff barrier prevented me), so I submit a visiting list for the prison's approval.

My spiritual director is proposing a visit over Christmas, which I discuss with the Catholic chaplain on the first Sunday in December. She directs me to my counselor, whom I practically never see, so I write him a cop-out. I'm confused about what rules apply to this visit and am anxious to be assured that I've done everything I need to for the necessary approvals to make it through the proper channels in time. When I haven't received any kind of response in two weeks, I approach the chaplain again. I simply assume that I can talk with her as a friend. This brief conversation demolishes me.

She seems to be telling me that she won't help me because I should be taking care of the matter myself, but the help that I need is information about how the system works, which I can't seem to find out from anybody, and which she apparently could readily have given me when I first asked two weeks ago. I feel put down and shut out, as if relegated to nonpersonhood, frustrated, and helpless. It hurts me so deeply that I'm quickly unable to talk coherently through my pain, see no point in burdening her with my tears, and leave to seek comfort in the solitude of the chapel library. She follows me, demanding that I return to her office. I accede, but it doesn't help to try to explain what's wrong; she seems to feel attacked and defensive. I ask if she'd please just call an escort to take me back to the hospital–where I retreat to my bed and cry for the rest of the day. When a caring nurse invites me to tell her about it, I say, "I died." That's how I feel: Dead. Demolished. Annihilated.

The chaplain comes to see me in the afternoon and gives me a great deal of time, which I appreciate, trying to talk through our problem, but we can't seem to resolve it. We can't seem to comprehend each other's point of view. The more we share, the more distanced I feel by the growing sense that her whole response to me is dominated by a need to control. There's no trust left in the relationship, no safety. Later, when I apologize for falling apart on her, she doesn't receive it at all, doesn't even acknowledge it. She continues to provide chaplaincy services for me; she makes arrangements for the visit; we remain on cordial speaking terms; but I no longer feel, or desire, any personal access to her. It's as if a door that I'd thought was open has been slammed in my face. And I'm afraid that it's mutual; I've become as difficult for her as she has for me.

I try to work on my feelings, but I'm depressed and don't surface from it. I'm fragile. I find myself in a strange, new emotional state that's numb and tired and unmotivated. I have to push myself to do the simplest tasks. I try to participate in some of the many Christmas season activities but don't have any resources for socializing with strangers.

My spiritual director arrives on December 24. The visiting room procedures are a hassle–especially around my refusal to provide an inmate registration number–but I'm allowed to visit, and I really value the time with Hugh. When he returns on Christmas Day, we have to cope with the chaos of crowds, including the relocation of about half of us to a depressing basement room. No windows. No microwave popcorn or other vending-machine treats. It's depressing just to look around at all the prisoners who are elderly and infirm; some are in wheelchairs; at least one is blind. *What* is the imprisonment of these people accomplishing for society? It's hard for me to stay focused on our conversation.

Then there's the mid-morning count. Visiting room officers ordinarily conduct counts without interrupting the visits, but this situation is apparently too complicated for them. They announce that all prisoners are to line up in the hall. Oh, no! I don't cooperate with that kind of regimentation. But how can I refuse when it would mean all sorts of unpleasantness in the midst of everyone's Christmas visits? My whole body tenses with the impossibility of the choice. There's no conscionable alternative. Finally deciding that I can spare the others by taking the pain on myself, I rise slowly, holding myself tightly together, and walk to the door. Which devastates me. I can't function any more. I apologize, in tears, to my spiritual director, leave as soon as I can be escorted, go back to bed, and cry for the rest of another day.

I can see that I've lost my resiliency. I keep getting wound tighter and tighter until I'm stretched so taut that I'm brittle. Often I find myself trembling from the tension and spilling over into tears. Sometimes it immobilizes me or breaks out in sharp remarks that I immediately want to undo. It's a terrible strain to deal with anything difficult or to make any non-routine decision. The arena of what's difficult seems to be spreading to encompass almost any interaction with the prison or anyone in it.

I recognize that what I'm doing wrong is fighting the pain, trying to push it away, not yielding to it and simply letting it flow through me. I'm forcing myself, by a great act of will, to stay both vulnerable and in relationship with the people I'm vulnerable to, and my emotions, which are like a whimpering child in the face of pain, brace themselves against the onslaught—which, of course, makes it worse.

But what would it mean to *accept* the pain? I keep insisting that things are *not* okay and *should* be different. Part of me keeps feeling that I should be protesting the overall prisonhood of prison, because it's *wrong*. How many little, cumulative injustices can I tacitly accept before I lose my integrity?

On the second weekend in January, Anna and another friend from Denver visit. Special as it is to see them, the attendant interactions with the prison push me to the limits of my (severely limited) tolerance. On Sunday I'm told that I can't leave the hospital floor without signing out. Signing out is apparently a general requirement for leaving the floor, but it hasn't been expected of me, since I'm always escorted; at least two staff people, in addition to the one with me, always know where I'm going. Now that it's suddenly being demanded, I will not agree to an authoritarian ritual that serves no useful purpose. An inmate worker chooses to sign me out in order to facilitate my last visit—and I don't leave the floor again at my own initiative.

Staying on the floor is my gift to the prison. I've found, in spite of my strong desire to be as generous toward it as possible, that I can't offer it much in the way of cooperation; I'm conscientiously unable to retreat from any principled position that's become clear to me. But I can, and do, offer it all my gray areas. Though I'm not willing to sign out, I *am* willing to avoid confronting the prison with the issue. I let go of outdoor exercise. I let go of Mass. In a way, my life is simplified.

February 5. There's been a second woman in the prison since before Christmas, in the room next door to mine. We've visited a little. Now that the floor is suddenly becoming crowded, I'm not surprised to hear that she's being moved in with me. I've tried to be prepared for the possibility. She's both quiet and accommodating, letting me keep the bed by the window and choosing to spend a good deal of her time outside of the room. Still, it takes me two days to adjust to the disruption of my life and space.

I'm so upset the first day that I can't eat. Then I decide to continue fasting for another day in the hope that it will help me pull myself together. It does. I begin to open up both spiritually and emotionally to that happy, gentle, receiving, little-girl space—where both prayer and appreciating people become spontaneous and effortless—that fasting commonly brings me to. I wonder if this isn't my very best spiritual self.

But, if so, there must be other ways of getting to it. Fasting is no long-term solution. I'm already becoming physically ill and don't want the prison to feel forced into responding. I resume eating, trying to understand what it is about fasting that's so beneficial. I think that it's the letting go of control. The less I'm able to do, then the less I have to be responsible for, to keep trying to discern and figure out, to balance faithfully between being relational and being firm about *other* things I stand for. I always feel the responsibility acutely, and it's exceptionally heavy here, particularly because the demands of relationality and of resistance to injustice—which go together when I'm being punished—seem to keep pulling me in opposite directions.

I'm grappling—as I have been for years—with the spiritual challenge to accept my own inadequacy. Weakness is the only door through which God's mercy and grace can enter, the only space in me that leaves room for God to work. Passionately as I want to, I know that I'll never accomplish perfect service for God. In fact, I decided recently, it's only those things that I know for sure I can't do that I'm able to do, because I turn to God, depend on God, and let God do them for me. And I'm well aware of the danger I'm in as soon as it looks as if I might be getting something right, because my pride tries to jump in and claim it from God. So weakness is really my salvation. I conclude that I need to be *happy* in my weakness—remembering that the answer to my sinfulness is not perfectibility, but rather the forgiveness of God.

At the same time, I'm continuing to try to figure out my proper relationship to the prison—which is complicated not only by the mixture within the institution of humane and coercive aspects that call forth distinctly separate responses from me; but also by the sense I've developed here that the institution can be related to as a "person," as an organic individual with whom one interacts in openness and fluidity. What, then, is the place of resistance? I've been feeling as if the prison has been so generous to me that I owe it something in return and *can't* fairly make trouble by not cooperating, and yet I keep bumping into things that I conscientiously *have* to resist.

The internal tension is excruciating. It reaches the breaking point during a long conversation with the captain about his new pass system, which replaces the escort requirement for us women to leave the hospital floor. He tries to persuade me to use it, making the huge concession of waiving the inmate registration number, but not the sign-out requirement. The more I search for a response, the harder the dilemma tears at me: Relationality impels me to affirm his personal concern and generosity about the number by accepting it. At the same time, principled integrity demands resistance to the depersonalizing assumptions of the system embodied in the sign-out requirement.

Argggggh!! Anguish and impossibility. There's no acceptable choice, no space of any kind in which to be myself, nothing I can do, or not do, that doesn't violate my own values and integrity. I'm torn apart and immobilized. Can't pray. Feel as if my whole personality is disintegrating. This is the bottom of the pit. It's Ash Wednesday.

On Thursday I discover one step that I can take: I can write to the captain, explaining how I feel. So I do. On Friday I realize that I now have some space again, because I don't have to make a further choice until the captain responds. In fact, he never responds; I'm left with the default option of not using the pass system, which I can live with. And I eventually recognize that I *did* do what I could relationally.

In the early days of March I begin to come up with some answers. The question is: What is the appropriate Christian response to a fundamentally evil system run by ordinary—well-intentioned and fallible—human beings? I'm clear about the evil of the assumptions underlying imprisonment: that it's just and acceptable for some fallible human beings to lock up other fallible human beings; that society has a right to enslave and dehumanize individuals with whom it disagrees; that cages and human beings can go together at all. I need to keep calling those assumptions into question. At the same time, I need to keep relating with the people, who are neither more nor less human than I am.

It occurs to me that the institution of slavery is an excellent parallel. A humane prison is like a benevolent slaveholder. What is the appropriate response of a slave to a benevolent master? He or she would be caught in that awful dilemma between wanting to be helpful and kind to a good person while feeling impelled, on principle, to refuse to work for or be obedient to that same person as the instrument of the evil system. I think that that's essentially my position here. A humane prison is perhaps particularly in need of being challenged, precisely because the humanness masks the underlying evil. I need to refuse to accept the evil assumptions, no matter how subtly hidden.

So my noncooperation has nothing to do with how kind and generous either a prison or the individuals within it are. The proper response to their kindness and generosity is at the relational level, in my friendliness and patience and that sort of thing. I don't owe them anything in any case, no matter how much they do for me, other than the "debt of mutual love" (Romans 13:8, *JB*). I'm already trying to give them everything I have to give, even if they're *not* being good to me. My *choices* don't belong to the interaction between me and any individual, but rather to that between my principles and the assumptions of the system.

I think that keeping this distinction clear would free me from most of the relationality-resistance dilemma; relationality and resistance could coexist again, which I've seen as their most natural and powerful state: I relate caringly to the people as people at the same time that I respond with principled choices to situations presented to me by the people as instruments of the system. Of course, I've been doing this all along, but my emotions have gotten horribly entangled by confusing the relationality with the principled decision-making process. I'm *not* failing in generosity because I feel compelled to refuse to cooperate with a fundamentally evil system.

These conclusions raise a new question: Why do I cooperate as much as I possibly can? That's always been my basic ground rule. But what's *good* about cooperating with a fundamentally evil institution at all? Shouldn't I be *basically non*cooperating? The answer probably is that I should be noncooperating with the system's *security* functions—including one or two, especially strip searches, that haven't been problems for me in the past.

By mid-March I'm praying a little again. I'm folding prayer cranes. I'm struck by how people outside the prison keep praising me for my strength, when I don't feel strong at all. But perhaps the key is that I'm willing; I really am willing to be used by God, to endure whatever I have to. It turns out that I'm not really able—I'm just a whimpering child having a hard time—but I'm *still* willing. Maybe it's important for people out there to see that willingness. Maybe it says something about faith in God.

A television producer in Colorado is interested in interviewing me for a show he's putting together about political prisoners. We have a good conversation on the telephone, and, though I'm very camera-shy, I'd like to accommodate him. But I finally decide that this is one area where I *can*, appropriately and relationally, be generous to the prison; I don't have to make it deal with reporters. It would have no choice if I agreed to the interview, and I feel that it's enough for it to have to deal with me.

March 23. The officer walks into our room after mid-morning count, pulls open the curtain between our beds, wakes up my roommate, and tells us that we both have to leave while she shakes down the room. What's most remarkable about this situation is that it hasn't confronted me before in my entire four and a half months in this prison. I'm beginning to suspect that God had a hand in holding it off until I was internally prepared. It's utterly routine. The officer is probably shocked that I refuse. But I've been clear for some time about not cooperating with shakedowns. I'm not willing to move.

I stay pleasant and friendly, explaining my position in extensive conversations with two different officers. A lieutenant arrives. Everyone keeps telling me what a small thing it would be for me to obey this simple, ordinary order, but, of course, my not obeying it becomes a very big deal. I'm handcuffed, lifted into a wheelchair, and taken to a seg cell at the far end of the hospital floor. The handcuffs are removed. I remain limp throughout. Two women strip-search me, deprive me of everything I was wearing except my underpants and glasses, and dress me in pajama bottoms, a T-shirt, and hospital slippers. They take my bra. They take the elastic band out of my hair. They leave me in an unusually cold cell without a blanket—or much else in the way of basic necessities.

My little girl, as usual, feels like withdrawing. I refuse lunch and burrow under the sheet and thin, polyester bedspread, wondering if I should protest all the routine dehumanization by refusing to pick up the pieces of daily life, including eating. It's helpful to receive, very soon, a caring and relational visit from the duty officer (a supervisor who makes rounds and troubleshoots), which gives me an opportunity to articulate my feelings. She leaves and returns with the warden: "I come in to do some paperwork and find you in the hoosegow!" He thinks that I just got tired of cooperating; how could I *never* have encountered that order before in all of my months here? He wants to know what else might come up that he isn't prepared for.

I promise to think about it for him, and surprise *myself* by discovering that there are *twelve* different categories of things I consistently refuse a prison. I realize that it makes me more vulnerable for him to know that I may be even more of a potential problem than he'd thought, but not only do I really want to give him everything I can in the way of openness and honesty, it's actually a good thing for me to be vulnerable.

Shortly after he leaves, I suddenly see with great clarity that I have to eat, both because that's a form of cooperation that I *can* conscientiously give the prison, and because it will keep me in a position of powerlessness, of utter vulnerability to whatever the prison might do to me, free from any temptation to try to pressure it in any way. Powerlessness is absolutely at the heart of who I'm called to be, especially in the midst of any witness. Reflecting on some of the incidents in Pleasanton and San Diego where I'm afraid I may have been too assertive, I think that the thing to watch out for is having some sort of "handle," which is a temptation to power. The more powerless I am in fact, then the easier it is to stay truly powerless in spirit.

At dinnertime I explain that I'm willing to eat if I can brush my teeth afterward, and the officer brings me a toothbrush, toothpaste, pencil, and writing paper. The duty officer made sure that I got toilet paper. But nobody brings me a blanket before morning, though I've asked twice. The cell is so cold that I'm unable to fall asleep all night. I have a strong suspicion that I'm being deliberately punished with the cold, which would be a violation of BOP policy as well as simply cruel, but I can understand how people might be needing an outlet for frustration over my noncooperation. I choose to accept the excessive punishment without complaint or negative feelings, as an expression of my compassion for them. Praise the Lord for the grace!

By March 25, the day after Palm Sunday, I've already—rather miraculously, in spite of all the deprivation—experienced Easter. The most wonderful thing is that my spirits have come all the way up! The upsurge almost certainly began when I knew that I had to eat, and by now I feel really good emotionally, for the first time I can remember since mid-December. All sorts of things that have tended to drive me crazy aren't driving me crazy any more. I'm smiling a lot at everyone who comes by, and finding human interactions as easy and natural as I would normally expect to find them.

There's something very solid and grounded about this good inner place, which I don't understand very well yet, but the one thing I'm sure of that's behind it is clarity. I'm finally free of a mass of ambiguity and confusion, in a situation where I'm very clear that I'm doing the only possible right thing, where I know who I am and am at home with myself.

The whole time in solitary turns out to be a retreat for me. I receive enough colored paper in my current mail to be able to fold the last of the 1,000 prayer cranes. There's a lot of turning to God and gentle reflection, with sparkling little insights bubbling up through it. I'm learning increasingly to lean on Jesus. I've been praying more and more to Jesus by name, because I'm so aware of ungodly spiritual forces out there that I want to name whom I'm talking to in case someone else is trying to claim my prayer; and it's somehow drawing me into a more specific relationship. I'm grateful for all the grace in my life, and feel dancy, bouncy, springy, deep-down *happy*.

April 4. Am groping around in a gentle, forgiving, emerging understanding of the struggling human community—all of us fallible, incomplete human beings who keep making mistakes and keep spilling our pain over onto others, and yet who keep trying—sometimes trying very hard in the face of huge obstacles—and that somehow it's through us (all of us), inadequate as we are, that each other is helped along the personal and spiritual journey—I mean, humankind isn't working its gradual way toward God through the inspired leadership of a few unique saints so much as through the daily interactions of ordinary, wounded, stumbling friends and family and neighbors—I mean, daily life and you and I and everyone else, broken as we are, really are the vessels for God's work in the world—are good enough, and chosen, for God's work, in the midst of all our imperfection. . . . Anyway, it sort of dissipates the problem of evil—I mean, it puts it in perspective or something—that the gradual evolution of humankind, over centuries and millennia, toward greater spirituality is itself evidence of the inevitable triumph of good (happening in tiny little, ordinary, daily ways), which no specific outbreak of evil can gainsay.

The DHO sentences me in early April to fifteen days in disciplinary segregation. Almost as soon as I've completed the DS time, I'm moved back into a double room with my former roommate. She takes the bed by the window without consulting me, which, of course, is fair; she deserves a turn. But it's very hard on me. She uses the TV room and also goes outside; the view from this window is all the nature I have. Still, I can see a good deal of it from my half of the room if we keep the curtain open between us. I adjust. I reclaim my personal property, start replacing my prison-issued clothing, which was all thrown into the laundry when I was locked down, and gradually reestablish my little corner of existence in the space available.

But my season for peaceful coexistence with the prison seems to have ended. On May 7, a third woman is scheduled to arrive at the institution, and my roommate and I are moved into a triple in anticipation. I'm upset by the disruption—and affronted by the transparent lies of staff about its purpose—which leaves me emotionally shaky and barely able to cope. I force myself to cooperate, prepared to do my best to handle the situation, but discover before the day is out that the new woman, whom I'll call Diane, and I are incompatible as roommates.

Most significantly, I have a deep psychological need to keep the hall door closed, to protect my sense of personal space and ability to concentrate, and to discourage casual socializing from the men on the floor, who are naturally attracted to the only women in the prison population. She has an equally deep psychological need to keep the hall door open, because she's somewhat claustrophobic and fights the anxiety of aloneness by gathering as much social life around herself as she can.

The situation is impossible. We talk about it and try some compromises, which don't work. We're both fragile. I feel (again!) squeezed out of any space in which I can be myself or live any semblance of my own life. I try to pray, sitting on the floor between my bed and the outside wall, where I can feel a little bit private with the hall door open, but I'm still assaulted by the noise. I already know that I can't *sleep* well when the door is open even a crack, and have repeatedly explained to officers and nurses that, if they open my door for count in the middle of the night and don't reclose it all the way, I'm inevitably dragged awake by the cumulative unquietness in the hall. My new roommate isn't sure that she can relax enough to sleep if the door is even partially closed.

The first night *I* can't relax enough to sleep. We're doing our best to accommodate one another, but the tension in the room is so thick you can almost see it. I don't go to bed until sometime around midnight and am awake again before 3:00. This is not going to work. When the 3:00 A.M. count has cleared, I get up and "move out," taking a blanket to sit on in the hall by the door. An interim solution, which won't meet my needs. But it doesn't violate any rule, so it gives both me and the prison some space while I try to talk with people about the necessity of separating me and

Diane. We can get along amicably enough, but we have to have different doors.

Prison staff are already aware of the problem and have so far been entirely unsympathetic. It's no big deal to them. But the nurse who saw me awake at 3:00 invited me to come talk if I'd like, so I meet her at the nurses' station. She listens attentively and seems genuinely interested in working on possible solutions. I'm keeping an eye on the time, not wanting to cut the conversation short but intending to be back at my door before 5:00 A.M. count. I'm not willing to cooperate directly but try to avoid the issue by being where I'm supposed to be ahead of time. And then the count is announced early. I'm ordered to go to my room. I'm so caught off guard by being confronted with the direct order I'd expected to avoid that I search inside myself for a way to comply. But I can't do it. I end up in lockdown again. The whole prison undoubtedly thinks that I set myself up for it. I didn't. But maybe God did. It's an acceptable resolution of the problem for the time being.

I'm treated much more humanly than the last time and start receiving the things I need right away. But I find myself much *less* accepting of unnecessary deprivation. There's lots of inner protest. I feel sort of defiant, sort of on the edge of refusing any longer to accept unreasonableness in general. Though it keeps feeling as if I'm being less flexible and accommodating toward the prison than it's been toward me, I think what's actually happening is that–after having reached a lot of internal integration when I was locked down before–I'm finally coming up against the *prisonhood* of this prison. I'm seeing more and more starkly how apt the benevolent slaveholder analogy is, and recognizing how much more resistant I need to be than I've thought. I've been confused and pacified, probably even manipulated, by the superficial humanness–which is probably genuine, but is doing everybody a disservice by masking the underlying evil assumptions and enabling staff and prisoners alike to keep accepting the fundamental inhumanity of the situation.

What's most fundamentally and horribly wrong is the mindset that considers some group of human beings to be inferior, less than human, giving you permission to treat them in ways that would horrify *you* if anyone did it to your "peers." It's the attitude that enables slavery and lynching and apartheid and any form of genocide, and it may be worse than deliberate cruelty, because it *sanctions* cruelty in the name of kindness; the perpetrators of cruelty pat themselves on the back for being so wonderfully kind and human. Our whole world is riddled with this sickness, but prison is one of the places where it's *legally* authorized and so goes largely unchallenged.

I need to resist *prison itself, on principle.* And that includes asserting my own judgment in matters of daily life, *not* deferring to unreasonableness as long as I possibly can. I've been deferring all along here, trying very hard · to adjust to everything I could, and it wasn't until the prison expected me to adjust to something impossible that I was finally freed from the automatic tendency to take what it thinks as a starting point. What it was asking of me didn't make any sense. What it expects of prisoners frequently doesn't make any sense. I'm unwilling to obey unreasonable orders; why do I keep going along with unreasonable requests and persuasion? When I let myself be victimized by the prison's choices for my daily life, then I'm caving in to the prison's assumption that I'm less than human. I need to stand up for my humanity, for the humanity, the *personhood,* of prisoners in general.

On May 14, I'm sentenced by the DHO to fifteen days in disciplinary segregation. On May 29, an officer unlocks my door to announce that I'm moving. I ask where to. He gives me a room number. I ask with whom. "The two other women." I refuse to room with Diane. He locks my door again.

On June 4, I'm told again that I'm moving in with the two other women. The DHO must have sentenced me to something other than DS time. The officer unlocks my door and encourages me to consult with everybody. The nursing supervisor is so persuasive about the prison's need to free up a single room for someone coming back from the outside hospital, and so willing to make the roommate situation as livable as possible for us women, that I'm swayed toward cooperating—even though I'm certain that the move would end up being *very* temporary, because there *isn't* any way to make the roommate situation livable and I'd soon be unable to tolerate it. But the more I talk with Diane, the clearer it becomes that she isn't sure she can handle even a temporary move, and I'm swayed toward refusing for her sake. I actually go back and forth between her room and the nurses' station several times, persuaded to change my mind each time.

When she breaks down in tears, though, I can't stand her pain and end up losing control with the officer, yelling at him that *no* one is thinking about *her* needs *except* me. He gives up on me and locks me down again, mad at me now and accusing me of selfishly holding out for a room to myself. I feel bad about the yelling and write him an apology.

However, I suddenly understand the overall roommate dynamic and realize that making room for Diane's pain was the right choice; she feels put down by my inability to live with her choices, no matter how accepting I am of her personally, so the tension of our trying to room together would be very destructive for her. The other woman, too, is much better off without it.

I know that the prison is going to transfer me. What prison wouldn't transfer you after a performance like that? And the warden really has no alternative. It's now obvious to me that I can't, under any circumstances, move in with those two other women and also that the nursing staff will not accept my presence here under any other conditions. But I suspect that God created the whole situation for me. I need to go. I need to get out of this Orwellian, two-faced prison, where I'm forever hurting people's feelings by resisting assumptions they can't even see, and where nothing I say ever seems to register with them. Maybe my resistance, at least, will make sense somewhere else. Here, now, I just feel like a nuisance.

June 7. The warden comes to see me. He's not pleased by what he's heard of my behavior. I confess that I feel bad about it. He thinks that it's time to transfer me. I entirely understand. He asks if I'd rather go to Pleasanton or Lexington. I've always left such choices to the system, but I do have a preference, and I answer his question: Pleasanton is the only place that's been really brutal with me. I'd rather go to Lexington.

I have a great peace about it now, and a strong sense that things are falling into place in general. There's loads of evidence that God is supervising my navigation in the dark. In fact, I'm beginning to see God's hand in my life in a mammoth kind of way that seems logically impossible: orchestrating complex events—which develop through independent decisions by many autonomous individuals who have no knowledge of or concern for my spiritual growth—to adjust my circumstances at the precise point where I'm ready for and in need of the next step that the change enables me to take on my spiritual journey. I know that I'm not at the center of the universe. God must be doing the same for everybody. And my rational mind can't comprehend how it could possibly be. But I'm increasingly convinced that it is.

I'm returning to some of my little-girl awareness of God as a friend in the room with me, a friend with whom I simply talk about whatever's on my mind. I'm trusting all sorts of ordinary things specifically and deliberately to God and am full of thanksgiving for all the answered prayers. I realize that I'm blessed with so many answers precisely because I'm asking God for so much specific help.

I do a lot of reflecting about relationships, starting with trying to understand my yelling, which surprised and embarrassed me, because I think of myself as a person who doesn't yell. I wonder if part of the problem in prison is coming smack up against stark unreasonableness and inflexibility while I'm still naturally, humanly, unconsciously assuming reasonableness. The effect is heightened here, because people act and talk as if they're being reasonable. I keep pouring energy into relating as fully and honestly as possible with whatever people are presenting to me, only to discover, over and over again, that their agenda is entirely different from what they've been presenting. Is relationality happening at all? I feel as if I'm flailing around in quicksand.

Even worse, the people themselves keep turning out to be different from how they've presented themselves. I've been disillusioned by individual after individual, with whom I thought I was relating, whom I've found to be nothing like her or his persona. And my own straightforward presentation of myself keeps getting twisted into someone else's projections. It seems as if people who are liars and opportunists themselves just assume that everyone else is, too. Maybe most of the people they know are. They assume that your motives are selfish. They assume that the consequences of your choice must have been the *reason* for your choice. Principles don't even make sense to them. What possible basis do we have for communication?

I've worked harder on relationship than anything else here, and now I'm wondering if there ever *was* any from the prison's side. I have almost no friends on the staff here, which is extremely unusual in my experience. I've received a lot of "professional" attention, and some people at the very beginning spent chunks of time trying to figure out what makes me tick, but most of them were apparently just looking for handles to get me to do what they wanted me to do.

The state of my emotions suggests that I'm feeling massively betrayed. I feel much worse about this place than I would have if it hadn't presented itself so positively, because the level of *sham* is so overwhelming. I suspect that it isn't even intentional. People may well be lying to themselves as much as to me. But that doesn't make me feel any better about it. Part of what's so very hard for me is the apparent impossibility of showing people how dehumanizing some of their unintentional behavior is. It's as if that just doesn't compute in their world view.

The problem is much bigger than prison. Children are treated in a lot of similarly dehumanizing ways. And the elderly. Homeless. Welfare recipients. Even ordinary hospital patients. The powerless in general. They become nonpersons who are related to only functionally by people who are only doing a job. I ultimately conclude that the major reason Rochester has been so very confusing and difficult for me is probably that it's much more similar to the larger society than I've come to expect of prisons, which are usually more unmasked. The subtle, perhaps largely unconscious masks are difficult for me in the overall society, too.

June 19. The officer wakes me up at 1:30 in the morning to move me to a different room, saying that the cell is needed. I cooperate, half asleep for the move and thoroughly awake for hours afterward. The following afternoon I'm moved back. No explanation. My tolerance for this kind of inhumanness is slipping, and I don't like the sharpness that creeps into my emotional responses. I'm having an especially hard time with repeated instances of being lied to by staff. I write a long letter to the warden—a sensitive, respectful letter—as a way of expressing and working through some of the feelings I'm struggling with about the prison. I recognize the need to reach an internal place that enables me to leave lovingly.

The one chaplain who makes me feel cared about at least pastorally, the Lutheran, brings a young intern to meet me, and our conversation about God and faith and prayer brightens my day. It's healing for me to see the nurses being gentle and caring with the very needy patient locked down across from me, whom I've been embracing with a lot of yearning prayer. One of them obviously loves him the way I do and warms my heart by giving him truly personal attention. By the time my property is packed out on July 1, I think I'm ready to leave even in that final sense of having worked through my feelings.

The warden stops at my door for just a brief greeting, cordial on both sides–perhaps an appropriate farewell between us.

On July 2, I leave on the marshals' airlift.

12

Transcendence

The airlift from Rochester arrives in Oklahoma City at approximately the same time on Tuesdays that the airlift from Oklahoma City arrives in Lexington, so I end up with a week in the county jail in Norman to wait for my connection. I'm put in a room with a woman who turns out to be the proud possessor of a *comb!*—which she passes on to me at her departure. I'm rich indeed. I share it with my new roommate and our friends next door and anyone else who asks or seems to be in need. When the jail moves my roommate out in order to lock me down, I insist that she take the comb. How could I hoard it behind my locked door when so many others can use it out there? I'm richer still.

From Oklahoma City we're routed to Lexington by way of New Hampshire, so it's late in the day when we arrive. I had loads of time for reflection in the county jail and am clear now that I need to noncooperate with strip-searches. At Rochester I finally reached the point of no longer responding to "Haines!" or "Inmate Haines!" at all. And I've been clear for quite a while that I need to wait to eat until I have a vegetarian diet. My re-entry into the prison is far from routine.

The first thing that happens in R & D is the strip-search. The lieutenant who's called in to handle my refusal is new to me. She's angry at my noncooperation and aggressive with my last name. She arranges for something resembling a riot squad. Being strip-searched against your will is a pretty ghastly experience in any case, but this is the first time that it's been done to me in the presence of men—and the whole incident is *video-taped.* I'm mortified. But there's nothing for me to do about it. I've gone limp. I endure. They don't hurt me physically. Essentially, they just change my clothes, taking away *everything* personal, including my underpants and glasses, and dressing me in an institution uniform several sizes too large.

They cuff my hands behind my back, carry me all the way to segregation, deposit me in a cell, remove the handcuffs, and lock the door.

I lie still on the bare mattress, wondering how long the name barrier might keep me utterly impoverished. But soon a different lieutenant comes to the door and calls, "Jennifer." So I'm able to respond. I'm willing to change into segregation clothing, including underwear, and ask for bedding and other basic necessities. The officer puts some effort into recovering my personal property from R & D, and is finally able to bring me my glasses sometime around 11:00.

In the morning I make a little sign for the window in my door: "My name is Jennifer." The door windows here are covered with wire mesh instead of Plexiglas, so I thread the sign through the mesh. Now, anyone who might be willing to use the name I answer to will know what it is, so I won't be totally shut off from communication before it begins. I was surprised when the lieutenant called me Jennifer last night. But I realize much later that my explanation in R & D must have been passed on to him, and he undoubtedly saw it as the easiest means to gain my cooperation.

The first day officer turns out to be the same one who consistently refused me my name last summer. He greets me with "Miss Haines," which I'm still willing to respond to. Then he tears the sign off my window, with a mischievous little smile as if it's all a game, and I'm suddenly no longer willing to compromise at all. I'll respond to "Jennifer." I go back to bed, hoping that I might actually be able to catch up on some sleep. I ignore all requests at my door for attention; none of them is addressed to "Jennifer."

Toward the end of the morning, the segregation lieutenant comes in. He locates my hands under the bedclothes, pulls them out, and cuffs them, saying, "It's only a cell move." Oh. This is the first I've heard of it. I'm not talking, and he simply assumes my noncooperation, pulling me, gently enough, out of bed and carrying me, with the help of an officer, into another cell. A second officer brings my bedding and other property. How I wish I could just remain passive! But I *have* to ask for toilet paper. I'm feeling very vulnerable and wonder if I should request to see a chaplain.

"Jennifer."

It's the Catholic chaplain, who knows me well. I'm so glad to see him! He tells me that the lieutenant called him to ask if he might be able to get me to talk, and I explain the whole problem. He evidently explains it to the lieutenant, because I'm suddenly given my name back. What a relief! Even at the time it occurred to me that the officer who pushed me beyond compromises by destroying my little sign may have been doing me a favor. Now everyone who is willing to calls me Jennifer, and most of those who are not come up with acceptable alternatives, such as, "Good morning." If they're standing at my door, it's obvious whom they're addressing. A couple still refuse, and some forget, which also hurts, but I have space in which I can move again.

The following morning I mention to the PA making rounds that I need a vegetarian diet.

"We don't have any vegetarian diets."

"I had one when I was here before."

"That's history."

"The doctor ordered it for me."

"Doctors don't order nonmedical diets. You have to write a cop-out to the dietician."

I write the cop-out, knowing that it will have no effect whatsoever. I'm dutifully attending to the proper channels, but I've learned that the communication the prison will hear is the fact that I'm not eating, and the person who will respond to my dietary needs is the segregation lieutenant—who was, deliberately I'm sure, listening in on my conversation with the PA.

Knowing all this makes me uncomfortable. I don't want to have any power, and I'm not interested in effectiveness. My original refusal to accept less than a vegetarian diet was a simple attempt to keep my choices conformed to my integrity. I wasn't concerned with what the prison might do. I just wasn't willing to participate in my own victimization by a policy that discriminates against vegetarians in the hole. But I've learned that the prison's response will be to give me whatever diet I'll settle for, which is clearly a lot simpler than force-feeding me indefinitely. So my passive noncooperation becomes both powerful and effective. Whatever I'm willing to accept becomes the criterion for what's provided. That doesn't feel right, but I can't see any way around it unless I don't accept anything at all.

The lieutenant responds more quickly than I expect, before the end of the third day, which is a Friday. He appears at my door to announce that I'm wanted in the clinic, and he'll take me there *without* handcuffs! I would have been willing to walk if he'd come in and cuffed me, but I guess he wants to make very sure that nothing obstructs my cooperation. The ordinary humanness of unrestrained movement feels great.

A doctor whom I haven't met before examines me. My physical condition is not serious. She says that she'll work with the dietician on a vegetarian diet for me and meanwhile, to get me through the weekend, she'll prescribe a liquid nutritional supplement. I politely decline the supplement. I'm not willing to accept anything but water until I have an adequate diet, and my experience suggests that I'll survive the weekend even if the prison denies me water.

The doctor picks up the telephone, calls the dietician, works out the diet, and tells me that I'll have a lunch tray. Lunch is already over. I make a quick detour through the lab to give blood and urine samples and arrive at the seg sally port at nearly the same time as the tray. (It has to wait for me to be strip-searched by two female officers, which is no fun for any of us, but I appreciate the absence of both men and fanfare—the seg lieutenant is low-key and down to earth and manages with a minimum of fuss.) It's a good, vegetarian meal. The speed with which that diet materialized boggles my mind. If it was *that* easy to order and prepare, what was the point of all that business about liquid food supplements?

I'm struck again that you get what you settle for. It's incredible! The dynamic is backward–reminding me of our bizarre court experiences in 1984. Those who are compliant and patient and go along with the program get shortchanged, while the problem children end up with the privileges.

At the same time, it's refreshing to see that my nonverbal communication *communicates* here. My actions make sense again. I'm already feeling more myself than I did in Rochester. I'm glad to see many staff people–who seem glad to see me, too–showing me how very many more meaningful personal relationships I developed here in five months than I did there in eight. I like my counselor, whom I knew as an officer last summer. I like the segregation lieutenant. Though he's remarkably unexpressive and we've never really had a conversation, he's pretty well figured me out and responds appropriately. My special friend among the prisoners is in a cell across the hall, and it's a delight to connect with her again.

But most of my attention for the next several weeks is engaged by a massive integration of all the learning from my years of interaction with the prison system, in which all sorts of pieces fall into place and I *finally* understand how it functions and what my vocation requires of me within it.

It *does* function backward from me, entirely on the basis of pragmatism, while I depend solely on principle. It has no principles, though individuals within it may, and is willing to use any means to accomplish its goals. Even its own rules are used if they work and dispensed with if they don't. Its overall goal is control: to pacify every prisoner into compliance. Those who are compliant to begin with, it ignores. Most of the rest can be controlled by the threat of punishment and, if necessary, the punishment itself. That leaves only a few who require individual attention. They end up with a special program: whatever they'll settle for, the minimum that pacifies them, along with a lot of punishment usually. I've been pacified now with my name and my diet.

So it's clear that there's *nothing* relational in the institution's behavior. Values like generosity are meaningless to it. It isn't doing me any favors when it gives me something that wouldn't ordinarily be available, like a vegetarian diet, but is merely using whatever means are effective to satisfy its own agenda of eliciting all possible compliance. My willingness to eat is precisely the return that it wants. If it tries to make me feel further obligated, I need only refuse the "favor" to discover how ardently the prison wants me to accept it.

Of course, I have myself to keep acting on the basis of principle. But I need to stop expecting any reciprocation or relationality from a prison.

An institution is *not* a person. I need to save all of my relational energy for individuals. And it hits me that our different *moral* assumptions were the reason I so misinterpreted Rochester, and it me. Principle is the highest level of moral functioning. I naturally assume high levels of others, so I never imagined that the prison was operating on the very low level it was. And those who operate on lower levels, involving more self-interest, can't even *comprehend* the higher ones. No wonder we couldn't communicate! We speak different languages.

In spite of this snowballing awareness, though, the prison's concessions to me still *feel* not only like favors, but like favors demanded and won—which is not the way I choose to be. I keep wanting to back off and say, "Forget it. I'll do without."

Even worse, no amount of noncooperation on my part prevents any of the abuses I'm sensitive to from happening all around me all day long to everyone else. The name thing. The handcuff thing. How much more like an object can you treat someone than by slapping cuffs on a personless pair of wrists through a low hole in a solid door that requires both of you to bend over where you can't even see each other? And my current cell overlooks the seg rec yard, which, in spite of already being securely enclosed by building walls, has recently had installed in the middle of it a row of little rec cages, which are an abomination!–like kennels. They're worse than Pleasanton's!

I want to scream. It's inhuman! It's immoral! It's utterly unacceptable. It's getting harder and harder for me to stand by while it happens. I'm complicit through everything I accept from the system, and especially through the things it gives me that aren't offered to others–the things that keep me pacified. Why am I accepting those things? Why am I still cooperating with daily life? Because I haven't been pushed over the edge yet. I'm still waiting for an irresistible compulsion before I further withdraw cooperation.

I've been on disciplinary segregation status since July 17–for not responding to some order that never made it past the name barrier, in addition to the initial strip search–which hasn't changed my already restricted circumstances. I'm managing fairly comfortably within them, making productive use of my solitude and experiencing that communion with God around daily life that was such a blessing at the end of my Rochester time. There are lots of prayers for little things, and lots of answers to be thankful for.

On August 1, the prison thoroughly unsettles me: My counselor's nonappearance keeps me from making a promised phone call. A nurse refuses to deliver vitamins that were ordered by a doctor, because I won't give her an inmate registration number in response to my name–even though I'm the only Jennifer Haines in the institution and the only person in the cell that has my name on the door (of course, the number is on the door, too). I decide that I can do without; I don't need *anything that* badly.

In addition, there's a shakedown. I'm not being handcuffed or removed from the cell these days, but I still feel the violation of my space. And what's really getting to me about these common and utterly routine dehumanizations is the way the staff takes them for granted—as if it's really okay for nice people who love their kids to invade someone else's space and rifle through her property and deprive her of things they wouldn't think of doing without themselves. It's the *attitudes* that are so excruciatingly wrong—relegating us to the status of objects, or of animals. I'm ready to scream, "IT'S *NOT* OKAY!!!"

I ask myself: What difference does resistance make? The things that hurt keep happening, and hurting, whether I resist or not. Maybe the really important thing I'm doing—and never do well—is carrying the pain. If I could only let it hurt as much as it hurts without wanting to scream at it or lessen it or *do* something in response to it, then maybe I'd be making the room for God in the situation that my calling is all about. I keep wanting to protest. I guess I'm back at that place of having to remind myself that nothing I do is going to change the *situation*. And ultimately I have to stop fighting the pain of *that*—of knowing that all this dehumanization is likely to go rolling right along, generally accepted by everybody.

Ah! I'm being thrust onto the threshold of a new understanding about my vocation; I'm only just now reaching that point in my prison experience where it can begin to take hold. Until now, I've been so absorbed in working through various aspects of my own pain—especially the ongoing struggle to discern the most godly response to one immediate challenge after another—that, though I've been praying in personal and general ways all along, I haven't had enough inner space for letting the pain of those around me become the wellspring of my intercession.

I remember how, at Rocky Flats, I had to struggle through my own pain first, before being released into powerful intercession for all those affected by the pain of the situation. Here, that liberation has come with understanding how the system functions, which has given me so many answers all at once that I suddenly feel relatively comfortable in my own groundedness and find my attention filled with the abuses I see against others. My first reaction is to want to do something about them, which is natural enough, but I learned long ago to let go of expecting that I can accomplish anything external. External work may be appropriate, but whatever we do is more or less limited and will not eradicate all the pain. We're freest for faithfulness when we have no investment in making any difference at all. The work I'm called to is internal, in any case. And the beginning of that work, the true intercessory prayer for this particular situation, is this letting in of all the pain I see around me.

But bearing the pain is not enough. I need to *accept* the pain, which means facing all the evil in the situation, acknowledging that it's as bad and as intransigent as it is, and still choosing God. The triumph of faith is to trust God in the *presence* of evil. That's what happened in me in such a powerful way at Rocky Flats. Because I love and choose God, the evil causes me great pain. Being vulnerable to love necessarily means being vulnerable to pain. The key is not to fight either the evil or the pain, not to hope that I can make them go away, but simply to keep choosing God in the face of them. Choosing God is, in itself, the answer to evil. It's all that's required. God is the only one who can overcome evil, even within our own hearts.

In fact, the whole struggle between good and evil takes place within individual hearts. The individual heart is where evil originates–evil is the sum of all of our not-God choices–and yet it's also where evil can always be transformed into good by the action of God. Within the heart is where God acts. So persons always have an infinite potential for good, for making God choices, and relationships have an infinite potential for being a channel for that. The hope that I now experience at Rocky Flats, because I meet God there, is present in the same way in every interaction with an individual, because God is present to the interaction.

Now I suddenly see what was wrong in my thinking that I could relate to a prison as to a person: a prison doesn't have a heart open to the action of God. Only human hearts can change the not-God choices that have been built into an institution. The institution itself is dead. It *can't* make God choices. It hits me that *this* is why I've always held up relationship as more important than law and structure. Within and between persons is the only place where God acts, the only place where the kingdom can come.

All of this means that whether or not I further withdraw cooperation should depend simply on whether my cooperation is putting obstacles in the way of my prayer. It's not a matter of being pushed over an edge by a final straw, but rather of keeping my inner space clear for the flowering of the freedom to love. I feel in a pretty "safe" place now for discernment– though I trust God somehow to keep me on the path even when I'm not. This assurance has been one of the great graces of the past year; at some point, it seems that I just *knew* it: I don't have to worry about my incapacity, especially with respect to discernment, because *God* will keep me faithful, as long as I truly desire to do God's will.

Another shakedown leaves me feeling more offended than wounded, closer to anger than pain, and I know that something is wrong. Am I cooperating too much? But I realize that the first thing I'm doing wrong is not truly praying for those by whom I feel oppressed. One can be angry only if one feels helpless, and one can't feel helpless if one is praying– truly praying–trusting God.

Humanly, the dilemma of my situation has become impossible. I'm essentially no longer accepting my prisonerhood: I'm a human being first; I expect to be treated like one, and when I'm not, I'm offended. There's something right about that point of view. Simple human dignity demands that one not just lie down and take this kind of treatment. Yet frequently there's no nonviolent alternative. Whether one cooperates or not, a strip search or a shakedown is dehumanizing, and so are the attitudes behind it. So really the only thing I have to work with is my own internal space.

I've known that praying for those who hurt or dehumanize others is necessarily included in intercession for my current situation, but I've stumbled over how hard it is to relate to their pain. *They* don't relate to it. They couldn't do what they're doing without numbing it out or walling it off. Yet my entering into their pain is what empowers my prayer. Now I suddenly recognize that it's precisely through praying for them in the midst of the dehumanizing act, in the midst of my own pain—whether for myself or others—that I touch theirs. My pain is surely only a shadow of theirs, because of the terrible things they're doing to their own immortal souls, killing something of their own God-sensitive spirits.

August 11. I'm bathing at the sink in my cell. It's early evening. The duskiness in the cell gives me some visual protection, but who knows when a male staff person might come to the door and turn on the light? So I've covered the door window with a piece of paper, held in place by the suction of the ventilation system. The regular male officer has told me that the paper is okay. The regular female officer happens by and declares that it's not. She dislodges it by poking at it with her pen. I insist that I need privacy for bathing. She denies it. I replace the paper anyway to finish the bath.

But now I'm feeling angry again, even mildly outraged, running all sorts of "How dare you?" responses through my mind. I'd been thinking, long before, that if anyone ever did deny me privacy for a bath, I'd probably just stop bathing; everyone else is allowed privacy for bathing in the shower rooms. But that might well leave me feeling that it's completely impossible to live as a human being in here. I'm close to retreating into greater noncooperation, both as a withdrawal of assent from the prison's inhumanness and as a way of giving myself enough internal space to regain my free, loving center in God.

I still haven't been really praying for those I feel oppressed by, though, which is my first responsibility. So I try. Within hours the same female officer initiates another shakedown, only four days after the last one; and in spite of managing to do some praying in the midst of that, I end up feeling harassed and vandalized, on top of my earlier feeling of violation. I have a strong sense that the cosmic purpose of the two incidents on top of each other is to convince me to pull back. I stop eating.

I know that I'm in too emotional a space for making any ultimate decisions, but fasting has the great advantage that you can choose it one meal at a time. I spend all of the first day working on my emotions. I'm determined, first of all, to get past the anger. It's crucial that I keep enabling the most fundamental response to the prison system that my calling requires of me, which is to remain friendly, open, and loving, no matter what. And I do move beyond the immediate negative stuff, to where I'm experiencing everything as pain, feeling very fragile and vulnerable.

Now I'm ready for prayer again. I believe that prayer always has to come first, preceding any decisions, but I couldn't do much of it until the fast had begun to settle and open me up spiritually—as fasting predictably does. I'm clear that I have to continue fasting until I return to a strong prayer space, and then at least until I can *really* pray for the officer who's been the most difficult for me lately. Praying for the oppressor seems to be the crux of my work just now, and I realize that, in God's perfect providence, circumstances may well have pushed me into fasting precisely because I needed fasting to facilitate the prayer.

At the same time, I sense that this may have been my final step into noncooperation with the ongoing inhumanness of the BOP. I have no idea what would enable me to start eating again short of my release from prison. I'm terrified by the possibility that I might die before then. I don't really think that I *will* die, but I can't bear even to imagine abandoning everyone who loves me, especially after they've been waiting so long and so patiently for my release.

On the evening of the second day I receive a visit from a doctor who's new to me. He asks why I'm fasting, and I find myself going on and on about God and faith and prayer. He's a good and gentle listener. My choices come incoherently, but now I'm able to explain them. Rationally, the reason for withdrawing cooperation from daily life is that every time I pick up the pieces and go on with living after an assault or invasion by the prison, I accept the dehumanizing way in which the prison is treating me, as if I were saying that it's okay. Of course it's not okay.

Emotionally, my withdrawal from complicity, from accepting any pacification program, frees me from frustration and anger. It frees me to love and forgive.

Spiritually, it's probably enough that fasting removes the barriers to living in my spiritual reality. But there's also a deeper reason having to do with carrying the pain of the world—my prayer vocation, which I keep discovering that I still live in very limited ways. I'm just beginning to understand what fasting has been for in the whole Judeo-Christian tradition. So far, I've experienced only its self-purification aspect—becoming free from distractions and irrelevancies to be more fully present to God. There's an atonement aspect that I've never entered into. I see a new desert opening up before me now, a desert filled with physical pain and the darkness of unknowing, "the valley of the shadow of death." If I can embrace *that* pain, it somehow will give me a handle on embracing the pain of the evil in the world, and especially in the prison system. It will become an act of redemption for the prison system, taking all of its evil with me, willingly, to the cross, where God can somehow transform it.

By the third day I can tell that the fast has become a fully spiritual one. The anger and sharpness are gone. I'm more and more in tune with my godly self. I'm no longer feeling terrified, probably because the only thing

I'm really afraid of is making a disastrous mistake, and it's clearer every day that I'm not doing that.

On the fourth day the doctor has me moved up to the hospital floor. On the way I run into my prisoner friend, who's now in the general population, in the medical unit directly adjacent to segregation. The officer who's escorting me allows us a wonderful hug. It's the first time ever that we haven't had at least one locked door between us. I'm still locked in in the hospital, but the environment is *much* more human than the hole, which was one of the doctor's reasons for moving me, well before I'm sick enough to require it medically.

A nurse tells me that my water will be turned off, but the doctor corrects her. The policy has been changed here: A "hunger strike" is no longer reason in itself for having one's water turned off (apparently, it still was last summer, even in the hospital, so my running water then must have been an exception); a specific medical reason is now required. This doctor has joined the staff since I was here before, but he's certain that my protest then was instrumental in persuading the prison to reconsider its policy. Isn't that amazing? It blows me away whenever I hear that something I've done might have had some effect on something.

My hospital room has its own shower, which would be exciting except that there's no hot water. I try it once, decide that I can't afford to squander any more irreplaceable calories, and do without bathing again for many days.

I continue to feel better and better emotionally and spiritually. There's some real grace around the mystical act of deliberately joining my physical discomfort with the evil of the institution and bringing them to God together. Twice, the physical discomfort simply vanishes. The fast is not only enabling me to be my best self in the face of the evil of the prison system, but it's even directing me into profound ways of integrating and transforming the experience. I sense that some kind of culmination of my whole prison journey may be about to happen.

At the same time, I'm growing sicker physically and am increasingly aware of the dilemma between physical health and spiritual health. Surely God doesn't want me to damage my body? And yet I have no fear any more, certain that I'm safely within God's will. Since the fast is now clearly spiritual, there's always the possibility of a spiritual endpoint to it, and by staying constantly open to God's guidance, I trust that I'll know what I need to do.

I'm beginning to get a glimmer of what it means to pray for the oppressor. I realize that I've never really done it before. I've thrown the torturer or the warmaker into my prayers as an almost hypothetical human being— about whom I knew nothing personally and for whom I could simply assume God's love in the absolutely general sense that everyone is a child of God. That kind of general prayer doesn't touch the reality of the situation at all. One needs to be able to pray for those persons by whom one feels *personally* oppressed, who are deliberately doing hurtful things that one feels the pain of, and who are entirely unrepentant. One has to love them not hypothetically but *actually*, in the midst of the oppression and pain and moral blindness—somehow to reach through all that and touch whatever it is in them that's lovable, that God loves.

I feel as if I'm somehow groping for the essence of God's love for us: God's love for the prodigal, which is all of us, of course; God's love for the hypocrite. I lie here imagining the segregation unit as a whole—which concentrates the essence of the prison system as a whole, which in turn concentrates some major portion of the larger society—a machine for inexorably grinding into the dirt individuality, humanness, and personal dignity. I think of the perfectly ordinary people who run that machine calmly, routinely, even self-righteously, and who will keep right on doing it into the future and feel good about themselves in the process. And I dimly sense that whatever key breaks open my heart to *them*—the way it's so easily broken open by the poor and vulnerable, making me yearn to gather them up into my arms—will somehow integrate for me the reality of the evil and the joy of God.

I'm aware that there's nothing particularly remarkable about my spiritual life these days, no profound prayer or great revelations. But there's something incredibly sustaining going on. I feel it in my groundedness and security and lack of fear; in my quiet happiness; in the ease with which I deal with minor irritations, taking them immediately to God and feeling them lifted right away; in my constantly growing conviction that I'm doing what I have to do even though I don't understand it at all. I seem to be somewhere beyond my little-girl spirituality, in a place that's just as open and receiving and contented but much less bubbly or "feely" and more other-oriented.

I keep praying that God will purify my motivations and not let me do anything out of pride or stubbornness or vainglory, that I'll do only God's will, that God will show it to me and make me willing. In fact, I think that this spiritual focus is in itself purifying my motivations. *This* is the way to fast in prison—or anywhere—not as a protest or reaction against something, not as a statement, not simply as a withdrawal from complicity, though that element is still in there; but as a process of "in-tune-ment" with God and "at-one-ment" with the world—letting God lead, minute by minute (though God has a way of doing that anyway). The spiritual fast doesn't get hooked by any subtle hope for outward change; its whole attention is on inward change.

I like and trust my doctor. He's very gentle, very respectful, very informative. About a week into the fast he wants me to have an IV, and I passively allow it. It runs continuously from now on. Though I know that it's undergirding my health, it's not the most comfortable thing to live with. The worst problem is my fear of infection, especially since I don't trust the sanitary practices of many of the nurses. The fluid bag has to be changed every eight hours. The tubing and the dressing are changed irregularly, and the needle has to be moved to a new site every third or fourth day. Some nurses are better at finding a vein than others.

There are at least two occasions when the site infiltrates, one of them scary. The evening shift nurse, who's making rounds, thinks that the needle doesn't look secure and pushes on it a little. She's gone before I notice that my hand is starting to swell. I push my call button. The hand is swelling visibly. I walk to my locked door and knock on it. I know that the call button turns on a light in the nurses' station and another one over my door. The hall is deserted. No one comes. I'm afraid of fooling with the computer that's monitoring the fluid. I knock on the door again. My hand is beginning to look inhuman, balloon-like. I'm tense with the need for someone who knows something to come help me. No one comes. It may be twenty or thirty minutes that I wait. I can't stand it any more. I pull out the needle and let it drop, dripping fluid onto the floor. Then I lie back on my bed, exhausted from the tension, keeping pressure on the vein with my other hand to stop the bleeding.

When the nurse finally returns, she remarks lightly, "Oh, we generally count on the inmate workers to let us know someone's call light is on." The inmate workers were serving the evening meal. I thank the Lord that I wasn't having a heart attack. She turns off the machine, sticks a band-aid over the little hole in my hand, and mops up the floor with a paper towel. Then she readies her equipment to start a new IV. No handwashing, no gloves, no sanitation of any kind. I can't stand that either. I refuse the IV. Later I let someone else restart it.

It's not long before the doctor approaches me about a feeding tube: a naso-gastric tube, which runs through the nose into the stomach. It would provide a liquid nutritional supplement (nothing ground up in a blender as the Pleasanton captain threatened in 1989) on a continuous basis through a computer monitor like the one on my IV. I don't want a feeding tube but finally decide that I don't have to refuse outright. I can leave the medical choices to the medical people, responding, as I do to an IV, with passive nonresistance. Well, I soon find out that I can't.

Inserting a naso-gastric tube is normally a cooperative process: a nurse threads the tube through your nose into the back of your throat, where you swallow the little bulb on the end of it, as if it were a pill, by drinking water. I'm not willing to participate. The nurses raise me to a sitting position by adjusting the bed. One of them threads the tube through my nose, while the other holds a cup of water to my lips: "Swallow. *Swallow!*" I don't deliberately do anything at all, but my body reacts involuntarily. When the foreign object hits the back of my throat, I gag. It doesn't go down by itself. I feel as if I can't breathe, and I cough and squirm and cry out and become increasingly panicked. I've never before been so utterly unable to remain passive. I actually let the nurse try it three separate times with different tubes, but I'm more and more out of control, gagging and jerking away and crying, and now my fingers are going all rigid–the nurse explains that I'm hyperventilating–which has *never* happened to me before–nothing like *any* of this has ever happened to me before–and I finally push his hand away. I refuse the tube outright.

Afterward, I realize that refusing the tube is really the only response that's consistent with my fasting: If I'm willing to put anything other than water in my stomach, I'd choose for it to be my diet.

The nurse tries to change my mind by assuring me that I'm going to get the tube whether I cooperate or not. But I'm now clear about my own choice and prepared to endure whatever the prison might do to me. I presume that there's a way of *forcing* the thing down your throat, which must be what doctors do when a patient is unconscious. If they're holding me down anyway, my lack of control won't matter. For the rest of the afternoon, I expect to be strapped down. Nothing further happens.

I've been gifted for some time now by lots of long conversations with many people who are concerned about me and looking for ways to encourage me to eat. I wondered before I left Rochester if one reason for the transfer may have been that God wanted me in a place where there was more possibility for witness. Now, for practically the first time this sentence, I'm in a position where all sorts of people are asking questions that elicit long conversations about God and faith and prayer. Maybe the most important ingredient is the strong place of faith I'm in. In any case, I'm feeling more whole, more fully who I'm called to be, than I've felt for a long time. Praise the Lord!

In addition, the deep and widespread concern, a lot of which feels truly personal, is a blessing in itself, building a warm, positive feeling for this place in the midst of my accumulated sense of dehumanization. I feel cared about by many staff people, including the doctor and several nurses. The chaplains are wonderful. One of the Protestant chaplains is a particularly helpful listener–willing and able to be present to whatever a person's need or process might be without adding any agenda of her own–so her presence is a great gift to my ongoing search for discernment. The Catholic chaplain is also warmly and supportively available, and he's able to arrange for me to make a pastoral phone call to my spiritual director. My counselor is concerned for me, too, and facilitates a personal call.

The nurses allow me to take a bath in the tub room down the hall. They even find me some shampoo and lotion. I luxuriate in feeling clean again. I expect that I'll soon have too little energy to repeat the procedure.

Meanwhile, my spiritual saga keeps growing more and more splendid. By the end of August I realize that I'm fully reaping the spiritual benefit that I'd glimpsed as a potential fruit of this fast: praying for the workers here, as I do for the workers at Rocky Flats, as I do for all my friends. The barriers are all gone. I can stand in the presence of the evil and love the people in the all-embracing love of God. (That inner freedom is sustained by the fast, though. I still can't imagine how I could live in this inner place in seg if I were also eating, because of the way my complicity drags me down.)

At the same time, I'm finding that the spiritual potential of the fast is way beyond my first glimpses. Wonderful emotions are welling up in me: an outpouring of little-girl love and trust toward the people around me; the delight of waking in the morning, refreshed and contented, to the presence of God. I'm surrounded by goodness and blessing, not only from God but also from the prison staff. I feel on the verge of a new perception of my oneness with these people that's far more than a spiritual exercise but is deeply experiential. I also feel close to some kind of breakthrough into joy. It seems as if whole new realms might be opening up for me.

Sunday, September 1. I have very little energy, though I still feel better physically than I would have imagined I could this far into a fast. The doctor tells me that I look "brighter" than yesterday. A nurse says that my vital signs are better. Where are the resources coming from? I'm beginning to suspect miracles.

But I'm also beginning to wonder if it's selfish of me to enjoy so much spiritual blessing, while my situation causes pain and worry to all those around me who care, including a lot of prison staff. Two of them have broken into tears on approaching me. I wonder if there's a way I can start eating as a gesture of generosity toward everyone who's worried about me, both inside and outside the prison, including the medical people, who've been good to me, and especially the doctor, who will otherwise feel painfully compelled to force a tube down my throat.

I feel as if I need a *reason* to eat, but the more I think about it, the more I wonder whether generosity might not be reason enough. I don't need a "way" to be generous; I could just be generous. It wouldn't wipe out any of the reasons against, and I can see all sorts of potential problems down the road, but here and now, leaving the future to God, maybe it's good and enough.

I'm not ready to make a final decision until I've had a chance to think it through with the doctor and the Protestant chaplain on Tuesday, after *another* long holiday weekend. But then I'm sure. I'll break my fast. I do it as a free gift, to the prison staff in particular, simply because I can see that there's an unselfish thing I can do. And it hits me at some point that *this* is *really* loving the prison staff—concretely and actively.

I begin eating on Tuesday evening. Food is remarkably uninteresting to me when I've been away from it for a long time, but I receive the first bite sacramentally, and then embark on a cautious program of readjusting my body to digestion.

On Wednesday I feel worse physically than when I was fasting, but the real shock is that I discover I'm depressed. What am I doing wrong that a right choice—surely it was a right choice!—could lead to such lousy feelings? I'm used to right choices being confirmed by great feelings. I try to thank God for the situation anyway, trusting that God is using it in some way I don't see. And suddenly it hits me that my decision to lift the pain from others has, naturally and appropriately, brought all of it back to me. Now I'm bearing my own pain–argh! Maybe this pain of eating–which is sort of enigmatic, but includes having taken on a lot of responsibility and opened myself up to a lot of difficulty–rather than the pain I'd anticipated of fasting, is what I have to offer in that mystical prayer act of atonement.

Early Thursday morning the IV infiltrates the surrounding tissues and has to be removed. I don't want it replaced and ask the nurse to let me talk with the doctor about it. She agrees to leave him a message. But another nurse strides in toward the end of the morning with a barrage of arguments for why I have to have it and an order from the doctor to restart it. I feel shortchanged by the doctor's lack of response to my request and pushed around by the nurse's authoritarian assertiveness. My depression overflows, and everything in me sort of abdicates. I capitulate passively on the IV, but continuing to cooperate while I'm also being coerced is more than I can handle. I can't eat. I was doing it as a gift to others, but it's become too painful and difficult for me. Maybe I'm not strong enough to be that generous.

Now I'm utterly miserable. I've lost all my emotional freedom and my spiritual groundedness. I have no basis for making choices and no possible way forward. I *can't* not eat, because the pain it would cause everyone who loves me would be more than I could bear; I can't eat, either, because the tension of trying to cooperate is tearing me apart. The Protestant chaplain helps me sort through my feelings, but I'm not able to move beyond them. For twenty-four hours I do nothing but cry, except when I'm asleep. My eyes sting from it. I can't talk or smile and can hardly even look at anyone. I ignore all my meals.

The doctor visits me on Friday, which helps, because he's very gentle and compassionate, comforting me, not pushing me at all. He apparently never got my message about the IV, and wouldn't have ordered it if he had. The Catholic chaplain visits, too, and then offers to come back with Communion: "Would that help?" How special! I break into a warm smile and answer simply, "Yes."

I'm able to stop crying after that and do some more coherent reflecting; but I'm distressed that I can't see any choice apart from the weight of its consequences. I've known all along that eating would mean becoming healthy enough to return to seg–probably by way of the compound, where I wouldn't last twenty-four hours, because there's a stand-up 4:00 P.M. count–and I've expected that I couldn't cope with seg without fasting. Now I'm finding that I can't even cope with the hospital. Nonetheless, clarity gradually emerges that I can't not eat. Period. So I might as well assume that I can live with whatever consequences I have to.

The doctor returns to offer me an alternative. My emotional collapse must have been as instructive for him as it was for me. In order to relieve me of as much emotional stress as possible, he's willing to keep me on the hospital floor for the rest of my sentence. I'm a little hesitant about it, because it feels like a special privilege, but I probably *do* need it, so I accept, gratefully. Then he simply visits with me for a long time, during which my spirits fully revive. I think he's a rather wonderful human being. I eat dinner, feeling deeply touched by the humanness of everyone's response to me.

The rest of my sentence is apparently not a very long time. Everyone has been telling me that my release date is October 22. I've been extremely hesitant to believe it, because it seems highly unlikely, depending on my receiving *all* of my "good conduct time." I don't want to set up myself and all my friends for a massive disappointment. But maybe Rochester gave me credit for the fifty-four "good" days that Lexington forfeited in the course of many DHO hearings. They're not officially taken until the end of the first year, and whatever *isn't* taken then can't be lost later. And could Lexington be giving me credit for the days that Rochester forfeited? My Rochester case manager told me in May that I'd be getting out in October. My paperwork when I returned to Lexington reiterated it. And during my fast, it was repeated over and over again. Even a judge in Denver, who called the prison with concern about my condition, was told that I'd be released then.

My counselor eventually clinches it for me. I share my hesitations about counting on a date that might change, and she assures me, "There's no way you can lose that date now." I begin to count on it.

It's occurred to me to wonder whether I may have plumbed the depths of the prison experience now. Maybe I've learned all that I need to from it and am ready to "graduate." If so, the ideal means would be the closure of Rocky Flats, which I'm praying for with a kind of luminosity, as if it may be truly meant to happen.

When I started eating, I was still on disciplinary segregation, from another of those incidents in seg when I didn't respond to an unacceptable form of address. The DS time ends on September 7, a Saturday; when the seg lieutenant returns after the weekend, he gives permission for my door to be unlocked. The IV is removed on the eighth.

Now I embark on my best attempt at "normal" life. Everybody's agenda, including mine, is to hold me together for the rest of my sentence. The prison is truly doing everything it can for me. I appreciate it and feel both compelled and determined to cooperate with daily life in response. Daily life on the hospital floor really is relatively human. The rooms are comfortable, with amenities such as mirrors. The windows are small and very high, but the back hall, where I exercise every day as soon as I have enough strength, boasts a bank of huge windows overlooking a sweep of natural scenery beyond the prison buildings. I enjoy some spectacular sunsets. I'm able to use the telephone. The nurses are caring and relational, though often busy. I'm almost moved into a double, but the prospect of having to live with a television so distresses me that the prison relents. I'm very grateful.

But I'm still painfully aware of the prisonhood of the place and continue to feel pushed around by what happens to others.

I make friends with a new arrival, who's here for a court-ordered psychological evaluation and whose health is precarious both physically and emotionally. After she's been on the floor for some time, she's suddenly locked down because she's unsentenced. Theoretically, though absurdly after the fact, she's being separated from us convicts for her own protection (a juvenile in an adult facility would be locked down for the same reason), but the last thing she needs is to be isolated from her only support system. I can't stand it. This place is too full of thoughtless, senseless, routine, impersonal *dehumanization*! I fall off the emotional cliff edge, where I've been balancing pretty precariously myself, into no longer cooperating with daily life. I stop eating. It's not a deliberate choice. It's just that nothing else is possible for me under the circumstances.

I experience a lot of dizziness and nausea very quickly. On the second or third day, I fall on the way to the bathroom, not from blacking out so much as from suddenly losing all muscle control. My legs simply crumple beneath me. Somehow, I recover enough to use the toilet and make it back to bed. Then my friend's door is unlocked again, and I'm able to resume eating. I'm trying *very* hard to hang in there with minimal cooperation until October 22, which is close now.

I've begun to recognize an overall pattern in my spiritual growth in response to an evil. I first identified this pattern in my experience of Lenten prayer at Rocky Flats, and then in responding to my trial and illegal conviction: At first, you're immersed in the pain of encountering an overwhelming evil, drowning in it, not able to see beyond it. Then you surface, through faith, to a place of standing face to face with it, no longer acting as its inferior but as its peer, acknowledging the enormity and intransigence of the evil and consciously choosing God in its presence. The final step is God's. God lifts you to a place of transcendence, into a spiritual reality so far above the pain and evil that they recede into insignificance in the distance. And the greater the evil that God lifts you above, the more you comprehend of the much greater greatness of God.

With respect to the evil of the prison system, I finally reached the surfacing stage this summer in segregation. So I was ready for the culminating step. I could see that God might have been using my long fast as a vehicle for it. But the fast brought me only part way. I haven't reached the mountaintop yet. I'm still expecting that I'll reach it, somehow assuming that that will happen before my release. And during the last week, as I write a lot of letters (in anticipation of being able to mail them from the outside) in which I share extensively about this exciting spiritual dynamic, I begin to ask myself *how* I think God is going to consummate it in the next few days.

I'm a little surprised that my unit staff hasn't approached me about release planning yet, but I trust that my end of it can be taken care of on the last day, which is Monday, October 21. On that day, though, I'm no longer patient enough to keep waiting for them to come to me. By mid-morning or so, I ask one of the nurses to call. He reports back only that a unit staff person is coming over, and I know that the news is bad.

Very bad. I'm not being released any time soon. "Oh, there was an error in your paperwork," I'm told. No big deal, they seem to be saying; these things happen. After positively assuring me that I couldn't lose the October date, and allowing me to count on it until the very last minute (when would they even have informed me if I hadn't asked?), they're suddenly extending my sentence by two months or more with all the casualness of correcting a spelling error.

I fall off the final cliff. The cruelty is beyond my tolerance–cruelty so casual and routine that they're apparently not even aware of it themselves. It's their *attitude* that hits me the hardest, the attitude that sees no need even to apologize, that takes the whole situation in stride as if it were a little thing, as if the pain that it inflicts on a human being is of no account. *This* is the epitome of the prison system's dehumanization. If someone other than me had been the object of it at this point, my reaction would probably have been the same.

There's a flurry of activity as my unit staff attempts to provide explanations for me. Someone produces a computer printout of a sentence computation, which claims that the first fifty-four "good" days were forfeited on March 5. That's a lie. I have conclusive evidence that no changes were made in the computer before September. In fact, the printout itself suggests that the changes were made on October 3. I accept that the failure to make them earlier may have been an error. I accept that there's nothing I can do about it anyway. I tell my unit manager that he doesn't have to try to make sense of it for me; I'll do the time.

But I'm no longer eating. I *can't* cooperate with this cruel and inhuman system another minute! I may well have been unable to in any case; I was only barely managing to hold myself together until the twenty-second as it was. Now, when the "good" days that were taken during my second year are entered into the computer, my out date will fall near the end of December. I know that the prison will have no choice but force-feeding to keep me alive that long. I accept it. There are no choices left to me at all. I'm clear and at peace with resting in the inevitable.

It's still distressing to feel my body using up its resources and becoming ill. I want to take care of it but am utterly dependent on the prison now to make the right medical decisions at the right times. I'm very thankful that I trust my doctor. I pray that he doesn't let my condition become too dangerous before he intervenes.

My spirit, though, is soaring.

—— ✖ ——

October 29. And oh! was Sunday ever a spiritual feast! I kept feeling such love pouring out of me toward the people around me!—simple, childlike, all-embracing, unconditional love—God's own love pouring right through me. What a gift! There's a growing trustingness, too—growing out of my trust in God's care for me and spreading to the prison staff—including a desire, and even the ability, to trust their good intentions toward me in spite of any evidence to the contrary. The prison is sending all sorts of people to visit me now, so there are lots of uplifting conversations about God again. And I wonder if I'm headed back up to that mountaintop—which really would be the spiritual culmination of my prison experience, I think.

God is so amazing! I can't even understand why a fast seems to open me up to such gift. The spiritual potential wasn't even part of my own motivation for fasting. Maybe it has to do with the letting go of control. But God's action is still so sovereign—just spontaneously pouring God's own Self into me, as into an empty cup that's just sitting there.

October 30. Now I've discovered the full spiritual potential of this fast, and it's truly monumental. It is the culmination of my prison experience, the next step after absorbing the evil, the step that transcends it. It's that act of atonement that I was beginning to have some sense of during my last fast—where one embraces the evil, gathers it to oneself, and carries it to the cross, willingly, lovingly. That's what all that love God's been pouring into me is for.

I came to the full measure of willingness yesterday, when I realized I had to stop hoping that the prison might save me from some of the consequences of my choices, and let go of it (the hope—especially that the prison might intervene sooner rather than later). I need to accept all the potential consequences of my choices, and leave the prison free to do whatever it chooses to do, without putting any expectations on it. It's incredible how that frees me up. I need to bear all the suffering of an indefinite fast, and I need to come to terms with death. I really don't think it's going to happen, but I've just discovered again how coming to terms with death helps one to really live. I did the accepting consciously. The pain related to death, of course, is in all the pain it would cause all my loved ones; I feel safe in God regardless; but when I'm doing the only possible thing I can do, when there are no choices, then I'd better stop being afraid of, or wishing away, the potential pain.

And then I had a mystical experience: I imagined myself standing face to face with the specter of death himself, the grim reaper, and I realized that I had no strength to face him with, but Jesus did (does), so I turned to Jesus, whom I then saw right there at my left side, and as we stood together, it was as if we were lifted up onto a mountaintop as the specter of death got smaller and smaller and farther away in the distance.

Jesus has already conquered death; death is insignificant in the presence of Jesus. The experience was just exactly like the one I had after my trial, when my awareness of spiritual reality was like standing on a mountaintop from which material reality looked tiny and distant and insignificant. So I'm already beginning to experience the mountaintop aspect of this fast, precisely because I'm willing to accept all the suffering of it.

    And that willingness has done something else for me, too: it's turned me from a sort of preoccupation with my own needs—I don't really need anything except to endure, and if I'm simply doing that, what is there to attend to?—opening up lots more space in me for others. I'm suddenly very free—and available to God—and full of praise and thanksgiving.

    I now know without a doubt that this is God's will for me in an utterly specific way. This is what I need to be doing for God, as well as for my own wholeness in God. I don't know that I've ever been called to such an important work—which, of course, I'm entirely incapable of, so God's had to prepare me for a long time, gradually drawing me along, and then pouring in supernatural graces, and then it's still God who does the actual work, but oh! I praise the Lord! for finally having brought me to the place where I can offer unreservedly the one thing that's always mine to offer, which is the willingness to be used.

— ✄ —

I've been aware that if a fast is spiritual and centered and in God's will, it *can't* lead to my death unless my death is in God's will. I'm experiencing that reality now with new depth. A vision that first came to me earlier in this sentence, I think when I was fasting on milk, returns often: I'm being lifted and carried by God (not that I picture God anthropomorphically; the vision is symbolic), as you might be lifted by a strong adult if you were very weak, held by one arm under your upper back and the other under your knees, resting your head on the strong adult's shoulder. I feel the dependable strength of God holding me; I relax into it, trusting. I have a wonderful, warm sense of being okay, knowing that everything will be okay, that I'm safely within God's will and care for me. Yet I haven't a clue as to whether I'm going to live or die. It doesn't matter. I've lost the dividing line. I realize that there's no significant difference between life and death as long as one is safely within the will and care of God.

The Catholic chaplain brings me a truly momentous gift. Accompanied by a few prisoners, he *celebrates* Mass in my hospital room and anoints me with oil for healing. I'm deeply touched.

Of course, friends everywhere are holding me in prayer, and many are calling and writing to the prison in their concern for me. My situation is highly visible.

The doctor would have given me an IV some time ago, but I've told him that I don't want one. IVs scare me. Isn't it strange that I can be so afraid of infection when I'm not afraid of death? What I'm actually afraid of is that someone, including myself, might make a disastrous mistake. I don't want to die by mistake. If I'm going to be forced anyway—I'm refusing a feeding tube but know that it's inevitable—I'd rather skip the IV. I've never fasted on water only for more than seven days without IV support before and have no idea what my body can handle. It's doing better than I would have expected, but I grow progressively weaker, gradually giving up such energy-demanding tasks as bathing and combing my hair. I spend all my time lying in bed. I use a wheelchair to get from the bed to the toilet and sink, but even that becomes a serious strain. I eventually ask for a less effortful alternative, and a nurse—now more worried about me than before—provides a bedpan.

November 1, a Friday, is the twelfth day of my fast. The doctor visits me toward the end of the day. I've been seeing quite a bit of him, and we've had some extensive conversations. He knows that I'm not trying to kill myself. He asks, "Now what are we going to do about this goal we both have of keeping you alive?"

"I'm afraid it's up to you."

"All right, if it's up to me, then I'm going to do the safest thing, and the safest thing is an n.g. [naso-gastric] tube. Since you won't cooperate with it, I'm going to have you strapped down. And I'm going to keep you strapped down unless we can come to an agreement that you won't pull it out."

"I understand."

"I'm not going to do it tonight. I'm going to the ballet tonight. I'll be back first thing tomorrow morning. But I'll give you a chance to decide to eat breakfast first."

I don't say so to the doctor, but I'm very, very thankful. I really do want the prison to intervene, preferably before my condition becomes any more precarious.

Saturday is very hard for me, because nothing happens at all. I finally realize that the doctor's whole story was a threat; even he was lying to me. I suspect that he was ordered to. I don't see him again until Sunday.

At some point during the weekend, I mention to a nurse one of those sudden pains in my heart that's unrelated to activity and different from the occasional pain of the mitral valve prolapse. She immediately wheels in the EKG machine and catches enough of the remaining flutter for the doctor to diagnose what happened: the heart beat out of rhythm, pushing blood back into the chamber it had just left; such arrhythmia isn't serious in the auricle, but would be if it involved the ventricle. His concern over my condition grows. I'm already concerned about my heart. I suspect that it's my most vulnerable organ.

On Sunday we have a long conversation about feeding tubes. The head doctor has recommended a gastric tube, inserted directly into the stomach through the body wall, which requires an operation. My doctor explains it in some detail. I'm clear that I'm not willing to cooperate with any part of it, including an IV for anesthesia. And I share my fears: I'm afraid that my heart may be unable to handle anesthesia; I'm afraid that it may be unable to handle the stress of my being forced; and I'm afraid of unnatural holes in my body. But I've abdicated all choices. The prison will do whatever it decides to do, and I pray that I'll survive it. The doctor, who's clearly not happy about having to force me, says that the operating theater has to be arranged for, and it won't happen today or tomorrow.

By Tuesday morning, the scenario has changed again. Apparently, the feeding-tube decision hasn't been finalized in high places, and the doctor is determined to provide some medical intervention today. He tells me that he's going to give me an IV, whether I cooperate or not, as soon as the authorizations have been completed. I've known for a long time that a court order is required to authorize force-feeding, and I'm beginning to suspect that the same must be true for a forced IV. (Maybe *that*'s why Rochester turned on my water—especially considering the holiday week-end—instead of forcing me.)

But he also has a new question: if my release date were moved into the immediate future, would I be willing to eat in order to enable my body to handle the flight home? (The only eventuality that can legally prevent release once the sentence has been served is medical inability to travel.) No. I truly can't imagine any possibility that I can eat again as long as I'm in the custody of the BOP. The compromises that he suggests are unacceptable. But there is one compromise I could make: I could accept an IV. I'm not refusing the IV as a matter of principle. I just don't want it. I could give in on that.

Later the same morning my room is suddenly full of bigwigs: the head doctor, the head of the records office, someone who must be an AW, my unit manager, and one or two others. The BOP has given me credit, they tell me, for those fifty-four "good" days that caused most of the confusion; I gather that approval for this had to come from farther up in the hierarchy than the warden. My out date is now November 13, eight days away. They promise me that I can count on it. I've had plenty of proof that I can't count on anything in the BOP, but I look around at all their smiling faces, and I'm sure that I can trust them. I agree to accept an IV.

Afterward I realize what tremendous grace there was in the timing working out so neatly that the doctor was never compelled to force me. I'm very thankful for his sake and praise the Lord.

Meanwhile, one of the chaplains has called Denver to encourage either Anna, who is a Sister of Loretto, or Hugh to visit me. Anna arrives on Wednesday, and special arrangements enable her to spend two or three hours in my hospital room each afternoon for several days. She brings me a message from Hugh: "I'm one hundred percent sure that you should be eating now." Anna's sure, too. It unsettles me. I'm one hundred percent sure that I *can't*. But I have profound respect for the wisdom and guidance of my spiritual director. What is he seeing that I'm missing? I decide that I must at least try to talk with him about it, so I ask the Catholic chaplain if he can arrange a pastoral call. He's still working on it when the answer reaches me unexpectedly through, of all things, the IV.

So far, it's a standard IV, feeding me salts and some sugar. For twenty-four hours, shots of albumen are added to it to prepare me for a more nutritionally fortified kind of fluid, which I'm ready to begin on Friday evening. But I'm dismayed when the two nurses who come in to start it turn out to be the two, of all those in the hospital, who make me feel the most unsafe: the one who put an IV needle in the crook of my elbow last year, and the one who mops up the floor and empties my urine pan without washing her hands. I can hardly bear to let them touch me. Apparently they're planning to move the needle, which I wasn't expecting, and they tell me that the tubing will have to be changed every twenty-four hours, presumably on the same shift, which is rather likely to cause infiltration and require moving the needle again. Even the most skillful nurses are barely able to find a usable vein on me any more, and the extensive possibilities for infection terrify me. It's suddenly too much for me to cope with. I refuse the new IV, in tears, helplessly caught between my earlier agreement to cooperate and my fear of the nurses. Tense with the inner struggle, I cry for the rest of the evening. And it begins to trickle into my consciousness that it's pretty silly to be going through all these agonies over the IV when I *could* eat. What's the big difference between letting the prison feed me through an IV and feeding myself? The current IV is already infiltrating, very gradually, which I avoid mentioning until the next shift, when the nurse insists on removing it. There are several day-shift nurses whose sanitation I trust enough to allow them to replace it, but I discover that the two most skillful ones—the day supervisors, at least one of whom has always been on—are both off for the entire holiday weekend. The nurse who tries can't penetrate a vein. My doctor has left for vacation. God is obviously trying to get a message through to me.

All right. I break my fast—again cautiously, hoping that I can stabilize my system enough in four days to be able to fly without endangering my heart—and end up laughing with God at the final joke on me: The need for me to eat at the end there was simply to remind me of who's in control. I didn't have everything figured out. I wasn't performing some heroic feat of endurance or principled consistency. Whether I could or couldn't eat in the custody of the BOP wasn't the ultimate question after all. God was working at an altogether different level.

God's purpose for the fast had been to complete in me the spiritual culmination of the whole of my prison experience. God accomplished it. So I was ready to go home. So the prison made the arrangements for me to go home. God's agenda was fulfilled, and the few remaining days before I left were of no significance.

Afterward, it occurred to me how crucial it was–through all those years of struggle when I was perennially searching for the most godly response to one unfamiliar and confusing situation after another–that I *didn't* have it all figured out. If I had approached new situations with predetermined responses of which I was certain, I would have turned every potential interaction into concrete, closing out both relationality and God. As it was, my openness to ongoing guidance, even when I thought I knew the answers, kept making more room for the flexibility of grace than my logical, controlling mind could imagine beforehand.

—— ✂ ——

The prison flew me directly to Denver on a tiny chartered jet that was equipped with a space where I could lie down for the whole trip. It arranged for Anna to meet the plane on the airstrip with a van. I arrived home without physical trauma and feeling very cared for by the prison. How wonderful it was finally to be reunited with so many friends whom I hadn't seen for so long! I quickly regained normal health and strength by indulging in a lot of good food. I entered into Advent with a quiet, gentle retreat at St. Benedict's. I celebrated Christmas with my family in New York. And God's agenda for Rocky Flats emerged with the new year.

Inklings of it had appeared in the spiritual reality that I'd recognized in myself before I left prison. I knew by the end of this sentence that the prison experience was complete and finished for me as a place of learning and spiritual growth. So how could it possibly serve God's purposes for me to return to it? But how could I possibly not return as long as Rocky Flats was producing nuclear weapons? The only resolution that I could see between spiritual and material reality would be for Rocky Flats to close. But I knew of no rational reason to expect any significant change there in less than ten years–the earliest time mentioned in government proposals to relocate its function elsewhere. Its plutonium processing had actually been suspended, for safety reasons, since before my arrest in December of 1989, but resuming production as soon as possible had been the plant's top priority throughout my entire two-year prison term.

In early January of 1992 the government announced that Rocky Flats was being withdrawn from nuclear weapons production. My inner compulsion to pray there had already disappeared. A decade of witness was over. Finis.

Epilogue

The spiritual journey continues, of course. Now that I'm praying neither at Rocky Flats nor in prison, I've had to discern all over again the rhythm for my daily life that best expresses my prayer vocation. I'm still living in the inner city, as part of the Catholic Worker community. I still attend Mass six days a week. Folks from the Catholic Worker have been gathering for weekday prayer at noon since early 1993.

That was the year in which I originally wrote this book. It was also a year of seriously escalating street violence in Denver, to which I responded with a mid-morning prayer vigil at public buildings downtown. By the fall of 1994, there was much less street violence in the local news, and I was beginning to stumble into a fruitful daily schedule.

My weekday mornings were already enfolded in prayer. I get up early, when I wake up naturally, usually around 5:00. That gives me plenty of quiet time before 7:30 Mass. In the summer I enjoy walking then, my favorite contemplative activity, at the loveliest time of day, when I'm particularly fresh, alert, and receptive. The public vigil encouraged me to continue praying through the morning but was itself active and distracting enough that I felt ready that fall to replace it with open, unstructured time for hidden, silent prayer in the place where I live, in the heart of the city. I try to attend to God in contemplative stillness. I pray rosaries. I reflect on scripture and devotional books. I'm particularly inspired by the lives and writings of saints and mystics. Sometimes I fold prayer cranes.

Violence increased in our Catholic Worker neighborhood in 1995, as drug dealing drifted into it, so at the end of the summer we moved our noon prayer into the park kitty-corner from the apartment where I live. Prayer there has the same power for me as prayer at Rocky Flats—celebrating God's light and hope in the midst of darkness. It also makes us even more available to our neighbors.

Afternoons now are for work, especially manual work at the hospitality house, including deep cleaning, minor repairs, sorting and organizing, and lots of gardening in the summer. Evenings, which are short, and flexible chunks of time on the weekends are for correspondence and other relational things.

It's a lovely schedule in theory, though I find that the balance rarely works out the way I expect it to. In spite of having pared down my activity to the minimum essentials, spending no time at all on what fills the days of most people—no income-earning work, no parenting, no school, no TV or other entertainment, no hobbies, clubs, or meetings—I still never have enough time. Loving God and sharing God's love with people are the only two priorities of my life, and I feel as if I repeatedly fall short in both of them.

Part of the problem, of course, is my own inadequacy. Prayer is extraordinarily difficult, no matter how much time is available, and I still feel like a beginner. I'm perennially distracted, especially by my own overactive mind, and tempted into easier and more tangible ways of serving God and God's human family. But prayer is the work God has called me to. I know that the world needs it desperately. I need it. There's nothing more important in the whole of life on earth than our ever-growing relationship with God, and whatever use God may make of us through it. Everything outside of God's will for us is worthless, and everything within it, no matter how great our incapacity, is made valuable by God. If I've learned anything along the way, I've learned that in the midst of all my inner poverty, the one thing I have to offer is my willingness to be used. So I keep trying to offer it.